WHEN DEADLY FORCE IS INVOLVED

WHEN DEADLY FORCE IS INVOLVED

A Look at the Legal Side of Stand Your Ground, Duty to Retreat, and Other Questions of Self-Defense

Bruce M. Lawlor

ROWMAN & LITTLEFIELD
Lanham • Boulder • New York • London

Published by Rowman & Littlefield
A wholly owned subsidiary of The Rowman & Littlefield Publishing Group, Inc.
4501 Forbes Boulevard, Suite 200, Lanham, Maryland 20706
www.rowman.com

Unit A, Whitacre Mews, 26-34 Stannary Street, London SE11 4AB

British Library Cataloguing in Publication Information Available

Library of Congress Cataloging-in-Publication Data

Names: Lawlor, Bruce M.
Title: When deadly force is involved : A look at the legal side of stand your ground, duty to retreat,
    and other questions of self-defense / Bruce M. Lawlor.
Description: Lanham : Rowman & Littlefield, 2017. | Includes bibliographical references and index.
ISBN: 9781442275287 (cloth : alkaline paper) | ISBN 9781442275294 (electronic)

∞ ™ The paper used in this publication meets the minimum requirements of
American National Standard for Information Sciences Permanence of Paper for
Printed Library Materials, ANSI/NISO Z39.48-1992.

Printed in the United States of America

CONTENTS

INTRODUCTION

If threatened with death, people will defend themselves and, if necessary, use deadly force to kill their attackers. Self-defense is part of what Sigmund Freud called the "deepest essence" of human nature.[1] Yet the law didn't recognize it as an individual right until sometime during the seventeenth century. Before then, only the king, or his agents, could kill another human being, and in the king's hands that authority knew no bounds. If someone, not sanctioned by the king, took a life, even to save his own, he was deemed guilty of "homicide by misadventure," and was required, at least, to forfeit all his worldly goods. He could beg for the king's forgiveness,[2] but with no guarantee of receiving it. Pardons were granted, or not, as was the king's want.

The evolution of self-defense is an interesting one. During the seventeenth century, Western intellectuals and political philosophers began to write about an individual's relationship to the state, as part of a cultural movement that came to be known as the Age of Enlightenment. It was driven in part by popular resistance to the fact that kings exercised absolute, unlimited control over the lives of their subjects. The king was accountable only to God.

In 1625, a Dutch jurist named Hugo Grotius proposed the existence of a body of unchanging rules that govern all human conduct. He said that every human being had certain natural rights regardless of his or her station in life, based on moral principles that God included in the scheme of things when he created the universe. Grotius called God's legal scheme "natural law."[3] Prominent among the individual's natural law rights was the right of self-preservation.[4]

At the core of Grotius's thinking was a novel, perhaps even seditious idea for the times, the notion that no monarch could take away an individual's natural rights, because they came directly from God. Grotius established limits and proposed there were things the king could not do. His ideas challenged the king's power, his absolute authority to govern his subjects as he wished. Hiding in a corner of that thought was another even more seditious notion, one that Thomas Hobbes would describe in 1651, namely that royal authority rested at least in part, if not on the people's consent, at least on their sufferance.

Hobbes reasoned that if natural law gave the individual certain inalienable rights, then the basis of the king's authority to govern his kingdom is a social contract between the individual and the state. The individual surrenders some of his rights in exchange for the state's commitment to protect his inalienable rights, and any other rights he and the king may agree to. Hobbes, like Grotius, believed that an individual's inalienable rights included a right of self-defense. He wrote: "If a man by the terror of present death be compelled to do a fact against the law, he is totally excused; because no law can oblige a man to abandon his own preservation. And supposing such a law were obligatory, yet a man would reason thus: 'If I do it not, I die presently; if I do it, I die afterwards; therefore by doing it, there is time of life gained.' Nature therefore compels him to the fact."[5] In short, Hobbes believed the power of self-preservation was stronger than the king's writ.

Hobbes's observations about self-defense proved to be true. As English society grew, the king didn't have time to hear every problem of his subjects, and more and more of the his power to decide such matters came to be exercised by English common law judges. Over time, they recognized reluctantly that on occasion people threatened with unlawful violence, had good reason, to take matters into their own hands. Begrudgingly, the common law began to fashion a limited, highly circumscribed, individual right of self-defense.

Having accepted the idea of self-defense, English judges wanted to make sure it was used only in situations where it was absolutely necessary, where no alternative means of avoiding the threat were available. To achieve this end, they crafted the concept of a duty to retreat, even in the face of unlawful, imminent danger. The doctrine became known as "retreat to the wall," the notion that individuals under attack had to have their backs against the wall, and no place left to run, before they could use deadly force to defend themselves.

The English approach to self-defense with its emphasis on "retreat to the wall" didn't fit well in the new world. The American frontier tested the idea of the state as protector of the individual, and found it wanting. American colonialists pushing westward learned the hard way that governments weren't always there for them in times of deadly danger, and that relying on the state to guarantee their personal safety, or that of their families, was a recipe for injury and death. When it came to protecting people from violence, governments weren't able to keep their end of the social contract.

So Americans began to ignore the crown's claims of authority, and rejected the common law's requirement to flee in the face of danger. As they marched to the Pacific Ocean, Americans created a new social contract. They accepted the government's authority when it was present, and capable of protecting them, against the murderers and thieves who preyed upon them, but in cases where it was absent or incapable, they retained the right to act in their own defense. The new social contract, they said, was based on the "inherent right of natural law."[6]

Self-defense, as a legal concept, is easy to describe, difficult to apply. Generally, a person who is without fault may use force, including deadly force, to defend against what he or she reasonably fears is an imminent unlawful threat of death or serious bodily injury, provided there is no reasonable alternative to avoid it.[7] When one begins to parse the words of this description, however, one runs immediately into a thicket of local laws and customs that influence how the words are interpreted and applied. The result is a bit of complexity and controversy that can lead to the appearance of arbitrariness, in what is really a well established, and stable system of legal analysis. The purpose of this book is to describe the system, how one goes about determining if a homicide is justifiable or excusable. It doesn't offer solutions so much as a description of the approaches taken to find them.

The limits of the king's authority to kill his subjects is once again the subject of debate, this time in the United States, as a rash of police killings has raised questions about law enforcement's use of deadly force. Although it's hard to believe, nobody really knows how often it happens each year, because the federal government doesn't collect such information, and even if it did, there's no requirement for local law enforcement agencies to report police involved killings. That is part of the problem. People intuit there's a problem, but there's insufficient data to understand clearly what it is.

The *Washington Post* set out to collect data on police killings during 2015, and concluded the number was 990. The *Post*'s analysis showed that about 25 percent of the time the person killed was having some sort of mental health crisis, or was running away, or that the police officer involved wasn't being attacked, or trying to protect anyone else from danger. The *Post* said 10 percent of the people killed were unarmed.[8]

The Guardian did the same thing for 2015, and it concluded there were 1,136 police killings. It thought that one in every ten people killed had a mental health problem,[9] and that 22 percent were unarmed when they died.[10] Based on the two studies, it appears reasonable to assume the total number of people killed by police in the United States each year is about 1,000.

While national data on the total number of police killings is imprecise, national data does exist for instances in which police officers are charged with crimes in connection with such killings. The first thing one learns is that criminal charges are very seldom brought. Between 2005 and 2015, the average number of police officers charged in connection with a civilian death was about five officers per year. In 2015, that number jumped to seventeen, primarily because of the pervasive use of video cameras. Somebody, a bystander or the police themselves, recorded the actual shooting on video.[11] The second thing one learns from the data is that even if criminal charges are rare, convictions are even more rare. Police officers brought to trial in connection with a civilian death are seldom found guilty. Since 2005, only thirteen officers have been convicted of murder or manslaughter for fatally shooting a civilian in the line of duty.[12]

Police shootings have become controversial because police officers invariably claim self-defense to justify them. They suggest the person killed behaved in a way that threatened them, or someone else, with death or serious bodily injury, causing them to fear for their lives, and justifying the use of deadly force to prevent the injury. At the same time, in an age of abundant information about almost any topic, people know more about when claims of self-defense are justified, and when they are not. It is very difficult for civilians to escape criminal charges, or be found not guilty, where the person killed was unarmed, or shot in the back, or mentally unstable, but not so much so, where the shooter is a police officer. Prosecutors, judges, and some members of the public tend to give police officers the benefit of the doubt, and therein lies the problem. There is growing concern, some of it legitimate, that police officers are getting away with murder, because the king isn't paying much attention to the killing of his citizens. Reform is needed, and perhaps the best way to achieve it is by beginning to apply the rules governing self-defense claims with an even hand, officers being judged by the same standards as civilians. From there, adjustments can be made by the various state legislatures to accommodate the unique circumstances in which police officers operate.

The U.S. Supreme Court decided the question of whether there is an individual constitutional right to bear arms in the cases of District of Columbia v. Heller (2008)[13] and McDonald v. Chicago (2010).[14] There is no longer a question of whether people can use firearms to protect themselves. They can. This book seeks to show how the law is likely to approach what happens after they do so. It describes a legal framework for thinking about self-defense that is applicable everywhere. It doesn't focus on the laws of any one state, nor does it compare the laws of one state with those of another. There are simply too many permutations in state court decisions to collect, discuss, and cross-reference all of them in a single volume.

Rather, it is a description of the approaches the states use to resolve common legal issues that arise in connection with self-defense claims. Some states may use one way to tackle a particular question, while other states use a different way to answer the same question. The approaches themselves are what are important because they provide a common language, a shared way to think about an issue, and a common methodology for how to address it.

Generally, on any given issue, a state will follow one of two possible approaches: a majority approach or a minority approach. That doesn't mean every state will apply the approach in exactly the same way as every other state that uses it, quite to the contrary. Individual states tend to tweak how the approaches are applied to fit unique local circumstances and preferences, and it is this variability in application that accounts for the law's perceived complexity. For example, take the idea of curtilage, a subset of the Castle Doctrine. It is a legal concept used to determine what portion of a residence is considered a home, thereby exempting it from the duty to retreat, another legal concept involved in self-defense cases. Some states apply curtilage to mean only the actual living space inside a dwelling. Other states say it includes other spaces as well, the porch, or the garage, or all the out buildings, or even the entire property. This book explains the idea of curtilage, and how it is used to make decisions, but does not attempt to identify what area it covers in each state. The point is that understanding the general concept enables the reader to find out how it applies specifically in their state, or circumstances. In that respect, what follows is the beginning, not the end, of understanding how self-defense works.

The book has fifteen chapters. Each chapter addresses a specific issue related to self-defense, and describes how judges and juries go about deciding what to do. Every chapter begins with a fictitious case narrative, describing the facts and circumstances of a deadly encounter in which the survivor claimed to have acted in self-defense. The main source of these stories is actual criminal cases in which the defendant was charged with murder or manslaughter. The people, cities, scenes, events, and timelines follow generally their description in the cases. Most of them have been modified, however, to provide additional descriptive details, and make them more interesting. The legal reasoning, however, what was decided and why it was decided, reflects the actual decision in the case, providing a pathway for the reader to better understand how specific questions relating to claims of self-defense are answered.

Usually State Supreme Court opinions address many different legal questions, and include the facts necessary to decide them. They are long on legal analysis, short on storytelling, and generally make for very dull reading. I have taken some license to make them more readable, and thus more memorable as a framework for thinking about self-defense. That said, none of the people described in the narratives are invented or constructed from composites. Their names have been changed to allow for individual thoughts and dialogue that were not present in the legal opinions. The thoughts and words ascribed to them are fictional.

The case narratives also omit issues and facts irrelevant to the self-defense claim being discussed, and legal reasoning that wanders or is off point. On occasion, additional detail was added to some of the fact patterns to promote a better understanding of the issue, or make the narrative more interesting. The result is case narratives that are fictional, but based on fact. They focus tightly, in a more interesting way, on a specific issue related to self-defense. Hopefully, each narrative helps to explain the law, while the law helps to explain each narrative.

A final word of caution. What follows is a discussion of the general approaches the various states use to decide self-defense claims. It's not intended to provide legal advice for any given set of circumstances, and shouldn't be treated as authoritative for any particular state, or any set of facts. The stories used are fictitious, intended to provide a framework for thinking about a particular issue, and nothing more. It can't be stated too strongly that if you possess a gun for self-defense, you need to become familiar with the self-defense law of your state. This book is intended to provide you with information about what to look for.

I

NECESSITY

KILL OR BE KILLED

Most Saturday afternoons in Richmond, Virginia, are hot and humid in July. This July 11 was a little different. It was still hot, but a southwest breeze scattered white clouds across a blue sky, blowing away some of the humidity, pausing now and then to offer shade before moving on. It was almost 1:00 o'clock in the afternoon and the temperature was 83 degrees. In another hour, it would be in the 90s.

Jason Donohue drove his pickup truck south on Jefferson Davis Highway, heading away from the city, going home. He was an average-sized man, fairly thin, and in pretty good shape. His hair was thinning on top and he was wearing a new pair of eyeglasses, the kind with no frame around the lenses. They made him look like a computer geek from the 1990s but he liked them anyway, a change from what he'd been wearing, from fashion to function.

He wore dungarees, a gray T-shirt, and old tennis shoes. Around his waist, strapped to his right hip, was a single action Colt, western style revolver, in a leather holster. It was a little unusual perhaps, but Jason often wore the gun when he left the shooting range. Instead of putting everything away, he'd throw the range bag onto the front seat of his truck, drive home, and then spend the next half-hour cleaning the gun. If he stopped along the way, he usually left it on, ignoring the occasional stare from a stranger. Most people, pecking away at their cell phones, didn't notice it anyway. Jason liked handguns, handled them safely, trained, and practiced with them regularly, and he was a pretty fair shot. He possessed a concealed carry permit but he didn't worry about it. This was Virginia, after all, where, in most places, carrying a gun openly is fairly common.

Donohue drove along a part of Jefferson Davis Highway with four lanes of traffic, two heading north and two heading south. A small grass median separated the north and southbound lanes, keeping the cars apart, like a referee enforcing the rules. On the east side of the highway, mobile homes and open lots dotted the landscape. On the west side, there was a wall of large commercial and industrial warehouses. During the day, the area was a beehive of activity, people going places, picking things up, dropping things off, working their jobs. At night it was a ghost town, enclosed by chain-linked fences, locked gates, and empty parking lots. When Donohue saw The Red Stripe Food Market just up ahead, he decided to stop and buy some Gatorade. It was going to be a hot day in the garage.

Farid Qureshi was a native of Egypt. He'd been in the United States about ten years, landed his first job in Richmond, and decided to stay in the area. He met and married his wife, Khadijah, whose family also settled in Richmond. The newlyweds found a house they liked, had a son, and then a daughter. Farid and Khadijah worked hard, saved their money, and when they saw a chance to buy The Red Stripe Food Market, they jumped at it. The down payment wiped them out financially, but they were proud of what they'd done, what they'd accomplished, and it showed in how they ran their store. Everything was always neat and clean, and the shelves were kept stocked with goods that people liked and could afford. Khadijah cleared a space near the front of the store and placed a few small tables and some chairs for people to sit, have coffee, maybe a sweet roll, and talk. Farid put in Wi-Fi and was amazed at how it attracted customers. The Red Stripe became something of a neighborhood hangout, an Egyptian coffee shop minus the hookah smoke and Middle Eastern newspapers.

The Red Stripe looked like all convenience stores: a single story cement block building, facing the highway, big glass windows in front, littered with advertisements, a small parking lot between the highway and the store, not enough parking spaces. A big sign ran along the building's roofline announcing Red Stripe Food Market. Large red and white vertical stripes extended from both sides of the sign to the building's corners, stripes about two feet wide and four feet tall with unusually bright colors, making the place hard to miss from the road.

Like many other people, Jason began going to the Red Stripe because it was convenient, a quick stop a place to grab what he needed, and be on his way. Then he found himself liking Khadijah and Farid, the way they took care of the place, the way they took pride in it. They were an affable couple, with ready smiles, and an easy way about them. He started dropping by more often, lingering a bit longer, chatting up Kadijah, who teased him about being a cowboy. He became a regular, then a friend. In Jason's mind, the Egyptian couple had proved the American dream still worked. People willing to put in the effort could make something for themselves. For some reason, that made him feel good and he began to buy most of what he needed from them.

Jason found an open space in the parking lot and parked his truck. He turned off the engine, grabbed his keys, and slid out the door. A blast of afternoon heat hit him, washing away whatever he was thinking about, demanding his attention. It's going to be a scorcher, he thought. He hesitated a minute, thinking maybe he'd leave the pistol in the truck. That would mean he'd have to lock it up of course, which would mean he'd have to roll up the windows. If he did that, he'd pay the price when he came back from the store. It would be hotter than hell inside. The thought of getting into a boiling hot truck decided it for him. He left the gun on his hip, turned, and headed for the Red Stripe's air conditioning.

When he opened the store's front door, he was a little surprised at how many customers he saw. The parking lot was virtually empty, yet there were maybe a dozen people milling around inside, getting coffee, walking up and down the aisles, taking things off the shelves, putting them into shopping baskets. Must be locals, he thought, as it was pretty hot to be carrying groceries very far.

Khadijah was sitting at a small table with another woman. They were laughing and looking at a cell phone. Jason guessed they were looking at baby pictures. There was a small line of people at the checkout counter. Farid was standing behind it greeting customers and operating the cash register. A group of kids maybe eight or nine years old—were looking at the candy racks near the counter.

Jason walked passed the checkout line and went to the coolers in the back of the building. He found the Gatorade and picked up two quart-size bottles. The apples on the next shelf looked to be fresh so he grabbed a couple of those as well, turned, and walked back to the front of the store. He went to the back of the checkout line and waited. Farid looked up, recognized him, smiled, and pointed his finger at him. Jason responded with a thumbs-up.

There were two people in line ahead of him. A woman was standing at the counter looking through her purse. Jason knew what that meant, although he thought it one of life's little mysteries, an unwritten, immutable law he would never understand. It felt as if some women carrying large handbags in checkout lines always waited until they had all their purchases rung up before starting to look for their money. Everyone else has to wait, their irritation palpable, yet no one daring to say a word. Jason smiled to himself, having given up long ago trying to figure it out. It's just the way it is, he thought. The woman in front of him this time was special. When she finally found her wallet, she carefully inspected each bill before handing the cash to Farid. Then she plunged both hands back into the handbag, pushing aside this and that, searching for loose coins, determined to find the exact change, pulling coins from where they were hiding, and looking at both sides before laying them on the counter. Jason stood there waiting. The man in front of him stood there waiting. Farid stood behind the counter waiting. All three men watched silently, submissive, resigned. The woman kept burrowing for coins.

Jason saw the store's front door open out of the corner of his eye and turned his head slightly to the left to see a short man walk in out of the heat. He was wearing black pants, a black T-shirt, sunglasses, and a blue baseball cap. He had a beer belly. The man looked startled, taken aback, like he'd seen something unexpected. Apparently, the number of customers in the store surprised him too, Jason thought. The way the man was holding his arm straight down by his side caught Jason's attention. That's when he saw the revolver in the man's right hand and he knew this wasn't going to be good.

The man pointed the gun at Farid behind the counter and shouted for everyone to get down on the floor. The woman at the counter turned her head, her hands becoming still inside her handbag, saw the pistol pointed in her direction, and dropped to the floor, like a bag of cement, her handbag coming with her, scattering its contents in front of the counter. Other people in the store, attracted by the sound of the man's voice, looked toward the checkout counter. Understanding came like dawn, touching first the faces of those nearest the gunman, then reaching into the room's farthest corners. Eyes widened, heads turned quickly, back and forth, looking for escape routes, seeking safety. People began to crouch behind shelves, keeping their eyes on the man with the pistol, as if they could dodge what he might throw at them. The room filled with fear.

Gunshots exploded suddenly and people began screaming. Farid's arms flew up in the air and he fell backward onto the floor. One of the kids, between Farid and the gunman near the candy rack, ducked his head, like a baseball player dodging a wild pitch, and bolted for the door. He ran passed the gunman and out of the building, his friend right behind him, arms pumping, both of them running for all they were worth. Jason saw the gunman fire, but he didn't comprehend it immediately, his mind unwilling to accept what his eyes were seeing. There was no reason to shoot. No one had done anything. No one had said anything. No one was resisting. Why would he start shooting?

Farid, hit twice by the gunfire, fell to the floor behind the counter, landing painfully next to another boy who'd decided to seek cover rather than follow his friends and run for the door. Wide-eyed, the youngster was on his knees, staring at Farid, shaking uncontrollably with fear, terrified by the blood coming from Farid's chest, a bag of potato chips crinkling in his hand like a baby's rattle. Farid was having trouble breathing—too weak to move, and unable to help himself. He thought the gunman would come around the counter and kill him, but there was nothing he could do about it. He lay there and waited to die.

The gunshots swept away any doubts people may have had about what was happening. The store's customers dropped quickly to the floor, all at the same time, like "Ring Around the Rosie" all fall down. Jason stood frozen, staring at the gunman, still not understanding, why? The gunman turned his head to look out the window at the two boys running across the parking lot, and Jason made his move. He dropped the apples and Gatorade, drew his revolver, and dove behind a barrel filled with ice and soft drinks near the counter, hoping for some protection against more gunfire.

He tried to use his hands to break his fall, but landed hard. The impact bent the pistol's trigger guard, jamming the trigger back, as if it had been pulled. Normally, the gun was fired by thumbing back the hammer until it was in the fully cocked position, then pulling the trigger to release the hammer, causing it to fall and discharge the bullet. With the trigger jammed, he thought the pistol might not fire because when he pulled the hammer back it might stay in the cocked position. Crouched behind the soda barrel, Jason eased the hammer back as far as it would go and then slowly moved his thumb forward. The hammer moved forward with his thumb. The jammed trigger had released the cocking mechanism. He could shoot the gun by pulling the hammer back and then simply letting it fall forward.

"Drop your weapon," Jason yelled. "I'm armed."

Startled, the gunman's head pivoted quickly back from the door, his eyes resting on the barrel near the counter where he'd heard the voice. He ducked behind a shelf of canned goods and moved toward the back of the store. Jason could see flashes of the blue hat as the man maneuvered from aisle to aisle. He was going toward the other side of the building, trying to find a place where he could see behind the barrel, and get a clear shot at Jason. The blue hat moved two or three times seeking advantage.

Suddenly, the man opened fire and charged down the middle aisle, running directly at the soda barrel that Jason was crouching behind. He shot rapidly, jabbing his revolver in the air, pulling the trigger as he ran. Jason returned the fire, but his rate of fire was much slower as he thumbed the hammer of his broken pistol and let it fall forward, something he'd never done before. Screams from people lying on the floor mixed with the gunfire, adding to the chaos. Halfway down the aisle, there was a crossover aisle and the gunman moved to his left seeking cover. Jason didn't know if any of his shots had hit the gunman. He tried to count in his head how many shots the gunman had fired, and how many shots he had fired, but he had no idea. He thought maybe the gunman was out of ammunition, but then maybe that was why he'd sought cover. The gunman was reloading. All Jason knew for sure was that he hadn't fired all six of his bullets. He still had at least one, maybe two rounds left.

"I'm out of bullets. I'm out of bullets," the gunman yelled.

"Well, I'm not," Jason called back.

One of the customers on the floor yelled that the gunman was trying to reload. Jason didn't know if that was true, couldn't see what the gunman was doing, couldn't tell if the person warning him could see the man. He stayed still, afraid of being tricked into standing up, into becoming an easy target.

"Listen," the gunman yelled as Jason heard the snapping sound of a hammer falling on empty cylinders. The man was pulling the trigger of his pistol, trying to convince Jason his gun was empty. Jason didn't move, afraid that maybe it was a trick to get him out into the open.

The gunman lurched from where he was hiding and staggered toward the store's front door. He held the pistol in one hand, the other pressed against his stomach. Jason could see no second gun and the man appeared to be hurt. Jason left the soda barrel and ran after him, grabbing the back of his t-shirt just as he reached the store's door. The man still had some fight still left in him and the two men grappled. Jason struck him on the head with his revolver. The blow staggered the man, and Jason struck him again with the pistol, knocking him to the floor, sending his baseball cap flying. The gunman lay on his side, curled up in a ball, holding onto his stomach. Jason pointed his gun at the man, extending both arms in front of him, holding back the hammer with his thumb.

"You move and I'll kill you," he said. His voice was labored, out of breath like he had just run a foot race. The gunman looked up at him, closed his eyes, and brought his knees further up into his chest.

The store's customers began to get up off the floor. "Are you OK?" they asked. "Anybody hurt?"

"Call an ambulance! Farid's been shot," someone yelled. "Jesus, there's blood everywhere!"

Jason heard someone calling 911 on their cell phone. He sensed more than saw people starting to move toward him. He forced himself to look away from the gunman on the floor to see who it was.

"You need to stay back," Jason said. "Did you get through to 911?" he asked no one in particular, turning back to cover the man at his feet.

"The police are on their way," someone said.

"Shoot him," somebody else said.

"Yea, kill the son of a bitch," said another.

Jason's breath was still coming fast. He kept the broken pistol out in front of him, aimed at the gunman. He could hear Khadijah sobbing softly behind the counter where her husband lay in a pool of blood. Jason still couldn't understand why the man had shot Farid. None of them had tried to stop the gunman from taking the money. Why didn't he just take it? The man had started shooting for no reason. Jason wanted to know how badly Farid was hurt, wanted to know if he would die, but there was nobody there to tell him.

The gunman groaned and clutched his stomach. He was moving his feet, in pain, but he wasn't trying to get up. Jason could see now that he was bleeding from a belly wound and growing weaker by the minute. He wasn't going anywhere, wasn't going to hurt anyone else. Jason thought for just a minute about letting go of the hammer, just letting it fall, making the gunman pay for what he'd done to Farid, for what he'd done to Khadijah, but he didn't. He breathed deeply and slowly moved his thumb forward placing the hammer in a safe position. The gunfight at the Red Stripe Food Market was over.

The police arrived a short time later. They seized Jason's pistol, handcuffed him, and locked him in a cage in the back of a police car. They gave first aid to Farid and to the gunman, called for ambulances, put up crime scene tape, and blocked the parking lot entrances with police cars.

More police arrived and they began asking questions of the store's customers: what did they see, what did they hear, who did what, who said what, where were they standing, where was the gunman, where was Jason, who were other witnesses? They searched for bullet holes made by the robber's gun and by Jason's. They seized the store's video camera. They took written statements from everyone. They wrote everything down, measured everything, photographed everything.

Later, the police drove Jason to the police station, still handcuffed, and talked to him about what happened. They started the conversation by reading him his Miranda rights: his right to remain silent, his right to have a lawyer present. Jason chose to tell them what happened, and when the interview was finished the police had a pretty good idea of how the shooting took place. They decided to let Jason go home. They took off his handcuffs and drove him to his house. A police officer brought his pickup truck from the Red Stripe Food Market. They told him the matter was still under investigation, that is was still possible he would face criminal charges for what he'd done.

Five days after the shooting, the Richmond police chief said Jason was a "good samaritan. He saved many lives that day." But the prosecutor's office remained silent, only suggesting that based on a "preliminary investigation" the shooting *might* have been justified. The prosecutor assigned to the case made it clear that she would not make a final decision about whether Jason would be charged with a crime until she had personally watched the store's surveillance film, and thoroughly reviewed the final police investigation report.[1] She wasn't going to rely on what the police told her. She wanted to look at the evidence herself.

The police continued to work the case, going over it again and again, looking for other facts, other witnesses, other evidence that might support a murder charge. Some people described their efforts as trying to confirm that Jason acted in self-defense. Others described them as trying to disprove it. Eventually, the prosecutor was satisfied that all her questions had been answered. She reviewed the evidence one more time and decided that Jason had acted in self-defense. No criminal charges were filed against him. [2]

The police charged the gunman with attempted robbery, use of a firearm in the commission of a felony, and possession of a firearm by a convicted felon. There was no trial, however, because the gunman never left the hospital. Four days after the gunfight, he died of his wounds.

DECIDING NECESSITY IS THE GOAL OF EVERY SELF-DEFENSE INQUIRY

What happened to Jason Donohue following the incident at the Red Stripe Food Market is pretty standard in shootings. The police arrived, handcuffed him, and began questioning him about what happened. The handcuffing was for the police officers' safety, but it also had the legal effect of placing Jason under arrest. He could no longer come and go as he pleased, his freedom subject to how the police felt about what he'd done.

As soon as the shooting stopped, the official inquiry began. The main question on the day of the shooting was whether the police would hold Jason in jail or allow him to go home, but the inquiry's larger purpose was to determine whether he had killed a man unlawfully, or whether he was innocent of any wrongdoing, a man caught up in circumstances not of his making, and faced with a choice of either protecting himself with deadly force or accepting the likelihood of being killed or seriously injured. The initial police work at the scene as well as the subsequent investigation followed a predictable pattern focused on collecting the evidence and interviewing the witnesses.

There have been thousands of homicide investigations. The investigative path is well known and well worn. The issues that arise when there is a claim of self-defense are well understood, and the questions that must be answered to decide them are familiar to every homicide investigator and prosecutor. The entire investigation, the effort to collect evidence, interview witnesses, conduct tests, and research the law is intended to answer a single overriding question: Was it really necessary to kill the victim?

Necessity is the theoretical basis upon which self-defense rests, and it lies at the heart of every self-defense claim. The idea is that governments shouldn't punish people for trying to avoid getting killed or seriously injured, even if they act illegally, provided they play no part in bringing about the danger.[3] Self-defense acknowledges there are circumstances in which innocent people find themselves in danger that leaves them with no alternative but to kill or be killed. Necessity is the law's description of why a killing may go unpunished. It describes situations "when physical forces beyond the actor's control make 'illegal conduct the lesser of two evils.'"[4]

Necessity means unavoidable. It describes situations in which people have no alternative but to take a life. The basic question in Jason's case, and in every self-defense shooting, is whether the killing was unavoidable. In other words, was it really necessary for Jason to kill the gunman to protect his own life or the lives of the other people in the store? If the answer to that question is yes, then he can't be convicted of murder. In some states, the killing is said to be lawful. In others, it is said to be excusable, meaning that although the killing is illegal, the state will not punish the person who committed it.[5] Either way, no penalties attach and the shooter goes free.

A general description of self-defense is that a person who is without fault may use force, including deadly force, to defend against what he or she reasonably fears is an imminent unlawful threat of death or serious bodily injury, provided there is no reasonable alternative to avoid it.[6] There is a lot to unpack here, but the major questions relating to self-defense claims are familiar, having been the subject of much litigation.

As with all things, the devil is in the details in homicide investigations. Still, whenever a claim of self-defense is involved, the investigation tends to travel down a well-worn path, sprinkled with well-known issues. There may be others matters triggered by a unique or unusual fact pattern, but the issues discussed here are quite common, and appear usually in one form or another in virtually every self-defense case. They are important because how each one is decided can determine the case's final outcome, and because reaching decisions about what happened and why is not always easy. Often it is a very close call, with arguments on both sides of the question. Reasonable people can and do disagree about what is the right answer. Each of the issues commonly encountered in self-defense cases will be discussed in greater detail in later chapters, but for now, let's look at them briefly in the context of the Red Stripe Food Market shooting.

COMMON ISSUES IN SELF-DEFENSE CLAIMS

What the shooter was thinking, when he or she pulled the trigger, is important because self-defense is all about intent. Thus, the first issue in self-defense cases, a threshold issue, is whether the shooting was an intentional act or was it unplanned, in other words, an accident. Did the shooting occur because the shooter pulled the trigger with evil intent to kill the victim, or trying to save himself or someone else from deadly danger, or did the shooting occur by happenstance, an unintended consequence of some other act?

Determining whether the gun fired by accident is critical because self-defense requires an intentional act, pulling the trigger deliberately enables a shooter to avoid being convicted of murder by showing that when he fired the gun, his intent was not to kill the victim, but to avoid being killed or seriously hurt. Accidents on the other hand, by definition, are unintentional. If the shooting occurred by accident, there was no intent to kil, and there was no intent to avoid one's own death or injury. There was no intent to act at all, and if that is the case, a claim of self-defense cannot be made because why the bullet was fired played no part in the victim's death. Jason's actions at the Red Stripe Food Market were clearly intentional. He fired his pistol deliberately, not by accident, and his purpose was to save himself and others from harm, thus he was free to claim he acted in self-defense.

The second issue is whether the person claiming self-defense provoked the confrontation that led to the shooting. The shooter cannot provoke, prolong, or contribute in any way to the escalation of events that ends in the victim's death. If he or she does, then no claim of self-defense can be made because the law assumes that in the absence of the shooter's bad behavior, an escalation of the hostilities wouldn't have occurred, and the homicide wouldn't have been necessary. In the Red Stripe shooting,

Jason played no part in bringing about the dangerous situation. He didn't provoke the gunfight, didn't prolong it, and didn't contribute in any way to the gunman's decision to start shooting during the robbery. In short, he didn't make the situation worse. Responsibility for doing that rested entirely with the gunman. Because Jason was innocent of any wrongdoing in bringing about the final encounter, his claim of self-defense continues to be valid.

The third self-defense issue, another prerequisite for claiming self-defense, is the triggering threat. Self-defense is like a light switch. When there's an imminent threat of death or serious bodily injury, the light switch is on. When there's no such threat, the light switch is off. There is no in-between. There are too many ways one person can threaten another to list here, but generally, the threat must be overt and plain to see. It must be some observable act that makes it clear the shooter is in great danger, and unless he or she acts immediately to avoid it, the consequences may be death or great injury. The gunman's behavior in Jason's case, opening fire without warning, an act of extreme violence, clearly turned on the light switch permitting the people who were threatened to use deadly force in return. It supports Jason's claim that it was necessary for him to act.

The fourth issue asks whether the threat was imminent. In other words, did it require immediate action to avoid? To be imminent, the danger must be immediate, right now, about to occur, not something that might or will happen at some point in the future. Imminent threats are those requiring instant action to keep from getting killed or seriously hurt. A gunman shooting at unarmed and innocent people in a public place, as occurred at the Red Stripe Food Market, is pretty much the poster child for an imminent threat. Once the gunman opened fire the threat was more than imminent. It was extant. Jason's claim passes this test.

The fifth issue is reasonable fear. Did the shooter reasonably fear that his or her life was in danger? There must be more than just fear, however. Naked fear isn't reasonable. Just because one is afraid doesn't give him license to shoot anyone, no matter how afraid he might be. The facts must justify a reasonable belief in the shooter's mind that he or she is about to be killed or injured. Some threatening behaviors signal clearly that extreme violence is about to occur: the use of lethal weapons, attempted murder, or rape. Other threatening behaviors not so much: a man putting his hand into his pocket during a verbal argument, for example. It could mean nothing or it could mean the man is reaching for a knife. At a minimum the threat must be such that it transforms a person's undifferentiated fear into a fear focused on a specific danger.[7] It is the difference between "I am afraid to be in the mini-mart" and "I am afraid to be in the mini-mart because there's a man with a gun in there acting strangely." The threat that Jason, and every other patron, saw that day in the Red Stripe Food Market was violent and deadly. The facts justified people believing that they were about to be killed or injured, thereby satisfying the requirement that the shooter's fear be reasonable.

The sixth issue looks at whether there existed a reasonable alternative to the use of deadly force. Our description of self-defense says that deadly force may be employed provided there is no reasonable alternative to its use. This requirement includes the duty to retreat, but it is broader than just the duty to retreat. It reflects the law's strong preference for the avoidance of violence and the peaceful resolution of disputes whenever possible. It exists in every state, even those that have done away with the duty to retreat. If a person becomes involved in an escalating confrontation, there may still be an obligation for him or her to avoid a deadly response, even in states with stand-your-ground laws.[8] For example, if there is an easy, available way for a person who is threatened to avoid the danger, by simply walking away perhaps, then the pathway to safety must be taken because simply walking away is a reasonable alternative to shooting anyone.[9] There is no question of reasonable alternatives where no easy pathway out of the danger exists. Such was the case in Jason's situation. With the gunman standing between him and the door shooting at people, deadly force was the only alternative Jason had.

The seventh issue relates to de-escalation of the confrontation. Has the initial aggressor abandoned the fight, or is he unable to continue it, or has he somehow indicated he wants peace rather than further confrontation? If so, the light switch is turned off immediately, and with it the right of self-defense. The law deems the encounter over and the danger passed. Homicide is no longer necessary to avoid the threat because the threat no longer exists. At one point in the Red Stripe Food Market gunfight, the gunman shouted that he was out of ammunition. He pulled the trigger on his revolver causing the hammer to fall on empty chambers signaling he was unable to continue the fight because his gun was empty. This type of behavior might be viewed as an attempt to de-escalate the encounter, a gesture the gunman was ready to give up the fight. Unfortunately, it came too late because Jason had already shot him and no more shots were fired after the sound of empty chambers was heard. In other words, at the time Jason shot him, the light switch was still on.

The eighth self-defense issue focuses on the reasonableness of the force used to avoid the danger. The force one uses in self-defense can be deadly, but it can't be more than is necessary to neutralize the threat. It must be reasonable force, sufficient force to contain the danger, but no more. So what is unreasonable force? The Red Stripe Food Market shooting is a good case in point. The confrontation ended with Jason in control of the gunman. The man was wounded, lying on the floor, without a weapon. Angry customers urged Jason to shoot him, make him pay for what he'd done. But at that point he was no longer a threat. The danger had passed. Would it then be reasonable for Jason to use deadly force against him? Hardly. Had he done so the force would have been excessive for what was required, unreasonable, and Jason likely would have been charged with murder, justifiably so. As it was, Jason stood down, and by doing so perfected his claim of self-defense.

As stated above, depending on the facts of the case, there may be other issues involved in self-defense shootings. These eight issues are noteworthy, however, because they appear, in one form or another, in almost every self-defense claim, and they provide a good framework for beginning to think about how self-defense works. We will look at these and other issues later on. For now, the important thing to remember is all of these issues provide information and answers to questions that will help police, prosecutors, and the jury to decide whether it was really necessary for the defendant to kill, or be killed.

DECIDING WHAT IS REASONABLE

Necessity provides the legal justification for self-defense, but it can't exist without reasonable behavior on the shooter's part. The shooter must act reasonably before using deadly force, not provoking, prolonging, or contributing to the encounter. The facts must be such, or appear to be such, as to cause a reasonable person to believe that he or she is in mortal danger. The shooter's fear must be reasonable, that is, based on observable facts. The force used to protect oneself must be reasonable, not more than is necessary to avoid the danger, and if deadly force is used, there must be no reasonable alternative to its use. If the shooter tries to withdraw from a confrontation, after provoking it, his or her desire for peace must be made reasonably clear to the other party. In short, the need for reasonableness permeates every part of a self-defense claim. So how do we decide what is reasonable?

There are two possible approaches: a majority approach and a minority approach. Most states will use the majority approach, but a considerable number will use the minority approach. Either way produces the same result, a decision about what is reasonable behavior.

The majority of states follow what is known as the objective standard for determining reasonableness. It is an approach that relies on the eyes of a third person, not involved in the incident, to determine whether the shooter's behavior was reasonable, in other words acceptable. States following this approach say that reasonable behavior is what a prudent person would have done or believed in the same or similar circumstances. Where do these states find such a prudent person? They crowd source it. It's called a jury. Juries make up a cross section of the community's members, and reflect collectively its values, beliefs, and its judgment about what is reasonable behavior. So if the jury thinks, based on the facts, that a participant's behavior during the confrontation was acceptable, then it's considered reasonable. If the jury thinks it wasn't, then it's not reasonable. It's as simple as that.

A minority of states, but still a significant number, follow a different approach. They answer the question of what is reasonable behavior by using what is known as the subjective standard. This approach doesn't employ a mythical third person to evaluate what is reasonable, but rather looks at the event through the eyes of the shooter. It judges reasonableness based on two factors. First, is the shooter's belief honestly held? In other words, did he or she really believe there was a deadly threat? Second, do the facts, as they appeared at the time of the shooting support the shooter's belief in imminent peril?[10] If the answer to both questions is yes, then the shooter's behavior under the circumstances is reasonable. If the answer to either one of the questions is no, then the behavior is unreasonable. Neither the objective nor the subjective standard is a perfect approach, each having its strengths and weaknesses, nevertheless for the most part, each one works well and reflects the community's belief about what is reasonable.

The use of different approaches by different states to make decisions is not unique to self-defense cases. Actually, it is the norm for all areas of the law, the result of state legislatures adjusting commonly held legal principles to reflect local values, customs, and traditions. In most cases, the various approaches group themselves nicely into a majority view and a minority view. Looking at it nationally, however, having two approaches to decision making on virtually every issue in a case creates a complex, hard to understand mosaic of conflicting laws that in some cases can lead to different outcomes for the same fact pattern. The important thing to remember is that the issues involved in deciding self-defense cases, for the most part, are the same in every state, as are the approaches used to decide them. What changes is how each state applies an approach to its own unique circumstances and preferences. The point is that once a person knows the issues and the approaches, it becomes possible, even relatively easy in some states, to predict the likely outcome for any given fact pattern.

It is also worth noting that disparity in state outcomes for cases with similar fact patterns is less than one might think. It is certainly true that across the nation different approaches can lead to different results for similar fact patterns, but that is normally not the case. Where such differences do occur, oftentimes they are the result of state legislatures having enacted different self-defense laws. For example, states that require a duty to retreat are likely to have different outcomes from those that do not. The disparity that does exist is acceptable, a reasonable price to pay for living in a federal system of governance that allows fifty different state legislatures to have a voice in saying what is fair for their citizenry.

Finally, it's worth noting that self-defense is a matter of human judgment, and that nothing is certain when human decision making is involved. There is always some wrinkle in a case to capture the jury's imagination and potentially send it off in an unexpected direction. Different people have different experiences to guide them, and at times, they will look at the same facts and see different behavior, or see the same behavior and come to different conclusions about what it means. It can be a bane or a blessing for the people involved in the case, but regardless of whichever way the jury decides, justice is served if the decision falls within an acceptable range of outcomes. The great majority of decisions involving self-defense fall within the range of what is considered acceptable.

2

INTENT

THE ROLE OF INTENT IN SELF-DEFENSE

It was Saturday night, July 23, 2005, in rural San Miguel County, New Mexico. Michael Bowden and his girlfriend, Sandra Lacy, were watching a movie at Michael's place. Michael owned a small patch of land in the foothills of the Sangre de Cristo Mountains. Not many people lived out where he did. His nearest neighbor was probably a mile down the road. Michael loved the place; he loved the peace and quiet, the solitude. Few cars came out his way during the day, almost none after dark. It was the kind of place where you could sit out on the back deck at night and gaze for hours at the stars in New Mexico's sky. Michael and Sandra were enjoying a lazy summer evening. It was past midnight. Saturday had become Sunday. Nobody had to work the next day and they were just hanging out in the living room, talking and watching an old movie.

About 2:00 a.m., a car pulled into Michael's driveway. The car's radio was turned up too loud, its speakers vibrating in the quiet night, the rhythmic beat of rap music demanding attention. Michael got up from the couch and looked out the window at his driveway wondering who would be visiting him at such an hour. Whoever it was, they were making a lot of racket, a practical joke no doubt, maybe some of his friends thinking they were funny. He didn't recognize the car and couldn't see inside it. He watched the car back up the driveway, stop near the county road, rev up its engine, pop the clutch, burn rubber, and screech down the short driveway straight at his garage. The driver stopped just short of the garage door, as the car came to a screeching stop. Sandra got up, went to the window, and stood beside him looking out.

"Who is it?" she asked.

"I don't know." Michael said. They stood next to each other, silent, each wondering who the driver might be. Nobody came to mind.

The car turned around on Michael's front lawn, leaving dark tire tracks on the wet grass and fishtailed its way back to the county road. When it got there, it turned back toward the house, lined itself up on the driveway again, and did the same thing—revved up the engine, popped the clutch, squealed down the driveway, and slammed on its brakes just short of the garage door, the entire performance accompanied by the rhythmic pounding of rap music. This time the driver misjudged the car's stopping distance, turning the car violently at the last minute to avoid crashing into the garage, almost hitting a large propone fuel tank that sat next to the building. The near miss startled Michael and Sandra.

"God, he almost hit the gas tank Michael," Sandra said.

"He must be drunk."

Sandra reached out and took Michael's hand. He looked at her and saw fear on her face. She turned her head in the direction of the kitchen then she looked back out the window as if she were trying to decide what to do. "She's terrified," Michael thought, "she wants to run away, but there's really no place to go." Michael put his arm around her shoulders and pulled her tightly to him, making contact with the length of her body.

"It's OK. Everything's fine," he said. "Probably one of my idiot friends. I'll go out and see who it is."

"Maybe you'd better not, Michael. I don't like this. Maybe we should call the sheriff," she said looking toward the kitchen where a telephone hung on the wall.

"Don't worry. It's probably just a bunch of kids and a case of beer," he said. He was growing angry. This was no longer funny. Sandra was really frightened. Whoever it was needed to knock it off. Michael gave her a quick hug, broke away, put on his slippers, and went to the front door. He flipped a switch on the wall and two outside lights popped on, one over the front door, the other on the front of the garage, illuminating the driveway. "I'll be right back," he said, opening the door.

Michael stepped onto the porch. The car sat there for a moment, reacting to the lights. Then it drove slowly about half way down the driveway and stopped, the radio still pounding out music, the speakers still vibrating with each beat.

"It must be a long playing CD," Michael thought, "the damn thing just doesn't stop." He walked to the edge of the driveway and looked in the car's direction. Its headlights went from low beam to high beam, responding to his movement, the light striking him in the eyes, his hand rising quickly to shade them from the glare. He thought he saw two people in the front seat, but he wasn't sure that was all there were, maybe there were more people in the back seat.

"Hello," he yelled, waving his hand, shouting over the music hoping his voice would at least cause them to turn down the radio. There was no response from the car. It just sat there, idling, the radio thumping, ominous.

"Can I help you?," Michael yelled.

No response.

"Can you turn down the radio a bit, so I can hear you?," Michael shouted.

Nothing.

"Who is it?"

Silence.

Michael felt the first twinges of fear, realizing that if it were just a bunch of kids drinking beer, they would have scampered away when the lights came on, or if it was any of his friends they would have said something by now. His instincts kicked in. Something else was going on here, something not right, something potentially very dangerous.

He turned and walked quickly back into the house, kicked off his slippers, replaced them with his shoes, and went into his bedroom. He took a .25 caliber pistol from the dresser drawer, loaded it, and chambered a round. Sensing someone else in the room, he looked up to see Sandra staring at him, her eyes flickering from the gun to his face and back again.

"What are you doing, Michael? You're not going out there with a gun. We'll lock the doors and call the sheriff. I'm not staying here alone."

"Sandy, I don't like this at all. I don't know if there is enough time for the sheriff to get here. You'd better go into the bathroom and lock the door."

"I don't want to go into the bathroom and lock the door. That isn't going to help much if you get yourself hurt and they come breaking into the house. We need to call the sheriff. Maybe they'll go away. Maybe the sheriff will get here before anything happens. Michael, I'm getting really scared," she said.

"They're not coming into the house," he said, talking more to himself than to her, looking down at the gun in his hand. "I just want to get their license plate number. Then we'll call the sheriff. I don't want them coming back. Just stay here and I'll be right back, OK?" He asked it as a question, but Sandra knew it wasn't. Michael had decided he was going to get the car's license plate number, and there was nothing she could do to dissuade him.

Without saying more, Michael put the pistol into his pants pocket, left the bedroom, and went out the front door. He was frightened. He didn't know what the people in the car wanted, but whatever it was he didn't think it would be good. He hadn't said it, but in the back of his mind a voice kept whispering to him: they might want Sandra. He told himself that wasn't going to happen, no matter what.

Michael saw the car was still where he'd left, it about half-way down the driveway, except the music had stopped. The only sound was its idling engine. As he approached the driveway, the angle gave him a better view of the car's interior, revealing a man behind the wheel and a woman in the front passenger seat. The woman was waving her hands at the driver, as if she were angry with him. There was no one else in the car. Michael glanced quickly around the yard, scanning the bushes. Maybe someone else was hiding, waiting to ambush him. He saw no one. He looked back at the car, trying to read the front license plate, unable to see it clearly because of the high beams, Land of Enchantment…7…5…4… He put his hand into his pocket, gripped the pistol, and walked slowly to the middle of the driveway, trying to see the rest of the plate.

The car reacted to his movement, backing up slowly toward the county road. At the end of the driveway it shifted into park, its gears making an audible clunk. The driver opened the door and stepped out. He was about Michael's size, maybe a little heavier, and was wearing a light shirt, a dark vest, and blue jeans. He had long hair and a mustache. Michael didn't recognize him. The man walked quickly toward him. He didn't speak. Michael stood there waiting, uncertain about what to do, expecting the man to stop and say something, tell him what was the matter. Maybe he was at the wrong house, or maybe he was looking for someone else.

When the man was at arm's length, without speaking, he cocked his right arm and threw a punch directly at Michael's face.

Michael's reflexes took over. He threw up his hands and ducked, trying to avoid what he knew was coming. When his right hand came out of his pocket, the gun came with it. Before he could block the punch, the man's fist struck him squarely in the face, just below his left eye. Michael heard a loud bang, thought it odd for a fist to make such a noise when striking a bone, as his head snapped back. He lost his balance and fell, landing on his back in the middle of the driveway. He realized the gun was in his hand. The sound must have come from it firing. He had no idea where the bullet went. He hadn't been aiming at anything. He must have squeezed the trigger accidently when the man hit him in the face. He looked up from the pavement. He could see the man's back. He was running toward the car. Thinking the man would get in the car and run over him, Michael got to his feet and staggered his way around the corner of the garage, intent on putting something, anything, between him and the car. He heard its engine rev. Michael looked over his shoulder to see what was happening. The car was backing up, out onto the county road. He saw it turn and drive away toward town.

Michael went back into the house, his face bleeding, the gun still in his hand. He told Sandra what had happened and she called the sheriff. He never did get the car's license plate number.

Two hours later, just after Michael had finally gone to bed, there was a knock on his front door. It was the sheriff. They found the car at the local hospital. The driver had pulled over to the side of the road, about a mile from Michael's house, and collapsed against the wheel, shot in the chest. His girlfriend drove him to the hospital but he died of a single .25 caliber gunshot wound to the heart.[1] Thirty days later, the local prosecutor charged Michael with second-degree murder. Michael claimed self-defense. His case went to trial and when it was over the jury found him guilty of involuntary manslaughter.

INTENT DETERMINES MURDER, OR SELF-DEFENSE

There are two basic requirements to prove the crime of murder. Every murder has them: an act and intent to kill.[2] To convict Michael of murder, the prosecutor had to prove beyond a reasonable doubt that he committed an act that resulted in the death of another, and that the act was motivated by an evil intent to kill, that is by murderous intent. Often, murderous intent is described as coming from malice, hostility, or ill will toward the victim.

There is no question but that the prosecutor could prove the crime's first requirement. Michael threw up his hands to ward off a blow, pulling a gun from his pocket that shot and killed his attacker. In doing so, he performed an act that resulted in the death of another.

The second requirement for a murder conviction, whether Michael acted with evil intent to kill his victim, is another matter. When a person kills someone out of malice, hostility, or ill will, the killer is said to have acted with murderous intent, and it is this murderous state of mind, this evil intent to deprive the victim of his life, that makes him criminally liable for the death of his victim.[3] The intent to kill must occur simultaneously with the act that brings about the victims death, one the product of the other, the intent causing the act, the act flowing from the intent. The question in Michael's case was whether at the time he shot the car's driver he acted with malice, hostility, or ill will in his heart, that is, with a murderous intent to kill his victim. If the answer to that question is yes, then the prosecutor has proven both parts of the crime and Michael is guilty of second-degree murder. If the answer is no, then the prosecutor has failed to prove his case and Michael cannot be convicted of murder.

The role of self-defense in murder cases is to prevent the prosecutor from proving the second element of murder, namely that the shooter acted with murderous intent to kill the victim. Simply put, if Michael's intent when he shot the man in his driveway was to save himself from being killed or seriously injured, then his intent in performing the act was very different from the malice, hostility, or ill will that causes one person to kill another. If he didn't have murderous intent when the killing act occurred, then he can't be convicted of murder. Indeed, it is just the opposite. If his intent was to avoid his own death or serious injury, then Michael has a complete defense to the charge.[4]

At first blush, the facts of the case appear to support Michael's claim of self-defense. He didn't start the fight, didn't know his attacker, had never met the man. There was no history of bad blood between them, indeed, no history of any relationship at all. When the car's driver was shot, Michael was trying to protect himself from a blow aimed at his face, a blow that came without warning, so suddenly that there was no time to do anything but react. Given the victim's sudden, unprovoked violence, the unexplained randomness of his attack, and his very dangerous driving behavior in the middle of the night, a jury could have concluded that Michael acted in self-defense, based on a reasonable fear that he faced imminent death or serious bodily injury.

Yet Michael didn't fire the gun intentionally. When he reacted to block the punch being thrown at his face, his hand came reflexively out of his pocket, and the gun came with it. It fired when he flinched from the blow striking him under his eye. He didn't pull the gun from his pocket deliberately, or use it consciously to defend himself, or to shoot his attacker on purpose. He didn't aim it at anyone, and he didn't know where the bullet went after it was fired. The gun fired accidently, not by design, but as an unintended result of the circumstances. In short, Michael had no intent to shoot the gun, no intent to kill his victim, no intent to save himself from injury. He had no intent at all. The gun fired by accident. This conclusion had two important consequences.

First, Michael could not be found guilty of murder because he lacked the requisite evil intent to kill his victim. His thinking, good or bad, didn't motivate him to pull the trigger. Murderous intent played no role in firing the gun because there was no intent. The gun fired accidentally, unintentionally. Thus, the prosecutor failed to prove the intent requirement of murder, and Michael was innocent of that charge.

Second, Michael couldn't claim self-defense to protect himself from being convicted of crimes other than murder because self-defense is focused tightly on murderous intent in homicide cases. It is an all or nothing defense. If the fatal act is shown to be unintentional, then obviously there was no intent to kill, because there was no intent at all. Hence, there is no need for Michael to show what his intent was because whatever his intent, it played no part in the civtim's death.

OTHER UNLAWFUL HOMICIDES WITHOUT MURDEROUS INTENT

Once the charge of murder, and with it self-defense, is removed from a homicide case, juries are often told to re-examine the facts to determine if the defendant has committed some other crime, involving intent other than murderous intent, such crime usually being some form of man-

slaughter. All states recognize the crime of manslaughter. How they define it varies a bit from state to state, but generally crimes of manslaughter tend to fall into one of two categories: voluntary manslaughter and
involuntary manslaughter.

The crime of voluntary manslaughter involves an intentional act that
results in an unlawful killing, but the intent required for conviction is
something less than malice, hostility, or ill will toward the victim. It is the
intent to perform a violent act, knowingly and deliberately, resulting in
the death of another. The crime often occurs when the defendant is in an
intense, emotional state of mind, caused by some provocation sufficiently
strong to make a reasonable person act impulsively or without reflection.
It is an uncontrollable state of anger, usually referred to as "the heat of
passion,"[5] and is characterized by fits of sudden rage. A bar fight that
escalates out of control, or the spontaneous killing of a spouse's lover are
often cited as examples of voluntary manslaughter. In Michael's case, he
cannot be convicted of voluntary manslaughter because that crime requires an intentional act and Michael didn't pull the pistol's trigger intentionally.

That leaves involuntary manslaughter. Most states define the crime as
an unintentional death produced either by the commission of a minor
crime, or by some act of negligence. The defendant didn't mean to hurt
anyone, but nevertheless the victim's death occurred because of the defendant's actions. Driving a car at excessive speed and killing someone in
an accident, or shooting a gun without knowing who might be in the line
of fire are examples of involuntary manslaughter. In such cases, the defendant will be held criminally accountable for the unlawful death he or
she has caused. New Mexico's manslaughter statute follows this general
approach.[6]

Up until the moment of the shooting, the evidence shows that Michael
did nothing unlawful for which he could be held criminally liable. Possessing a gun is not a crime. Neither is arming oneself in anticipation of a
possible confrontation. Neither is throwing up one's hands to ward off an
expected blow. Hence, Michael is not guilty of involuntary manslaughter
based on the commission of a minor crime.

The only remaining question is whether he somehow acted negligent-
ly, and his negligence caused the death of the man who assaulted him. If
there was no negligence on his part, then the victim's death is considered

an accident: the unintended, unforeseeable, and unavoidable result of lawful and prudent behavior. [7]

So the question is, was Michael negligent? Negligence is the failure to behave as a reasonably prudent person would behave under the circumstances. Juries, as the community's conscience, are given great latitude, based on the facts, to decide what that behavior is. It is a matter of human judgment.

When the incident in Michael's driveway began, he and Sandra were inside the house. The victim was outside, sitting in his car. There were no threats against either Michael or Sandra, no menacing shouts, nothing thrown at the house, no attempt to break in. The car was being operated in a reckless, even dangerous manner, to be sure, but neither Michael nor Sandra appeared to be in any danger as long as they stayed inside the house. Under those circumstances, what would a reasonably prudent person do? Would such a person stay inside the house where it was safe, call the sheriff, and wait for a deputy to arrive, or would a prudent person arm himself, leave his place of safety, and go outside to confront trespassers who were acting strangely?

Reasonable people, reasonable juries, can disagree on the answer to that question. That's one of the risks associated with arming oneself and going to a dangerous place. One jury might see it as reasonable, while another might see it as carelessness. In Michael's case, the jury saw it as carelessness. It believed that Michael was negligent when he armed himself and left the safety of his house to confront the people in his driveway. A produent person would have locked the door, stayed inside, and called the sheriff. Based on that conclusion, it convicted him of involuntary manslaughter.

UNINTENTIONAL HOMICIDE AND SELF-DEFENSE

Across the country and fifty years earlier, a similar case unfolded in Buckingham County, Virginia. It was February 8, 1925 and seventeen-year-old Betty Jefferson was visiting the small farm of her uncle, Millard Jefferson. After lunch, around 1 o'clock, Betty and her cousin, Naomi Taylor, began walking home. They hadn't gone very far when they heard the clop-clop of a shod horse walking on the road behind them. They turned and saw Jeremiah Wilson coming toward them atop an old draft horse. He appeared to have just left Uncle Millard's farm. Betty and Naomi both knew Jeremiah. He was a good-looking young man in his early twenties who did odd jobs from time to time for local farmers. They both waved at him and he waved back.

The old horse caught up with them, and when it did, Jeremiah dismounted, took the reins in one hand, and began walking along beside them. He stayed close to Naomi, chatting her up about a county job he thought he might get in Buckingham, the county seat. He said his chances were pretty good and that if he got the job he would have enough money to buy some land and build a house. He would be quite a catch for some single woman. Naomi was smiling at him and seemed to be enjoying his excitement and his good fortune. That was all right with Betty. She didn't care if Naomi made mooneyes at Jeremiah all day long. He wasn't her cup of tea. She picked up her pace a bit, creating some distance between them, giving them some space to talk alone. She pushed herself along until she could no longer hear their chatter or the clopping of Jeremiah's horse.

"It was a good day for a walk," Betty thought. It was one of those rare winter days when the sun shone bright and the day was pleasantly warm. Winter had taken a step backward as if testing whether the time was right to welcome spring. Betty liked to be outside on such days. The air was cool and crisp, not cold, and she enjoyed walking along the country road. She passed a herd of cows standing in a familiar meadow off to her right, signaling that she'd reached the Brindlemarker Farm, almost half-way home.

The clop-clop of a horse's quickening step brought her thoughts back to Naomi and Jeremiah. She looked behind her and saw Jeremiah urging the old draft horse into a trot in her direction, his elbows flapping like a baby bird testing its wings. When he caught up with her he slowed the horse down and rode along on her left side.

"I heard you talking about the job," Betty said looking up at him. "Do you think you'll get it?" she asked.

"I expect so. They're supposed to tell me next Friday," he said. He took the reins in his left hand, and used his right hand to rub the top of his leg, the one next to Betty, like he had something to say, but was too nervous to say it. "You know, you and I need to become better friends," he said smiling down at her. "After I start this new job, I'm going to be making good money and we could have a lot of fun. We should be together."

"Jeremiah, we're already good friends. What are you talking about?" Betty said. She looked up at him, shielding her eyes with one hand, a visor against the afternoon sun.

"We should be better friends, you know what I mean," he said as he moved his hand from the top of his leg and began massaging his genitals.

Betty stopped walking and looked at him. "Sweet Jesus," she thought. "What's he doing?"

Jeremiah jerked the reins, stopping the horse beside her. "I just think you and I should have some private time together. Nobody has to know," he said, his right hand still between his legs, stimulating himself. He smiled at her. "What do you say?" he asked.

Betty was suddenly very frightened. She didn't know what to say, what to do. Nobody had ever acted that way toward her before. She looked back down the road. Naomi was not far away, walking toward them. Perhaps she could stall him long enough until Naomi got there, or at least within listening range. That would stop him.

"Private time? Well, that's something of a surprise, Jeremiah. I'll have to think about that. What about Naomi? You seemed pretty interested in her about ten minutes ago. Maybe you should have some private time with her?"

"Naomi? Naw, I'm not interested in Naomi. Her old man wouldn't give me no job. I just wanted to tell her I'm getting a better job. I don't need her, and I don't need her old man. Besides she's not my kind of woman."

"Well, what is your kind of woman?" Betty asked.

"You're my kind of woman, Betty. I need your kind of woman."

Jeremiah glanced back in Naomi's direction, measuring whether she was within earshot, and decided she was getting too close. "Let's talk about it later," he said, letting go of himself, and taking the reins in both hands.

"Later then," Betty said, turning to wait for Naomi, thankful Jeremiah had stopped rubbing himself, hoping he would just go away.

When Naomi got close enough to talk without shouting, she said to Jeremiah, "Thanks for catching up with her," as if he had done her a favor. She turned to Betty and continued: "I wanted to talk to you before you left. I forgot to ask. My ma wants to know if you can help next week at our house. She wants to have a birthday party for Uncle Millard. It'll be fun."

"I can certainly do that," Betty answered, putting her arm through Naomi's, walking close to her down the road, eager to be away from Jeremiah, and grateful for the diversion of Uncle Millard's birthday. Jeremiah nudged the horse forward and followed along behind them.

About a half-mile later they came to a fork in the road where the two women would separate, Naomi going to the left, and Betty going to the right.

Jeremiah was still close by, and Betty continued to have her arm through Naomi's. "Why don't I just come along to your house?" she said. "I can talk to your ma about the party." Betty nodded her head in Jeremiah's direction, trying to signal her cousin that she didn't want to be alone with him.

"Oh that's too much trouble," Naomi replied, oblivious to Betty's body language. "It's not going to be that big of a deal, plenty of time to talk about the party before it gets here."

"I really don't mind. Really I don't. I like being outside on days like today and we could visit along the way."

"Well, to be honest Betty, I was looking forward to a quiet walk. I don't ever get any time of my own. My brothers are always pestering me and as soon as I get home, ma will have a thousand things for me to do. I thought I could just relax a bit, enjoy the day alone for a change."

Betty was trapped. She didn't want to offend Naomi, and she didn't want to accuse Jeremiah of anything. He would just deny it and it would be her word against his. She'd been around long enough to know how that would go, particularly if she accused him of sexual misconduct. He would spread rumors about her, say she tried to seduce him, and she wouldn't be believed. She would be embarrassed in front of her friends. So she decided to take her chances.

"Of course, I understand," she said. "All right then. I'll come by tomorrow. Be careful and enjoy your walk home."

"You too," Naomi said.

Betty smiled at Naomi, turned loose her arm, glanced sideways at Jeremiah, and walked away. She took the right fork in the road, and continued on her way home, not looking back, praying that Jeremiah wouldn't follow her. She hadn't gone fifty yards before she heard the clop-clop of his horse behind her. Soon Jeremiah was once again walking along beside her, holding the reins in one hand, his other resting on his thigh nearest her. Betty didn't know what to say, so she decided to keep walking and say nothing. A bend in the road marked the end of the Brindlemarker farm, and she could feel Jeremiah watching her as they approached it. As they rounded the bend, the landscape changed from open farmland to woods. There was a barbed wire fence along the right side of the road. Behind it oak and red maple trees stood packed together, surrounded by thick, tangled underbrush. The ground sloped uphill from the fence and then disappeared, like a rampart guarding the highway. From the road, you couldn't see what was behind the hill.

Jeremiah turned the old horse in front of her, blocking her way. "Betty, let's you and I go into the woods behind that hill," Jeremiah said nodding at the side of the road. It was the first time he'd spoken.

"What for?"

"You know what for," he said, moving his hand between his legs, working it up and down, stimulating himself again. He kept his eyes on her, not smiling, not speaking, waiting for her to answer.

"But I don't want to do that, Jeremiah," she said.

The words were hardly out of her mouth when Jeremiah jumped from the horse and grabbed her by the arm. He held the reins in one hand and started pulling her toward the fence with the other.

"What are you trying to do? Pull me, the horse, and all through the fence?"

"I'm going to tie the horse. And then we're going into the woods."

"I don't reckon we are." She tried to pull away from him.

He dropped the reins, but kept ahold of her arm. Then he reached inside his coat, and pulled out a gun. "Yes, I am," he said, "and if you don't believe I'm going to tie this horse and then do what I say I am, you can take this gun and shoot me." He extended the pistol toward Betty, with the barrel pointed at his chest. "Go ahead, shoot me," he ordered, gesturing for her to take the gun.

Betty's eyes opened wide at the site of the pistol and she started to shake. Tears formed in the corner of her eyes. "Where did you get that gun? I don't know nothing about no guns," she stammered.

"You take this pistol or we go in the woods," he said squeezing her arm, pushing the gun at her. "Make up your mind, girl."

She reached out to take the pistol. Her hand was shaking and she was crying. When she grabbed the gun by its grip, there was a sudden bang, and she almost dropped it. Jeremiah staggered, fell to the ground, blood flowing from his chest.

"Oh, my God, oh, my God! Are you shot?" she cried.

"Yes, I'm hurt bad," he grimaced.

"Oh God, oh God. I didn't mean to, I didn't mean to, Jeremiah. What do you want me to do? I don't know nothing about guns. What do you want me to do with this?" she said holding up the pistol, not wanting it, but too afraid to let go.

"Take it. Go get some help. I need some help."

Betty ran back to the Brindlemarker farm, shouting for Mr. Brindlemarker to help her. The gun was still in her hand. By the time she returned with the owner, Jeremiah Wilson was dead in the road. Betty was charged with first-degree murder. The trial judge found, as a matter of law, that she had killed Jeremiah unintentionally, and based on that conclusion, found her not guilty of the murder charge, because she lacked murderous intent at the time of Jeremiah's death. He then told the jury that it should consider whether she was guilty of involuntary manslaughter. The jury did so, and found Betty guilty of that crime. She was sentenced to two years in jail, and she appealed her conviction. [8]

ELIMINATING SELF-DEFENSE IN HOMICIDE CASES

Virginia's homicide laws, and its view of self-defense, are similar to those in New Mexico. Self-defense is focused on the intent necessary to support a murder conviction, and it's an all or nothing defense. If a gun is fired unintentionally, the shooter's state of mind played no role in its discharge, and hence the shooter cannot claim to have acted in self-defense.

Knowing that based on the facts Betty was unlikely to be convicted of murder, the prosecutor began her trial by conceding that she harbored no malice, hostility, or ill will toward Jeremiah, and that she had not shot him with murderous intent. The trial judge, acknowledging that such being the case, Betty could not be convicted of murder, dismissed the first-degree murder charge, and ruled that her claim of self-defense was no longer part of the case.

The trial continued with the prosecutor arguing that Betty was guilty of involuntary manslaughter, because either she pointed a loaded gun at another person, a misdemeanor under Virginia law, or that she was negligent in taking the pistol from Jeremiah's hand. Betty was unable to tell the jury much about Jeremiah's threatening behavior toward her, or his sexual misconduct on the road, because the trial judge deemed such evidence to be part of her self-defense claim that had been eliminated by her acquittal of murder. Without the context of Jeremiah's behavior, the jury accepted the prosecutor's arguments and found her guilty of involuntary manslaughter.

SELF-DEFENSE AND INVOLUNTARY MANSLAUGHTER BASED ON NEGLIGENT CONDUCT

The appellate court found three problems with Betty's trial. First, the facts didn't support the prosecutor's claim that she had violated Virginia law by pointed a loaded gun at Jeremiah. Betty had not done that. Quite to the contrary, Jeremiah had done it to himself. He was the one who "suddenly drew the pistol from his inside coat pocket, presented it to the accused with the barrel pointed toward him and the handle toward her."[9]

Second, the facts also didn't support the prosecutor's claim that Betty mishandled the pistol when Jeremiah forced it upon her. All they showed was that she grasped the gun by its grip when he insisted she take it. There was no evidence showing how one should grasp a pistol under such circumstances, or what the standard of care might be in such a fact pattern, or what Betty might have done differently to be more careful. In short, there was no evidence to suggest that Betty's actions were somehow contrary to what a reasonably prudent person would do in the same situation. In the absence of such additional proof, the evidence shows that Betty grasped the pistol by its grip when it was handed to her, and such evidence does not support a finding of negligence.

Finally, the appellate courted noted that the standard for judging whether Betty was negligent should have been what a reasonably prudent person would have done if faced with the same situation as she faced. The question of Betty's negligence was to be determined not by what a reasonably prudent woman would do if handed a loaded gun with the barrel pointed at another person, but rather by what a reasonably prudent woman would do if handed a loaded gun with the barrel pointed at the man who was about to rape her. An accurate picture of that situation was not presented to the jury because it never heard about Jeremiah's misbehavior. His misconduct before his death provided important context for what Betty did or failed to do, and should have been part of the evidence presented to the jury about the circumstances in which she was required to act.

The court noted that if Betty had grabbed the gun from Jeremiah and fired it intentionally, she would have been acting in self-defense, because the facts showed that it was reasonable for her to fear that she faced death or serious bodily injury. [10] It stated that reasonably prudent behavior for a woman about to be raped is to grasp a pistol, if offered, and defend herself against unlawful violence. The gun may have fired by accident, but that doesn't change the fact that when she took it, she was acting prudently. The appellate court went on to conclude that, in the final analysis, Jeremiah's death was an accident, the unintended consequence of actions taken by an innocent person. It set aside Betty's conviction and sent her home.

3

PROVOCATION

THE SHOOTER'S BEHAVIOR BEFORE THE FATAL SHOT IS FIRED

Metairie sits between New Orleans and Kenner, Louisiana. It's an unincorporated area of about 160,000 people occupying the south shore of Lake Pontchartrain in Jefferson Parrish. It has no mayor, no city council, in fact no local government at all. If its residents ever decided to organize one, Metairie would be among Louisiana's largest cities, but they never bothered. Most people in Metairie thought local government would mean another layer of taxes and another group of politicians to feed. They were fine with things just the way they were, being a part of Jefferson Parish.

When it comes to taxes, the citizens of Metairie can be a little contrary at times. In 1990, they elected David Duke, a white supremacist and a former grand wizard of the Knights of the Ku Klux Klan, to be one of their two representatives to the Louisiana State Legislature. It wasn't as that they liked what Duke had to offer, as they hated his opponent's proposal to raise property taxes, the current level of county services being about right in their minds. Still, electing a Ku Klux Klan grand wizard to represent them caught peoples' attention, and, for a brief time the national media descended upon Jefferson Parish, set up its cameras, and talked about the Ku Klux Klan, forgetting the property tax issue in favor of suggesting that there was some greater meaning to Duke's victory.

At the center of Metairie is Fat City, a collection of restaurants, clubs, lounges, and other assorted entertainment offerings. It used to be a happening place, hosting crowded happy hours, gregarious bartenders, and many energetic young people. For a time, it competed successfully for the tourist trade with the French Quarter in nearby New Orleans. Then Fat City lost its luster, along with most of its tourists, a casualty of the massage parlor operators and drug pushers who moved in to take advantage of its live and let live lifestyle and the absence of a local police force. Hurricane Katrina came along in 2005 and unleashed its wrath on the area, battering buildings and taking what little was left of the tourism industry.

Like all urban areas, Fat City has its share of all-night mini-marts, catering to the grab and go crowd, accommodating people with no time or inclination to shop while the sun shines. It was about 4 o'clock in the morning on Friday, October 29, 1993, and Fat City was shutting down for the night. Jose Ibanez drove his Toyota Corolla into the parking lot of an all-night mini-mart and parked it in an empty space facing the building. Carlos Rodrigues was in the front passenger seat. Stacey Parker, Jennifer Baislain, and Alano Gomez were sitting in the backseat. Parked two spaces over, on the left of Jose's car, two women sat in a Ford Bronco eating snacks and listening to the radio. Carlos got out of the front seat and Stacey got out of the back, and the two went into the mini-mart to use the facilities and buy beer. Jose got out from behind the wheel and walked over to chat up the two women in the Bronco. Alano and Jennifer stayed in the backseat, talking.

Shortly thereafter, Charlie Taylor drove into the parking lot in a brand new two-door, blue Buick Regal Gran Sport. He pulled into the empty parking space on the right side of the Toyota. Tony Noles was in the front, sitting with Charlie. Kyle Keiler sat in the backseat behind Tony, and Daniel Vasquez sat next to him behind Charlie. Tony opened his door, leaned into the dash, and pulled the back of his seat forward, giving Kyle room to exit the two-door car. Kyle bent his way out of the backseat and went into the store, also to buy beer.

In the back of Jose's car, Alano Gomez decided he'd been sitting in the car too long and needed to get out, stretch his legs, and walk around. He pulled the door latch and hit the back door with his shoulder, unintentionally hitting it a bit too hard. The door shot open. Alano grabbed for the armrest, missed it, and winced as the door struck the side of Charlie's Buick with a loud thud.

Sitting behind the wheel, Charlie heard and felt the impact of the Toyota's door striking his car.

"Aw, shit," he said, turning his head and opening the driver's door. He got out of his car, took a couple of steps toward the back, and looked down. There, on the rear quarter panel of his brand new Gran Sport was a very noticeable dimple where the Toyota's door had jammed it, gouging away some of the paint, exposing shiny metal underneath.

"What the hell you doing, man? You just dented my car," Charlie said, looking up at Alano, who was now half way out the back door of Jose's car.

"I'm sorry, man. I didn't mean it. The door just slipped out of my hand," Alano replied.

"I don't care if you didn't mean it. I still got a dent in my car. So what now? You say you're sorry and walk away?"

Tony Noles, hearing the exchange between Charlie and Alano, got out of Charlie's car, closed the door, and stood near the front fender where he could see both Charlie and Alano. He made no move to intervene, didn't say anything, just stood there, arms folded, watching the argument. Daniel Vasquez stayed where he was in Charlie's backseat.

Inside the store, Kyle Keiler glanced out the window and saw his friend Charlie pointing at the side of his car and talking to someone from the car next to it. He looked upset and very angry. Kyle decided to find out what was going on. He left the store and walked between the two cars toward the two men.

"What's up?" he asked.

"This guy just jammed the crap out of my car," Charlie said pointing at the dent. "Look at it."

Kyle stepped past Charlie, moved the Toyota's back door to get by, bent down, looked at the ding, straightened up, looked at Charlie, shook his head, and looked at Alano.

"So what're you going to do to fix the man's car?" he asked.

"It was an accident," Alano said. "I didn't mean it. The door slipped. It's just a scratch. The insurance will cover it. If not, I'll pay to get it fixed."

"Good answer," Kyle said. "But we ain't interested in hassling with an insurance company. The man wants his car fixed. You need to fix it. How much money you got?"

"I don't have much cash, man."

"Well then, I think you got a problem. Let's be clear. I don't give a shit if you got it, or your friends got it, or where you get it, but if I don't see some money real quick to fix the man's car, I'm going to kick the shit out of you and your friends. Five hundred should do it." Kyle looked at Charlie. "You think five hundred will do it, Charlie?"

"Yea, that'll probably do it," Charlie said.

"Five hundred it is. OK fella," Kyle said turning back to Alano. "What's it gonna be? One way or the other you're going to pay. You can give him the money to fix his car or you can get your ass kicked."

"I haven't got five hundred dollars," Alano said.

"That's it," Kyle shouted, slamming Alano in the chest with both hands, pushing him through the Toyota's open door, banging his head against the car's roof as he fell onto the backseat. Kyle leaned through the door, cocked his right arm, and reaching with his left, tried to pull Alano from the car. Alano threw up his hands and leaned further into the car, trying to keep away from Kyle's fist. Kyle got a hold of Alano's leg and began dragging him out of the car. Alano grabbed Jennifer's arm and she held on to keep him from sliding across the seat. She began screaming, "Stop it, stop it, someone help us."

Jose, standing by the Bronco, talking with the two women inside it, heard Jennifer's scream. He looked over toward his car and saw a very big man on its far side, bent over, reaching into the backseat and swearing. Alano was leaning against Jennifer and kicking at him.

Jose recognized the man, had seen him in the bars around town, knew his name was Kyle. He'd been in the bar where they'd met Jennifer and Stacey earlier that evening. Kyle was somebody to avoid, a mean man, with a quick temper and a bad reputation, a tough man who liked to fight. There was a story that he'd fought with two police officers and was having the better of it until one of them hit him in the face with a billy club. Kyle was nobody to mess with.

Jose saw another man standing between the two cars. He was holding the Toyota's back door open, egging Kyle on, and yelling at Alano. He wasn't as big as Kyle, but he was still bigger than Alano. A third man was standing on the other side of the blue car parked next to his. Jose thought the blue car was probably Kyle's. The man stood there, arms crossed, watching. Jose couldn't see how big he was, but he seemed ready to join the fight. A fourth man was sitting inside the blue car. He was watching through the backseat window.

Jose's chest tightened. He knew he and Alano and Carlos were no match for these guys. There were four of them: bigger, heavier, meaner. If the others were anything like Kyle, someone was going to get really hurt, and it was likely going to be him or one of his friends. He ran toward his car.

"Get away from me," Alano screamed, kicking at Kyle with his free leg, holding onto Jennifer's arm, trying to keep from being pulled out of the car. "Jose, help," he yelled.

"Leave him alone. Leave him alone. Go away," Jennifer screamed.

Kyle seemed unfazed by the yelling. He batted away Alano's attempt to kick him, swore loudly, and pushed himself further into the car. He grabbed the front of Alano's shirt with both hands and started to pull. Charlie was behind him holding open the car door. "Get him," he shouted.

"You son of a bitch," Kyle growled, striking at Alano's face with his fist. His size and the car's small backseat made it hard for him to maneuver. He couldn't get much power into his punches, but he had the upper hand, and he could tell that Alano was weakening.

Carlos and Stacey were still inside the store. Seeing the fight break out in the parking lot, Carlos abandoned their beer at the counter and dashed out the door to help his friend. He ran between the two cars and hit the Toyota's open back door with his shoulder, breaking it free from Charlie's grip, and slamming it into Kyle's side, causing him to let go of Alano. The blow surprised Kyle and diverted his attention, but it didn't do much damage. Kyle backed out of the Toyota, stepped around the door, pushed Charlie out of the way, and grabbed Carlos. Holding the smaller man with one hand, he hit him several times in the face with the other, his arm pumping as fast as he could make it go. Thump, thump, thump, thump, thump.

Jose, who was almost to the side of his car, saw Kyle's rapid fire punches hit Carlos's face, could hear the sound of his fists striking flesh and bone. Carlos tried to defend himself, but the blows were too powerful and came too fast. There was a loud crack as Kyle's fist landed near Carlos's eye. Kyle let go of him and Carlos fell to the ground. As Jose yanked open the Toyota's front door, he could see Kyle begin kicking at his friend.

Jose reached under the driver's seat and grabbed a 9 mm semi-automatic pistol, equipped with laser sights. Gun in hand, he looked through the passenger side window and saw Kyle still kicking at Carlos on the ground. He backed out of the door, stood up, leaned over the Toyota's roof, and fired the pistol at Kyle.

The gunshot froze everyone in place. Kyle startled, then realized quickly what it was, and like prey sensing the predator, turned and ran for his life, jumping over Carlos and sprinting between the two cars toward the front of the store. Charlie ran after him. Tony Noles, who was still standing on the other side of Charlie's car, ducked down at the sound of the gunfire, then he too ran toward the store. Kyle and Charlie made it to the curb, turned right, and raced down the sidewalk toward the corner of the mini-mart. Tony joined them as they ran past him in the front of Charlie's car.

Jose steadied his arms on the roof of his car and fired again at the three fleeing men. Kyle felt the bullet hit him in the back, cried out, staggered, regained his balance, and kept on running. Jose fired again when they were almost to the corner. This time Tony Noles screamed and staggered, also hit in the back, but he too kept moving. All three of the men made it around the corner of the store.

Jose was terrified. He wasn't sure if he'd hit anyone. Three of the attackers had gotten away. His first thought was that they would be back, with guns. Kyle would be armed for sure, and if he had a gun the others probably did too. Then it would be three against one and he would likely die.

He saw movement coming from the blue car out of the corner of his eye. Looking in that direction, he saw the last man, Daniel Vasquez, trying to get out of the car. Daniel was in the back seat, leaning forward, pushing against the back of the front seat and reaching for the driver's door handle. The door opened and Daniel bent his way out of the car. He stood up, looked at Jose, his eyes widened, and he reached for something in his pocket. Jose, still standing behind the Toyota, pointed the pistol at him and fired twice. Daniel staggered backward, like he'd suddenly lost his balance. He half sat, half fell onto the driver's seat. He pulled up his legs, turned his body into the car, and closed the door. He started the car, shifted it into reverse, and pushed the gas pedal to the floor. The engine roared, the tires screeched, and the car shot backward a short distance across the parking lot before crashing into the store's gas pumps. There it stopped. Daniel reached down, turned off the engine, sat back in the seat, and died.

By now, Jose was so afraid he was having trouble breathing. He ran around the front of the car and found Carlos curled up on the pavement bleeding heavily from cuts on his face. One of his eyes was swollen shut. He helped Carlos to his feet, opened the Toyota's passenger door, got him onto the front seat, and closed the door. Carlos leaned his head back against the headrest and moaned. Jennifer and Alano were still in the backseat. Alano reached out and closed the back door. Jose jumped behind the wheel and started the car.

Jose looked up and saw Stacy Parker standing on the sidewalk in front of his car. "Let's go," he shouted at her, but she was paralyzed by fear, terrified by what she'd just seen, and just stood there staring back at him. Jose didn't wait. He put the car in gear, backed out of the parking space, and left the mini-mart. He drove east toward New Orleans. Not far from the store there was a small bridge that crossed a creek, and as he approached it, he could see that there were bushes on either side of the stream.

"Here, get rid of this," Jose said, handing the gun to Carlos, who rolled down the window and tossed it out of the car as they drove across the bridge.

Back at the mini-mart, someone called the sheriff's office and gave the dispatcher Jose's license plate number and a description of the Toyota. A short time later, Jefferson County sheriffs pulled him over and arrested everyone in the car. Jose cooperated fully, describing the incident and leading deputies back to the bridge where they found the gun.

Altogether, seven shots had been fired at the mini-mart. Two of them struck Daniel Vasquez. Each of the bullets passed through his left arm and penetrated his chest where they caused serious internal damage and bleeding. Daniel never made it out of the car after hitting the gas pumps. One shot hit Kyle Keiler in the back and one shot hit Tony Noles in the back. Both men recovered from their wounds. The other three shots were lost.

Jose told the police, "The fourth man got out of the car. He put his hand in his pocket. I was scared because ... you know they're in their car and I'm in my car. I carry a gun. I don't know if they carry a gun, you understand? He reached into his pocket, I was scared, you understand?"

A grand jury indicted Jose on one count of first-degree murder and two counts of attempted first-degree murder. He claimed that he acted in self-defense. [1]

INNOCENT VICTIM OR PROVOCATEUR?

A person who misbehaves in any way may not later claim that he acted in self-defense if he kills an adversary, even if it is to save himself or herself from death or serious injury. Put another way, a person who provokes a confrontation, prolongs an encounter, or contributes to the circumstances that lead to another person's death may not later claim the killing was necessary. The law holds people who misbehave accountable and denies them the right of self-defense because it assumes that had the misbehavior not occurred, the encounter would never have escalated to the point where it became deadly. In short, a shooter's misbehavior before or during a confrontation makes him or her at least partially responsible for the other person's death. With forfeiture of the right of self-defense at stake, a key issue in every self-defense case is whether the shooter was innocent or whether he or she somehow misbehaved before the final fatal act.

Misbehavior by a shooter and self-defense are incompatible, mutually exclusive. Deciding a self-defense claim is as much about judging what the shooter did as it is about judging what the victim did. Was the shooter's behavior leading up to the fatal act good or was it bad? Good behavior makes it less likely that deadly force will be used. It is behavior that sidesteps potential arguments, de-escalates confrontations, walks away from hostile encounters. It is behavior that suggests the shooter is innocent and wishes to avoid the confrontation.

Bad behavior, on the other hand, makes it more likely that deadly force will be used. Bad behavior starts arguments or prolongs them. It escalates confrontations and contributes to the buildup of hostile encounters. It inflames emotions, makes people hostile, and pushes them toward violence. Like good behavior, bad behavior can be anything, limited only by the range of how human beings might behave under enormous stress and by how third party observers, police, prosecutors, judges, and juries might feel later about their conduct. Bad behavior makes the shooter at least partially at fault for the victim's death because it makes it more likely that someone will be killed.

To illustrate how the law holds people accountable for bad behavior, suppose a man starts a fistfight with a stranger that soon escalates out of control. The stranger gets the upper hand, draws a knife, and is about to stab his assailant. Fearing for his life, the man draws a pistol and kills the stranger. The prosecutor charges the man with murder, and at his trial the man claims he acted in self-defense. He argues that he shot the stranger to keep from being stabbed because he was afraid of being killed. The jury accepts his testimony and believes that he held no malice, hostility, or ill will toward the stranger when he pulled the trigger, that his intent when he shot the stranger was not murderous, but rather a desire to save himself from death or serious bodily injury. The jury also believes the shooter behaved badly by starting the fight. So how does the case end?

The shooter's intent, why he pulled the trigger, is very important. He didn't shoot the stranger because he wanted to kill him. He wasn't motivated by malice, hostility, or ill will. He shot because he was trying to avoid being injured or killed, to stop a deadly attack. As we have seen, under these circumstances the shooter is not guilty of murder because he didn't have the requisite murderous intent for that crime. He didn't shoot the victim to kill him. He shot to save himself. At the same time, the shooter started the fistfight, his behavior was bad, and he is at least partially at fault for the victim's death. There are several possible outcomes that will prevent him from benefiting from his misconduct.

One possible outcome is the jury believes that when the shooter saw the stranger pull a knife, he became furious, lost his normal capacity for self-control, was unable to keep himself from lashing out, and killed the stranger "in the heat of passion." If such is the case, the shooter performed an intentional act that resulted in another person's death and is guilty of voluntary manslaughter for killing the stranger in a fit of sudden rage.

Another possible outcome is that the jury understands the man did not intend to kill the stranger, but believes that the killing occurred while the man was misbehaving in a way that amounted to some minor criminal offense. For example, the jury finds that in starting the fight, the man assaulted the stranger in violation of a misdemeanor assault statute. If that were the case, the man would be guilty of involuntary manslaughter.

Still another possible outcome is that the jury felt there was no minor crime involved but that the shooter's misbehavior was negligent in some way, and that his negligence contributed to the victim's death. That too would lead to a conviction for involuntary manslaughter.

A compromise has been struck. The man has been found not guilty of murder, a very serious crime with a long prison term, because he lacked murderous intent at the time of the killing but at the same time he is still held criminally liable for the stranger's death and will be punished for his part in causing it, albeit with a shorter jail sentence.

The point is that even though a jury may believe a shooter killed his assailant to save himself, if the shooter has also somehow misbehaved as part of the incident, then self-defense is taken off the table, becomes unavailable to the shooter, and exposes him or her to criminal liability for the misbehavior.[2] And that is true even if the facts show clearly that as the fight progressed the assailant was about to kill or seriously injure the shooter. Pleading self-defense is simply not an option for those who misbehave during the time leading up to the killing.

An important point to remember is that the shooter's bad behavior doesn't have to be the precipitating or penultimate event in a deadly encounter for it to prevent a claim of self-defense. In other words, it doesn't have to initiate the confrontation and it doesn't have to be the last thing before the fatal shot is fired. It can be remote behavior, not close in time or proximity to the fatal act, so long as it contributes, however minimally, to the escalation toward violence.[3] We will look at this issue of remote behavior in chapter 7.

EXAMPLES OF MISBEHAVIOR

Bad behavior can occur when a person acts in accordance with his or her moral or religious beliefs. Assertions of religious authority, such as an "eye for an eye,"[4] or claims of redress for wrongs inflicted, do not justify bad behavior. If you punch a loudmouth who cursed your spouse and end up killing him in the ensuing melee, you don't get to claim self-defense to save yourself. Your behavior will be judged by what the law says is permissible, not by what you believe is moral, or by what your religion says is the word of God, or by what you believe are good manners. To repeat, if you start a fight, or persist in an argument when you can walk away safely, or contribute to the circumstances that ultimately lead to someone else being killed, you have misbehaved, and regardless of how morally right you may think you are, you will not be given the benefit of claiming self-defense to avoid punishment.[5] Simply put, you may not "take the law into your own hands" and claim moral or religious beliefs to justify someone else being killed.

Bad behavior is usually thought of as doing something you shouldn't do, of crossing some line separating right from wrong, of doing something offensive to others. But what if the person killed consents to your bad behavior? Verbal disagreements that lead to the famous "let's settle this in the parking lot" challenge are all too common, and on occasion they escalate into life and death struggles in which one of the combatants is killed. Such contests are known as "mutual combat"; both parties having indicated their intent and willingness to engage in fisticuffs. The agreement, a shared readiness to assume the risk of injury, each party believing he or she will emerge unscathed from the battle, changes nothing. If someone dies, the spotlight will focus tightly on the survivor's behavior prior to the fatal act. Was the shooter compelled to fight, is it really reasonable for two people to settle their differences by going into a parking lot, or anywhere else for that matter, to engage in some form of mutually agreed to violence, is it OK for one person to kill another because the other agreed to the risk, is trial by combat a social policy the law wishes to promote? In short, was the killing really necessary? The answer to all of these questions is a resounding no. The law will not permit one to avoid the consequences of murder by asserting the dead person agreed to it. If it did, every murderer would claim his victim agreed to the risk and consented to his or her own destruction. "Mutual combat" is considered bad behavior everywhere and provides no justification for killing anyone.[6] People may not make up their own rules about life and death.

BERNIE GOETZ, NEW YORK'S SUBWAY VIGILANTE

Is breaking the law automatically bad behavior? Not when it comes to self-defense. Bernard Goetz, New York City's famous "subway vigilante," offers a case in point. In 1981, Goetz suffered a permanent knee injury when muggers attacked him in a New York City subway car. When Goetz got out of the hospital he applied for a concealed carry permit and the city turned him down. Undeterred, he purchased a .38 caliber revolver, and began carrying it with him back and forth to work, in violation of the city's ordinance. Three years later, on December 22, 1984, Goetz entered a nearly empty New York City subway car, his revolver in his pocket.

As the train sped along under the city's streets, four young men approached Goetz demanding money. Goetz refused, words were exchanged, and one of the young men reached for a weapon. Goetz drew his revolver and shot all four men. Manhattan prosecutors charged him with four counts of attempted murder, four counts of assault, four counts of reckless endangerment, and one count of criminal possession of a firearm. Goetz claimed self-defense. The case became a symbol of New York City's lawlessness, and Goetz became a hero to some, as a person who tried to fight back, and a villain to others, a violent vigilante who took the law into his own hands. At his trial, the jury accepted Goetz's claim of self-defense, found him "not guilty" of all charges except carrying a loaded, unlicensed weapon in a public place.[7] The judge sentenced him to eight months in jail.

There is no question that Goetz behaved badly. His carrying a concealed handgun was a clear violation of the city's ordinance. So why wasn't he disqualified from claiming self-defense? The answer lies in how the law views bad behavior in the context of self-defense cases.

Not every bad behavior triggers the forfeiture of a self-defense claim. Remember, a misbehaving shooter forfeits his or her right of self-defense because the law assumes that if the misbehavior had not occurred the confrontation would not have escalated into a deadly encounter. But it is a different story if it is clear that the misbehavior would have made no difference in how the situation escalated into a deadly shooting. There must be some nexus, some cause and effect relationship, between the bad behavior and the subsequent shooting for the law to attribute some fault to the shooter because of it. If no such connection exists, then the shooter's bad behavior doesn't matter. Thus bad behaviors that are connected somehow to the confrontation, behaviors that promote, prolong, or contribute to the encounter, leading to the victim's death, count. Other bad behaviors don't count.

Another way to look at it is to ask whether the shooter's bad behavior was part of the interactions between the shooter and the victim, the verbal back and forth that preceded the shooting, the shouting, the pushing, the threatening behavior. If it wasn't part of that point-counterpoint confrontation leading up to the killing, contributing somehow to its escalation, moving the participants toward physical violence, then it's irrelevant. It doesn't matter because it played no role in the circumstances that made it necessary for the shooter to use deadly force to protect himself or herself against a threat of death or serious injury. [8]

Bernie Goetz's misbehavior in carrying a concealed handgun in violation of New York City's ordinance had nothing to do with the decision of four would-be muggers to rob him. It wasn't part of the back and forth between Goetz and them. It didn't cause the four men to demand money, wasn't the reason they threatened to attack Goetz if he didn't hand it over, didn't trigger one of them to reach for a weapon. It just wasn't part of the confrontation until the very end, when Goetz had to choose between the use of deadly force and his own death or injury. The jury found he was justified in choosing deadly force, regardless of how he came to possess it.

Some would argue that if Goetz hadn't broken the law by carrying a gun, the shooting wouldn't have happened and in some sense that's true, but the argument is legally and logically inconsistent. It makes little sense to use a statutory violation to prevent a person from making his or her self-defense case to a jury unless the violation helped to produce the confrontation. If a person's circumstances are so extreme that he or she may ignore laws against killing, then surely they are extreme enough to allow the person to ignore laws of lesser importance. Without some nexus between the violation and the confrontation, minor statutory violations would end up promoting injustice. For example, there are city ordinances against eating food on the subway. Should the violation of such an ordinance prevent a person in Goetz's situation from claiming self-defense because he was eating a ham sandwich when the four thugs approached him? Of course not.

POOR JUDGMENT

Misbehavior can include poor judgment as well as physical acts. Suppose a man named Jim awakens in bed in the middle of the night to the sound of someone downstairs, inside his house. He reaches out and touches his wife. She is still asleep beside him. He gets up, looks into his son's bedroom, and finds the boy is in his bed, also asleep. Jim hears the noise again and his adrenaline kicks in. The neighborhood has experienced a rash of recent break-ins; one homeowner was beaten and property was stolen. Jim goes back into his bedroom and retrieves his pistol. He hears the noise again, this time in the dining room, right beneath his bedroom. He racks back the pistol's slide and lets it go, chambering a round, the sound incredibly loud in the still night, but Jim doesn't care. He hopes the intruder will hear it and run away.

The gun in front of him, his arms extended, the safety off, Jim leaves the bedroom and moves carefully down the stairs to the first floor. It is dark, but the streetlights are shining through the living room windows helping him see what might be there. The hallway at the bottom of the stairs runs straight from the front door to the back of the house where it ends in the kitchen. Jim looks across the hallway into the living room, walks softly toward it knowing where to step, avoiding noisy spots in the floor. He enters the living room, sweeping the gun, first to his left then to his right, looking for anyone, searching the shadows. No one is there.

On his left is an archway leading to the dining room, the table and chairs sitting silently in the gloom, the streetlights barely reaching them. Jim leans against the wall near the archway. He peeks around the corner, the gun still in both hands, extended toward the floor. At the back of the dining room a door connects it to the hallway, one step into the hallway, turn right and one step into the kitchen. Jim can see only part of the kitchen's interior. He moves around the dining room table toward the kitchen door, his heart racing, his breathing labored, audible.

He leans into the hallway and looks into the kitchen. It's empty, but the back door is open, a night breeze gently rocking it back and forth. It seems deathly quiet as if the house is waiting, watching, anticipating. Jim wonders how they got the back door open, defeating the deadbolt, doing it quietly without breaking anything. Softly he closes the door and locks it. He begins to relax, the pistol in hand now points at the floor. "They're gone," he thinks, locked out of the house. Suddenly another thought comes, "maybe they're not gone, maybe he's just locked them inside!"

Gun back up, both hands in front of him, Jim looks down the hallway leading to the front door. He needs to make sure whoever it was didn't avoid him by moving farther into the house by walking down the hallway while he was checking the living room. He leaves the kitchen and walks slowly, quietly, down the hallway toward the bottom of the stairs. He moves the gun upward, covering the stairs as they come into view. He reaches the bottom, looks up to the second floor where his wife and son are, his back to the living room.

Suddenly, there's a rushing sound from behind him, the sound of footsteps on the rug! Turning, Jim sees a figure coming at him from the living room. Quickly, he points the gun and fires twice. The figure cries ou and then falls to the floor. Jim moves to the figure lying on his rug, covering it with his pistol. Looking down he sees his wife in her bathrobe, a pool of blood already forming beneath her. By the time the ambulance gets there, she is dead.

The prosecutor charged Jim with murder. The police determined an intruder had entered his house but they never found out who it was. Jim genuinely feared for his life. He had reasons to be afraid, the neighborhood's crime problem, the noise awakening him in the night, finding his back door open, a burglar in his home. Once he realized someone was coming at him from the living room, he had almost no time to think about who it was, about what the threat might be, or about what he should do.

Had the figure moving toward him in the dark been a stranger, a burglar, no one would have questioned his actions, but it wasn't, it was his wife, in her bathrobe. She must have heard him get up, or perhaps was awakened by the sound of the round being chambered into his pistol, and followed him downstairs. Unless one assumes Jim intended to kill her, which he didn't, he obviously shot before he realized who she was. What does that mean?

One thing it could mean is that Jim was careless by shooting his gun not knowing the threat and not knowing the target. By pulling the trigger too quickly, he condemned to death his wife, an innocent woman who had done nothing wrong. The jury believed his behavior was unreasonable and negligent under the circumstances. Its conclusion extinguished his right of self-defense and Jim was convicted of manslaughter.[9] In the final analysis, he used poor judgment, and because of that he killed someone when it wasn't necessary.

GOOD BEHAVIOR BECOMES MISBEHAVIOR

This brings us back to the case of Jose Ibanez and the convenience store shooting in Fat City. The case turned on whether Jose behaved badly in response to the attack by Kyle Keiler. Jose fired three times, seven shots in all. The first time, he fired one shot at Kyle, when Kyle was kicking Carlos, a shot that missed. It stopped the beating at a time when Carlos was hurt, on the ground, defeated, defenseless, and vulnerable. The facts support a reasonable belief, and hence a reasonable fear, that Carlos was about to be killed or seriously injured. They also support a conclusion that when Jose shot at Kyle, his intent was to prevent his friend from being hurt or killed. Had he been charged with attempted murder for this shot, it seems likely the jury would have accepted his claim of self-defense and found him not guilty.

The second time Jose fired is problematic. He shot four times from behind his car, at the backs of Kyle, Charlie, and Tony, as they were running away, trying to escape. Carlos was no longer in any danger and Jose was safe, his car a barrier protecting him against possible attack. The danger had passed yet Jose rested his arms on the Toyota's roof, took careful aim, and fired four times at the three fleeing men, hitting both Kyle and Tony. Was the light switch still on? Were these shots really necessary? Not based on the facts. The confrontation was over.

The third time Jose fired he shot Daniel Vasquez twice in the chest, afraid he was reaching for a gun, one hand in his pocket, as he was getting out of Charlie's car. The two shots killed him, both bullets piercing his heart. When Daniel died, Kyle, Charlie, and Tony were gone, having fled behind the mini-mart. Daniel's behavior, his reaching into his pocket, is what is known as a furtive gesture and will be discussed later. Suffice it to say for now that when Jose shot him, he had no idea what might be in Daniel's pocket, and it is clear that Daniel had not participated in the fight. Under those circumstances was it necessary to shoot him? Again, based on the facts, the answer is no.

The jury concluded that Jose had misbehaved when he fired the second set of shots at the three fleeing men and the third set of shots at Daniel. He had prolonged a confrontation that was over and done, the men he was aiming at no longer dangerous to him or to anyone else.

Jose's bad behavior forfeited his right to claim self-defense, leaving the jury to ponder whether he was guilty of murder or of some other crime. It concluded that he feared for his life and the life of his friend Carlos when he fired the first time at Kyle. His intent when he fired that shot was not to kill Kyle but to save Carlos. But then he became enraged by the thought of Carlos being beaten, at the sound of the bones in his friend's face being broken, and unable to control himself, he seized the gun in a fit of anger and shot at those responsible for hurting Carlos. He shot at the three fleeing men and at Daniel "in the heat of passion." The jury found him guilty of one count of manslaughter and two counts of attempted manslaughter. The judge sentenced him to fifteen years in jail.

ALCOHOL AND SELF-DEFENSE

One final note about the presence of alcohol and shootings. While alcohol and guns are never a good mix, it is fair to say that if misbehavior and self-defense are incompatible, the presence of alcohol in a shooter's system at the time someone is killed is usually toxic to the shooter. Juries understand instinctively that decisions concerning the necessity to kill must come from the workings of a clear mind, not a cloudy one, and alcohol impairs one's judgment. Self-defense cases involving a shooter who has consumed alcohol are in remarkable alignment. Shooters with alcohol in their systems are punished invariably for misbehavior, regardless of whether they're found to be "legally drunk." The old adage, "if you drink, don't drive," applies in spades to self-defense claims. If you drink, don't carry a gun, and if you carry a gun, don't drink. If you do and someone dies, count on going to jail.

4

DEADLY THREATS

FISTFIGHTS GONE BAD

Mike Brighton lived in Meridian, Mississippi, for most of his fifty-two years. He was a slight man, worked hard, took care of his family, paid his debts, and generally got along well with everybody. He tried to enlist in the Navy when World War II came but the Navy wouldn't have him. He was a railroad worker and railroad workers get hurt. A couple of years before Pearl Harbor, working at the rail yard, he cut off three fingers on his right hand leaving just his thumb and forefinger. Mike thought he could do with his thumb and forefinger just about what anybody else could do with their entire hand, but the Navy didn't see it that way. He was classified IV-F, physically unfit for military service, and went back to work on the railroad, consoling himself that every day he helped the war effort by making the trains run on time.

Occasionally after supper, Mike would take a drive around Meridian, see what was going on, talk to friends, maybe stop and get a cup of coffee. The caffeine didn't bother him. He slept like a baby. Sometimes he just sat by himself in one of the local restaurants, his cup of coffee untouched in front of him, thinking about things, trying to figure it all out. He claimed the quiet time helped to keep him focused. What he was focused on, he never said.

October is a good time of the year in Meridian. Summer has turned off the heat, and autumn breezes blow in from the northwest announcing the approach of winter, or at least what passes for winter in Mississippi. Days

are warm and nights cool. The evening of October 10, 1942, was a bell
ringer. The sky was clear, a gentle breeze blowing, no humidity, and the
temperature was holding steady at about 65 degrees. Mike thought it
didn't get any better than that, and after supper he decided to take a short
drive into town just to see what was going on before calling it a day. He
got into his pickup truck and headed east on 8th Street, going nowhere in
particular, wondering who might be out and about, not expecting much,
the stores all being closed at that hour. Mike was proud of his pickup,
because it was one of the last ones delivered before the plant stopped
making them before converting from civilian production to supporting
the war.

Around 10:00 p.m. he found himself on Front Street, headed west,
back toward home. In the distance he could see The Crossing Café, lit up
as usual, summoning the railroad's night crews with promises of good
coffee, hot apple pie, a scoop of vanilla ice cream. He decided to stop for
coffee, see who might be there, maybe catch Jake O'Donnell. Jake could
be found at the counter, more often than not, chatting up whoever might
be available, whoever had the time to listen. Jake thought himself a real
Irishman, spoke with a brogue, praised the old country, damned anything
British, and ignored the fact he was born in Meridian and had never lived
anywhere else. He had an Irish last name, but not much else to do with
Ireland. Everyone knew that most of what Jake said was malarkey, but it
didn't matter. He was clever with words, had a good heart, and was
always ready at the drop of a hat to discuss his latest drama, usually
involving women, local politics, or both. An encounter with Jake was
always worth the price of admission, leaving Mike shaking his head,
grinning from ear to ear. So when Mike saw a spot right in front of the
restaurant he grabbed it, parked the pickup, and went looking for Jake.

The Crossing Café had two dining areas. In the front, near the entrance, was a lunch counter, a typical affair, like most small town diners.
The counter ran down the left side of the room. A line of stools stood in
front of it, fixed to the floor, like sentries guarding access to the food
supply. Behind the counter, against the wall, were shelves filled with
cigarettes, coffee pots, cups and saucers, plates of pastries, and all the
tools of the restaurant business. There was a large opening in the wall
exposing the kitchen behind it and a shelf upon which the cooks placed
orders of food for the waitresses to pick up and deliver to customers.
Service at the counter was designed for busy railroad men: get in, grab a

quick bite to eat, get out, get back to work. A corridor extended the length of the room between the counter and the outer wall forming a passageway to the back of the restaurant. There were hooks on he wall for people sitting at the counter to hang their coats on. In the back there was a dining room, with tables and chairs, a place for people who weren't in a rush, who had the time to enjoy a more leisurely meal.

Mike walked along the corridor looking for Jake until he reached the dining room. Despite the late hour, there were still quite a few people sitting and talking at tables strewn with half-filled coffee cups and messy dessert dishes. Mike couldn't see Jake but he decided to stay anyway. He turned around, walked a few steps back along the counter, picked out a stool, and sat down.

"Jake, around?" he asked Molly, a short, plump waitress who came to take his order.

"Haven't seen him. Probably won't. Saturday night, you know."

"Something going on?"

"Nah, not really. Jake doesn't come in a lot on Saturday. Got lots of business to attend to," she said with a laugh.

Mike smiled. "Yea, he's a busy man, alright. I wonder what he's up to?," he asked.

"Winnie Brown, I hear. What would you like?"

"Really? Hadn't heard that. That should be good. A cup of coffee, please."

"It will be," she smiled. "That it?"

"That's it."

"You got it," she said turning away and heading to a stack of white coffee mugs on the shelf behind the counter.

Bobby Randall was also out riding around in his car that night. Janice Newcomb and Della Ronkowski were with him. The ride was a treat for Janice and Della, not everyone could get gas for joy rides with the war on, but Bobby could. He was thirty-two years old, tall, muscular, good-looking, a strapping fellow, who worked hard and played hard. He was known for being a little hot-headed. If Bobby lost his temper he could brawl with the best of them. He and Mike had been friends until recently. Mike lent Bobby some money, helped him get a business started delivering firewood in town. Bobby's business did pretty well, but when Mike asked him to pay the money back, Bobby could never quite get around to it, became too busy to answer Mike's phone calls, or his letters. Finally,

Mike got sick of asking and sued Bobby for the money. The case was still pending before the local court. It had destroyed their friendship.

Bobby was heading west on Front Street when he passed Mike's truck parked near the curb in front of The Crossing Café. Spotting the truck, he turned around immediately and drove back to the diner.

"How about a cup of coffee, ladies," Bobby said.

"Sounds swell to me. What about you, Della?" Janice answered.

"Great, let's go," Della said.

Bobby found a spot across the street from the diner and parked the car. He and the two women got out and headed across the street.

Inside, Mike was enjoying his coffee, thinking about Jake and Winnie Brown. He smiled to himself again. Winnie was level-headed, a no-nonsense woman. Jake, on the other hand . . . well, Mike wouldn't describe him quite that way. He wondered how long the two of them would last. He paid no attention to the tiny bell over the front door announcing the arrival of another customer. Then he heard Bobby Randall's voice.

"Let's sit at a table, ladies."

Mike glanced up and saw Bobby with two women moving in his direction. He turned quickly back to his coffee, took a drink from his mug, no sense trying to talk to Bobby now, he thought, wrong time, wrong place.

Janice and Della led the way along the counter, down the corridor toward the dining room in back. Bobby trailed behind. The two women chatted about work, the war having given them chances to do things they'd never done before. Bobby said nothing. Mike didn't look up as Janice and Della passed behind him but sensed Bobby had slowed down, felt the tension rise, as if someone was staring at him. He shrugged his shoulders, not feeling right, nothing he could put words to, just an uncomfortable feeling, maybe of hostility in the air. Bad luck, he thought, picking the one place in Meridian where Bobby would show up.

"Refill love? Fresh pot," he heard Molly say.

"Thanks," Mike said, looking up at her, expecting another round of good cheer, but she wasn't smiling. She was looking past him, at someone behind him. He turned to see who it was, knowing it was Bobby, sensing the man's presence before confirming it. Sure enough, he was standing there, staring at him.

"Can I help you?" Molly said to Bobby, causing him to look away from Mike.

"Uh, sure. I'd like a cup of coffee."

"OK, I'll bring it right over to your table."

"I'll take it at the counter," Bobby said. He walked toward the front of the building and took a seat at the counter between Mike and the door, leaving Janice and Della sitting in the dining room. Molly watched him go, looked at Mike, and went to the stack of coffee mugs. She poured the coffee and set it down in front of Bobby. Then she pulled a pad of order slips from her apron and walked back to where Mike was sitting. She put the pad of slips on the counter in front of Mike and began writing.

"You need anything else?" she asked.

"No, I think that's it, thanks."

She kept her head down, studying the order slip, lowering her voice. "That guy's acting kinda strange. Something going on between you two?" she asked.

"Yea, he doesn't like me very much, but I'm leaving so there won't be any trouble."

"Did you know he was walking back and forth behind you?"

"No."

"Well, he was. Walked past you into the dining room, then turned around, and walked back past you toward the door, then turned around again, walked behind you and just stood there, staring at the back of your head. Maybe I should call the cops?"

"Nah, I'm going home. He'll settle down. My truck's right outside."

"You sure?"

"Yah, I'm sure."

"OK, here's your check."

Mike stood up and reached into his pocket for some change. He left a tip on the counter and walked past Bobby to the cash register by the door. As he stood there waiting to pay the check, Bobby got up from the counter and went out the door.

Molly came to the cash register, looked at Mike, raised her eyebrows, a question. "You sure about this?" she asked.

"I'm sure. I've known Bobby for a long time. He gets a little excited sometimes but he's OK. My truck is right outside. I'll be gone in two minutes."

"Ok, here's your change. Thanks for coming."

Mike smiled at her, put the change in his pocket, and went out the door. Bobby was leaning against the wall, beside the door, waiting for him.

"What in hell did you mess me up for down there?" Bobby said.

"I didn't mess you up, Bobby. I just wanted my money back, is all."

"You could have got your money."

"Bobby, I called and called you. I wrote you. I asked to come see you. You never answered. You wouldn't talk to me. What was I supposed to do?"

"You're a god damned liar," Bobby shouted, launching his fist at Mike's face, catching him off guard, hitting him just below his left eye. The blow staggered Mike backward, across the sidewalk, and up against the side of his truck, the truck helping him stay on his feet and blocking him from tumbling into the road. Stunned by the suddenness of Bobby's attack, Mike couldn't recover before Bobby was on him, punching him several more times, again and again in the face, one of the blows causing Mike's nose to spurt blood. Mike's hands went up instinctively, trying to protect his face, exposing his midsection. Bobby stepped back, took aim, and punched him squarely in the solar plexus, putting his shoulder into it. Mike gasped and collapsed onto the sidewalk, unable to breathe. Bobby continued to attack, kicking at Mike's side, at his hip, at his arms as he coiled them around his head, trying to protect it. Mike grabbed the running board on the side of the truck, tried to get to his feet, exposed his face again, and Bobby was there, punching him, knocking him back to the ground.

Dazed, bleeding badly from his nose and from a cut on his cheek, no longer able to resist, Mike drew his knees up into his chest, hunched his shoulders, and tucked his face, trying to protect himself. Bobby was standing over him, screaming, his words unintelligible, except for the cursing, "you lousy son of a bitch, … you lousy son of a bitch." Desperate to stop Bobby's attack, Mike reached into his pants pocket and grasped the .38 caliber Smith & Wesson pistol he sometimes carried. He got the gun out of his pocket, at the price of a kick in the ribs, pointed it in Bobby's general direction, and pulled the trigger. The bullet entered Bobby's right eye, a lucky shot, but Bobby was dead before he hit the ground.[1]

A Meridian policeman happened to be walking nearby and heard the gunshot. When he reached the scene, both men were laying on the sidewalk, pools of blood forming around them. Mike Brighton was indicted for murder and convicted of manslaughter. The judge sentenced him to two years in the Mississippi State Penitentiary. He appealed his conviction to the state's Supreme Court. The question in his appeal was whether the threat he faced justified the use of deadly force to protect himself.

UNLAWFUL DEADLY THREATS TRIGGER THE RIGHT OF SELF-DEFENSE

At the core of every self-defense claim is an act of unlawful force, a ferocious attack that creates mortal danger and threatens death or great bodily injury, unless the person threatened takes immediate action to stop it. When such unlawful force is used against an innocent person, the law's prohibition against killing falls by the wayside, and deadly force may be used in response to save one's life or to prevent great injury. So how do we identify an unlawful, deadly threat from other kinds of threats? What merits the use of a gun for self-protection?

It is obvious, but still needs to be said. People who shoot other people don't get to make the final decision about how serious the threat is. The law gives that job to the police, the prosecutor, the judge, and the jury. The point cannot be emphasized too often, because the facts determine how dangerous the threat is and what force is permitted in response to it, and what the facts are is influenced by who gets to decide them. Different police officers, different prosecutors, different judges, and different juries can look at the same set of behaviors and see different things, draw different conclusions. People bring their own backgrounds, life experiences, morality, political persuasions, and other individual characteristics to the process of judging threats and responses; unstated biases affect how they see things and influence how they decide them. One view of the facts is not necessarily more right than another, more fair than another, just different, a product of human diversity, of human decision making, but the difference can be terribly important to the people who must endure the consequences.

Fistfights provide a good example of how different people can reach different conclusions about threats and of how difficult it is to decide what is unlawful, deadly danger. Determining whether a fistfight has accelerated to the point where one of the combatants is in mortal danger is not only a difficult task, but also a subjective one. A teetotaler's terrifying nightmare may be an Irishman's joyful beer brawl. Understanding how the law handles fistfights is a good way to think about whether any threat presents an unlawful, deadly danger.

LAWFUL VERSUS UNLAWFUL THREATS

First, the unlawful force that justifies killing in self-defense, the ferocious attack that creates deadly danger, must be just that: unlawful. If the force is lawful, permitted by law, then self-defense is taken off the table, made unavailable to anyone who resists it. Police officers, for example, may use force in the performance of their official duties, their coercive behavior a lawful exercise of government authority. Former New York police commissioner Bill Bratton calls it "legal ugly." Government coercion is not pretty. It can get violent and people can get hurt, but it is permitted if it is lawful.

You are not free to resist a police officer with physical force, for example, even if you are the subject of an unlawful arrest, and even if you believe the use of such force is necessary to avoid a physical assault.[2] This kind of restriction on the use of force to resist police authority exists because there are procedures in place to determine whether the police have acted appropriately, whether they used lawful force, whether they were in the right, or whether they've made a mistake. The legal casebooks are full of court decisions condemning police misconduct, correcting police mistakes, setting aside wrongful convictions, proving that judges will rectify the wrongful exercise of police power. If the police have erred, the courts will say so, and they will fix it. It is that simple. So the law says that while the system is doing its work, it is best to keep everyone as safe as possible, and that is done by prohibiting the use of force against police officers in the lawful exercise of their authority. Public policy favors strongly the protection of police officers. If a police officer is killed or seriously injured while performing his duties, in the vast majority of cases the person responsible will be charged with the appropriate crime, stripped of his or her right of self-defense, and most likely convicted.

The law, however, is annoyingly consistent in one thing: every rule has its exception. The rule against the use of force to resist police authority is no different. There is a limited set of circumstances in which the use of force, even deadly force, against a police officer might be justified. It is based on mutual mistake.

To illustrate, suppose a police detective, let's call him Jim, wants to interview a witness, let's call him Pete, who saw a local gang member commit an armed robbery. Jim goes to Pete's house, running late, not having called ahead, trying to catch his witness at home. Jim is wearing casual work clothes, dungarees, an open collar shirt, and a sports jacket. He rings the doorbell, and when Pete opens the door, Jim mistakes him for a wanted fugitive, a man known to be armed and very dangerous, a cop-killer even. Jim reaches instinctively for his pistol. Pete, seeing the flash of Jim's gun, mistakenly believes him to be a gang member, perhaps a friend of the armed robber determined to prevent a fellow gang member's conviction, by silencing the main witness against him. He flees to another part of the house. Jim, his pistol now drawn, yelling for Pete to stop, runs after him. He sees Pete dash into a clothes closet, begins to point his pistol in that direction, but before he's in position to give further commands, or to fire, Pete shoots and kills him with his own pistol drawn from the closet shelf.

Let's look at the same facts from Pete's perspective. Pete is nervous about having witnessed the armed robbery, believing it to be a gang heist, knowing the danger of confronting gangs. He hears the doorbell ring, opens the door, sees a stranger not wearing a uniform, looking determined, saying nothing, reaching under his jacket, revealing a gun. Pete is terrified. He thinks immediately of the armed robbery, the gang, his testimony, the danger of being killed. He runs to the clothes closet where he keeps his pistol, and the stranger runs after him, gun in hand, yelling at him to stop. Pete grabs his gun, sees the stranger lifting his arm, starting to point his gun in Pete's direction, getting ready to shoot. Pete kills him.

Jim mistakenly believed Pete posed a deadly threat, Pete mistakenly believed Jim posed a deadly threat, both were wrong, one ended up dead. It happens. This fact pattern, the situation in which a police officer and an innocent civilian both misread the facts, is one of the few times when a claim of self-defense might prevail against the exercise of lawful police authority, but it is still a very hard case for the shooter to make. There must be no suspicion, not even a whiff, of the police officer's true identity, and the officer's behavior must be such as to convince a jury that he or she violated good police procedures or acted impermissibly.[3] Meeting these two requirements is a tall order, and not many fact patterns do. That is why most shootings of law enforcement officers end up with the shooter being convicted of murder.

ONLY DEADLY THREATS JUSTIFY DEADLY FORCE

The force that justifies self-defense must not only be unlawful, but also deadly, presenting an imminent threat of death or serious bodily injury unless action is taken to stop it. Trying to catalog all the possibly deadly behaviors, movements, gestures, conduct that might trigger self-defense is impossible. There are simply too many ways one person can harm another. They are as varied as the human imagination. Some threats are obvious and extremely violent—the use of lethal weapons, attempted murder, rape. Others are not so obvious—a man putting his hand into his pocket in the midst of a serious argument, a stranger moving toward a woman in a dark parking lot. Deadly threats can be anything that causes a person to fear reasonably that he or she is about to be killed or seriously injured. If the circumstances, in the minds of reasonable people looking at them after the event warrant a fear of death, then the threat is considered deadly and the right to use deadly force in response is justified.[4]

THERE ARE NO HIDDEN THREATS IN SELF-DEFENSE

The unlawful, deadly force that triggers self-defense must also be overt, plain to see. It can't be hidden from view, secret, unknown, or unknowable. One can't reasonably fear for his or her life in the absence of some observable behavior by another that makes clear the possibility of death or serious injury. There must be some threatening conduct, some observable action, some objective sign of unlawful, potentially deadly danger, putting the shooter at risk, creating reasonable fear, justifying deadly force in response.

Fear alone is not enough. You can't shoot someone because you're afraid of them, or because you're afraid of being in a bad part of town,[5] or because you're afraid something bad will happen. Something bad actually does have to happen.[6] The person who threatens you must behave in some way that actually puts you in mortal peril, or at least appears to reasonable people to put you in mortal peril.[7] If such behavior is nowhere apparent, then there is no danger of unlawful, deadly force against you, and no need to kill anyone.

THE SPECTRUM OF BEHAVIORS

One way to think about unlawful deadly force is to envision a behavior spectrum. At one end of the spectrum are behaviors that clearly are not deadly. Rudeness comes readily to mind. Today, it seems to be everywhere. The world is full of rude people, but you don't get to shoot one of them because he or she insults you. At the other end of the spectrum are behaviors that are clearly deadly, a woman fighting off an attempted rape, a homeowner confronting a knife-wielding intruder, a victim being robbed at gunpoint, attempted murder.

As you move from either end of the spectrum toward its center, it becomes harder to distinguish between behaviors that pose deadly danger and those that do not. Personal beliefs, life experiences, political preferences, and individual characteristics begin to play a greater role in the decision, influencing what is considered deadly, creating a lack of consensus about behaviors near the middle of the continuum. The crossover point, the line that separates deadly from non-deadly behaviors, is not fixed. It is located on the spectrum in different places for different people. Some people place it more toward the end where rudeness and insulting people reside; others place it nearer to the end, where rapists, armed intruders, and robbers dwell. Again, the teetotaler's terrifying nightmare may be the Irishman's joyful beer brawl.

The crossover point can also shift depending on various facts in the case; for example, the relative size and strength of the victim versus his or her attacker, the 100-pound woman facing a 200-pound man, or the victim's age or disability, the wheelchair bound octogenarian threatened by a younger person with full use of his or her limbs. In each of these situations, the disadvantaged person is less able to handle the threat, more likely to be overwhelmed, at greater risk of injury because of his or her relative size, strength, and ability to defend against the danger. Where such disparity exists, the crossover point, in most people's minds, tends to shift somewhat toward the end of the spectrum where non-deadly behavior exists, expanding the behaviors considered deadly. A 200-pound professial linebacker punching out a 100-pound woman is a different proposition from two 200-pound professional linebackers punching out each other. The ability to resist an attack can be as important in determining the deadliness of a threat as the amount of unlawful force used to carry it out.

There doesn't have to be a weapon present, such as a gun or a knife, for unlawful violence to be considered a deadly threat.[8] For example, fistfights can become deadly, turning from confrontations about physical dominance into confrontations about survival. If one of the fighters appears intent on seriously injuring the other and capable of doing so, the potential victim may defend himself, as best he can, to include the use of lethal force to avoid being killed or seriously injured.

ROUTINE FISTFIGHTS AND THE CROSSOVER POINT

Most fistfights begin with no weapon involved and the combatants more or less evenly matched. What ignites them can be almost anything: long-standing hatred, sudden dislike, some perceived slight, an inadvertent bump, or just being in the wrong place at the wrong time. They tend to follow well-established rituals, hostile words, insults, taunts, gestures of disrespect, the first shove, screaming and shouting, a cascade of reciprocating blows, until one of the combatants achieves dominance over the other. Once that occurs, the winner, having inflicted some pain, produced some humiliation, usually relents, backs off, and stands down. The fight produces no serious injuries, no permanent damage, both combatants somewhat bruised but physically okay, although one may be a little more arrogant, and the other less so. The contest usually ends with a few contemptuous words, perhaps an obscene gesture, a final indignity hurled in the loser's direction. Then it's over, the heat of passion cools, the confrontation ends without much more than a bloody nose or a split lip and bragging rights, no one needs to die.[9] That's how it usually goes.

But not always. Sometimes, the winner, having established his dominance and overcome his adversary's ability to resist, doesn't stop. He keeps going, attacking, changing the nature of the fight, putting his victim in deadly danger, his intent no longer about domination, humiliation, or even inflicting some pain. The fight becomes about killing or seriously injuring an opponent who can no longer defend himself. When that happens, the potential victim, if he or she is able, may use deadly force, if necessary, to fight back. The problem is trying to figure out when that point is reached.

Suppose there's a fistfight and one of the combatants, let's call him Bob, having won the fight, stands over his opponent, who is laying on the ground, let's call the loser Mike, screaming invective, and kicking at his legs. Mike is curled up into a ball no longer having the physical strength to prevent further attack, trying to protect himself against Bob's attack, as best he can. What happens next? Is the fight over? Is it done? Or is it the prelude, the run-up to another, more vicious assault, one that may kill or seriously injure Mike?

There is really no way to know for certain until Bob actually takes the next step. Then unfortunately, it may be too late for Mike. If Bob relents, Mike is likely to recover fully, in the long run no worse for wear and tear, albeit with a somewhat bruised ego. If Bob continues to attack, however, then Mike is likely to be seriously injured, if not killed. Suppose before the next blow lands Mike pulls a gun and kills Bob. What then? Is this fistfight somehow different from the vast majority of other fistfights that end without anyone being injured seriously? Was Mike facing an unlawful deadly threat at the time of the fatal shot? If so, he may claim self-defense, if not, he's likely to go to jail for a very long time. The people charged with finding the facts, the judge or the jury, will look at Bob's aggression and at Mike's ability to resist and decide where the combination sits on the behavior spectrum. Does it pass the crossover point to fall on the deadly danger end of the spectrum, permitting Mike to use deadly force to protect himself, allowing him to go free, or does it fall on the non-deadly side of the line, making Mike a murderer?

Facts unrelated to the actual fistfight will influence the decision. Was Bob a convicted criminal? Did he have a reputation for being violent? Did Mike know about his reputation? Did Bob seek out Mike to confront him? Did Mike try to get away? Was one of the two men bigger than the other, if so, by how much? Was one of the men physically impaired, if so how did it affect his ability to defend himself? Had either of the two men been drinking, if so did it affect his judgment (almost always yes)? All of these questions are important to the jury, seeking as it always does to determine if the shooting was really necessary. The law is not a lot of help in such cases, recognizing, on the one hand, that most fistfights end in not much more than bloody noses and bruised knuckles, but acknowledging, on the other hand, that occasionally they do become deadly and justify the use of deadly force by one combatant against another. [10] In the final analysis, it all comes down to what the jury thinks about what happened.

DECIDING WHAT IS REASONABLE

One important factor likely to influence the outcome is what guidance the jury is given about how to decide whether Mike thought he was facing a deadly threat at the time of the killing, and whether it was reasonable for him to fear that he was about to be killed or seriously injured. His claim of self-defense rests on how the jury answers these two questions. The first question focuses on all the facts of the case. It looks to see if they show the presence of mortal danger, or at least the appearance of mortal danger. The second question focuses on just Mike himself. It seeks to determine if he really thought his life was about to end.

The states generally agree about how to decide the first question; namely, whether the facts show it was reasonable for Mike to believe he faced an unlawful, deadly threat at the time of the shooting. Juries are told to decide what a reasonable person, or a person of reasonable courage, would believe if confronted with the same set of facts. But how, you may ask, does one know what an imaginary, objective, hypothetical, reasonable person, or person of reasonable courage, thinks about what happened?

There have been volumes of legal decisions written about this question. Generally, the law says that a reasonable person is one who exercises appropriate skill, care, and judgment commensurate with the circumstances. That sounds rather lawyerly, but what does it really mean? Stripped of all the legal mumbo jumbo, what it really means is that a reasonable person thinks and acts within limits, however the jury decides such a person should think and act under the circumstances.

That is not as arbitrary as it may sound. Juries are made up of a cross section of the community, some members are liberal, some conservative, some compassionate, some not so compassionate, some inclined to believe what prosecutors say, some not so much. They are an amalgamation, a fusion of the community's values and beliefs, and together, collectively, they represent the community's judgment about what is reasonable behavior and what is not. So if they say, based on the facts, a reasonable person, if faced with the same facts as Mike, would believe there existed a dangerous threat, then such a belief by Mike is reasonable. It may not seem very scientific, but that's the way it works, and on the whole it works pretty well.

There is less consensus among the states about how to decide the second question, namely, whether Mike really feared for his life. The majority of them follow the objective rule, the same standard used to answer the first question, what would a reasonable person, or a person of reasonable courage, fear if faced with the same facts? If the jury believes a reasonable person in Mike's position would fear that he was about to be killed or seriously injured by the threat, then Mike's fear is deemed to be real. If a reasonable person wouldn't entertain such a fear, then Mike's fear is deemed not to be real.

A minority of states follows what is known as the subjective rule to decide whether Mike feared for his life. They don't bother with trying to figure out what a reasonable person, or a person of reasonable courage might fear. Instead, they focus on what Mike actually feared at the time of the shooting. This approach tends to focus more tightly on the shooter's conduct, his personal characteristics, and his environment. If the jury finds Mike was genuinely afraid of being killed based on his conduct, personal characteristics, and the situation in which he found himself, then he had the right to use deadly force to defend himself against the threat.[11] If he wasn't actually afraid or his fear wasn't warranted by the facts, then his claim of self-defense fails.

REASONABLE PEOPLE CAN DISAGREE ABOUT REASONABLENESS

Now let's turn back to Michael Brighton and his fistfight at The Crossroads Café. The Mississippi Supreme Court's decision in his case underscores how different people can look at the same facts and come to dramatically different conclusions.

The Supreme Court observed that Michael was the target of a sudden and unprovoked attack by Bobby Randall. He was an innocent victim, facing violence not of his making, having done nothing to provoke it. He had the right to use whatever force he needed to protect himself from being injured, the only question being whether he had the right to use deadly force.

The court also noted that Bobby Randall had clearly won the fistfight using surprise to strike a first, debilitating blow, eliminating quickly Mike's ability to resist and establishing his dominance virtually from the outset. Mike was down, laying on his side, unable to get up, his defense limited to using his arms to protect his face from further blows. There were other factors the court thought were important. Bobby was twenty years younger than Mike, bigger, stronger, had the use of both hands, and had a reputation for having a violent temper. In contrast, Mike was older, smaller, couldn't make much of a fist with one of his hands, and knew of Bobby's reputation as a fighter, knew he faced a violent man who could easily beat him.

Reviewing these facts, the Supreme Court decided that Bobby's continued attack on Mike passed the crossover line and entered that part of the behavior spectrum reserved for deadly threats. By continuing to beat Mike as he lay on the sidewalk, unable to resist, Bobby changed the character of the fight, taking it to another level, demonstrating his intent to at least injure, if not kill, his victim. In the court's opinion, the confrontation ceased to be a mere fistfight about domination and became a deadly encounter in which Mike faced imminent death or serious bodily injury.

The court noted that deadly force is normally not permitted in fistfights, but there are exceptions. Under such circumstances, Mike's alternatives were either to suffer death or serious bodily injury, or defend himself with deadly force against his attacker. That met the criteria for an exception to the rule that bars deadly force in fistfights. The court vacated the jury's verdict and set Mike free.

The case demonstrates how reasonable people can look at the same facts and come to different conclusions. After listening to the witnesses and looking at the exhibits, the jury in Mike's trial decided that it was unreasonable for him to believe that he faced a threat of death or serious bodily injury. The Supreme Court looked at the same facts and saw something entirely different. The court's crossover point on the spectrum fell at a different place from the jury's. One has to suspect the two crossover points were near each other and that deciding if the threat was deadly was a close call for both the court and the jury. It is an example of how deadly threats are sometimes difficult to discern. Reasonable people will disagree about what is reasonable. Suffice it to say that whenever one combatant in a fistfight responds with a gun, he or she does so at great personal peril. [12] Deciding what is necessary is never easy when fists are flying.

5

VERBAL THREATS

HOSTILE WORDS

Jacob Merton lived off the bounty of Virginia's Shenandoah Valley. His first job was picking fruit. He loved it, and it led to a life that followed the valley's seasons. In the spring he sowed the fields, in the summer he quenched their thirst, in the fall he captured their harvest, and during the winter he rested and prepared to do it all over again. Jacob was proud that he worked the land, that he knew its habits. He prospered, and by the time he was thirty he had his own band of much sought-after field hands and a reputation for doing good work.

He chased Shenandoah's farmers around the valley, like Stonewall Jackson chased the Yankees during the Civil War. He kept his ear to the ground, listening for news of farming's inevitable casualties, broken fences, broken equipment, broken workers, all of which had to be replaced quickly to make sure the crop didn't suffer. He didn't rejoice in other people's misfortune, but he believed that Mother Nature stopped for no one, and he respected that, honored it really, by jumping in to help when people needed an extra hand.

Jacob lived with his wife, Beth, and their daughter, Martha, in Christians, a small village in the Allegheny Mountains, about ten miles west of Staunton, Virginia. The couple fit well into their community. The local wags called them "the lovebirds" because they seemed incapable of keeping their hands off each other. When they were together Beth often rested her hand on Jacob's back or on his shoulder, leaning into him just to be close. Jacob had the habit of reaching out and taking her hand when talking with others, making it clear to his listener, and to her, that she was part of the conversation. The women thought it was sweet. The men mumbled disparaging remarks, but secretly most of them envied the couple's relationship. Jacob and Beth just liked being around each other.

John Randall was a thirty-seven-year old itinerant field hand who worked as part of Jacob's crew. Born in Atlanta, the tall, lanky Georgian drifted north through the Carolinas and somehow ended up in Staunton. After a couple of odd jobs he happened to be in the right place at the right time. Jacob was looking for someone to build horse stalls and John was available. The job turned out well and Jacob made him an offer to work full-time. John had no family and few possessions, apart from his tools, so he accepted the offer, moved to Christians, rented a room from Beth's mother, Sarah Wright, and became Jacob's go-to guy for rough carpentry.

John was an experienced carpenter. He had built many things, some of them difficult to do for farmers in his native Georgia and in both of the Carolinas. He saw himself as a "seasoned" hand, with considerable talent, a man who knew carpentry, and how to get things done. He offered his opinions freely about almost anything having to do with the job, what should be done, who should do it. At times it irritated other members of the crew, but for the most part they just let it go. It was just John being John.

John wasn't shy about giving Jacob advice if he saw something he didn't like. He was older than Jacob, and in his mind older meant wiser, better even. He was always ready to teach his younger boss about life's lessons whether Jacob wanted to hear them or not. He was somewhat dissatisfied with his own position in the crew. He thought that, given his skills and experience, he should be doing more than rough carpentry work and that he should be helping to manage the jobs.

Jacob saw it a bit differently. Farming required a lot of rough carpentry: barns, chicken coops, silos, and fences. It was an important part of his business, and John was good at it. Just as importantly, it helped to keep him paid. If the business got large enough, and he needed additional people to help manage it, then perhaps John could move up, but that decision was for later. Right now he was satisfied to keep everyone busy. John's role in the work became a minor source of irritation between them. Occasionally, Jacob became tired of John's complaining and pushed back. It didn't happen often and never amounted to much. John would vent a little, then go back to work, and he always did what Jacob asked him to do, and did it well. That was good enough for Jacob.

One Saturday in early November 1950, Jacob found himself in Staunton enjoying a rare day off, a chance to relax and be with his family. It was near the end of the apple harvest and the crop had been good. His crew had been working non-stop at one place or another in the valley for almost ten weeks picking apples, and he'd decided to give everyone a couple of days off. They needed it. He was in town with Beth, Martha, and his mother-in-law Sara. The women wanted to take Martha shopping, and Jacob begged off a visit to the dress shop by claiming he needed to see a recent widow. The dead man's farm would need help bringing in the harvest and Jacob wanted to do the work. The widow told him she would think about it.

About 3 o'clock in the afternoon the family assembled at a local diner on the road back to Christians. Jacob got there first, ordered coffee and a piece of cake while he waited and enjoyed the time alone, just sitting with nothing to do. The others arrived soon after and also ordered refreshments. The adults had coffee and cake while Martha ordered ice cream. They were trading the latest gossip and Jacob had just finished drinking his coffee when he saw John walk through the door. He stood up and waived to catch John's attention. Then he grabbed an extra chair and began scooting his family members this way and that to make room for him at the table.

"Hi John. How's it going?" Jacob said smiling, glad to see one of the crew. His greeting triggering a round of "hellos" and "Hi John" from Beth, Sara, and Martha.

"It's going good now that I've got a day off," John said slowly, thick tongued, laboring to pronounce his words. His eyes were glassy. Beth was the first to realize he'd been drinking.

"Yes, this past week was a rough one," Jacob said.

"The past two months were rough ones," John said, "nothing but work. This is the first time I been to Staunton since September." He spoke more easily this time, but with a hint of irritation in his voice.

"You're right John, but you know the harvest season. Gotta make hay while the sun shines. The next couple of days we can take it easy," Jacob soothed. "Want some coffee?"

John looked passed Jacob at a waitress who was serving the next table. "You can take it easy boss man. I don't need coffee," he said. He raised his hand to catch the waitress' attention but she was serving other customers and didn't see him wave.

Beth looked at Jacob, furrowed her brow and mouthed silently, "He's drunk." Jacob shook his head at her and mouthed back "Not now."

While Beth and Jacob signaled silently back and forth, John kept trying to get the waitress' attention. Finally, he asked in a voice too loud to ignore, "Hey missy? Can I get a beer?"

The waitress took the last plate from her tray, set it in front of a customer, and turned in his direction.

"I'm sorry sir but we don't serve liquor here," she said.

"I didn't ask for liquor. I asked for a beer," John said.

"I'm sorry but we don't serve that either. We don't serve any kind of alcohol," she said.

"I've had beer here before," John insisted.

"I'm sorry but I don't think so. We've never served any kind of alcohol," she said.

"Well missy, I think you're mistaken." Jacob interrupted the exchange, touching John's arm. "John, don't bother," he said. "We were just leaving anyway. Got to get back home. You need a ride?"

"Where you going?" John asked.

"Home. I want to get back before dark."

"You got a car?"

"Nope, came by taxi. Going back the same way."

"Well, I do need a ride."

"How'd you get here?"

"Had to hitchhike. Don't make boss man wages."

"I bet that wasn't fun. We'll give you a lift. Let's go," Jacob said standing up, a signal for the others to follow. He glanced at Beth. She was watching John closely, an unhappy look on her face, her hands clenched tightly in her lap. Her mother Sara took the hint and began fiddling with her pocketbook, making ready to leave. Hearing Sara's pocketbook rattle, Beth stopped looking at John, picked up Martha's jacket from the back of her chair, and handed it to her daughter. The family pushed back from the table and headed for the exit. John got up and followed them through the door.

Jacob stayed behind, paid the bill, left a tip, and then went outside to the parking lot. As luck would have it, there were two taxis in front of the restaurant parked side-by-side, heading in opposite directions. The drivers were sitting behind the wheels, talking to each other through their open windows. Jacob walked over to the taxis and asked if either driver was interested in taking them to Christians. After a bit of back and forth about where in Christians, one of them agreed, and Jacob waved the others over to the car. Beth, Martha, and Sarah climbed into the backseat and Jacob and John got into the front seat. Jacob sat next to the driver so John could sit by the window. He thought the fresh air might do him some good, sober him up a bit. Off they went.

It was pretty quiet for the first two miles back to Christians.

Then Beth said: "John, could you roll up the window please? It's pretty windy back here." The road was dusty and some of it was blowing through the open window into the back seat.

"Don't see how that's necessary, Beth. It won't be but another thirty minutes," John said.

"John, please. It's blowing things around back here and it's dusty," she said.

"Don't seem necessary, Beth."

"Come on, John. Give the ladies a break," Jacob jumped in. "Roll up the window."

John turned his head and stared at Jacob. "You know boss man, I have to put up with you ordering me around when I'm working, but I'll be damned if I'm going to take orders on my day off from you or some backseat driver," he growled.

Jacob winced at the comment, but otherwise didn't react. He rubbed the palm of his left hand across the knuckles of his right, thinking. John was in one of his moods he decided. He wanted to complain about something. He wondered what it might be, but now wasn't the time to find out. He opened his hands, palms up. "Come on, John," he said, not making eye contact, his voice conveying a warmth he didn't feel. "There's no reason to talk like that. All she asked was to close the window."

"Well, lookee here? A knight in shining armor. You wanna joust boss man? I'll kick your ass," John said.

"I don't want to fight, John. You've been drinking. Let's just get home. And will you stop calling me boss man, and please turn up the window a bit so the dust doesn't come in?"

John didn't move to turn up the window and continued to stare at Jacob. "Not gonna happen, boss man. If you keep bothering me, I just may knock your head into next Tuesday," he said, curling his hands into fists.

Jacob's face reddened. He locked eyes with John. He wasn't going to put up with it. The man was disrespecting Beth, and him, in front of Sara and Martha. He glared back, unwilling to look away, accepting the challenge. The air inside the car began to drip with hostility.

The taxi driver wiped his mouth with the back of his hand. "OK, boys," he said. "Here's the deal. I don't care how far we are from Christians. Either both of you simmer down or I stop the car and all of you get out. I'm not going to have some kind of fistfight in here while I'm trying to drive. You all can walk back to Christians. You understand?"

"Fine with me," John said, not taking his eyes off Jacob. "Let's stop this piece of crap and we'll find out who's bossing who."

The driver slowed the car looking for a place to pull off to the side of the road. Realizing they were about to be left there, halfway to Christians, Jacob surrendered, dropped eye contact with John, turned away from him, and touched the driver's arm. "OK, hold on, I need to get the ladies home. There won't be any trouble. We'll be quiet. Just take us home please." His plea made, he wiped his face with both hands, sat back in the seat, crossed his arms, and looked straight ahead.

"I thought so," John taunted. "Not such a big shot when the chips are down, are you?"

Jacob didn't respond to the question and kept his eyes forward. John shook his head, disgusted, then turned back and looked out the window. Satisfied his passengers had calmed down, the driver continued on to Christians, the car enveloped in uncomfortable silence, the dust blowing through John's open window into the back seat.

When they reached Jacob's house, they climbed out of the taxi. Sara tried to make peace while Jacob paid off the driver. She asked John if he would wait while she picked up her things at Jacob and Beth's house and then walk home with her. He said he would wait in the yard, but she suggested that he come in the house with her and help her carry them. Before Beth could think of a reason to prevent it, John had agreed to go with her.

By the time Jacob finished paying the driver everyone had gone inside and settled in the living room. Jacob was the last one to join them. He saw John sitting on the couch, smiling, his legs stretched out in front of him, crossed at the ankles, arms folded across his chest, talking to Sara as if nothing had happened. He seemed to be back to his normal self. So Jacob went over and sat down next to him. That's the way it was with John, he thought. The man said what he had to say, almost always more bluntly than was necessary, but then he moved on, giving no thought to the hard feelings he'd left behind.

After a few minutes of listening to idle chatter, Jacob got up and walked through the dining room into the kitchen. He got a glass from the cupboard and filled it with wine. "Anybody like a glass of wine?" he called into the living room. No one answered, so he put the bottle away and stood there in front of the sink, sipping his wine, and looking out the kitchen window.

A few minutes later John came into the kitchen. "I think I'll have a glass of wine if you don't mind, Jacob," he said.

"No, I don't mind. Are you sure you want it? Sometimes wine and beer don't mix so well," Jacob said reaching for the wine bottle.

"You accusing me of being drunk?" John flared. He stepped forward and pointed his chin at Jacob. "You know, I'm really tired of your crap. You seem to think you're pretty big stuff, bossing people around all the time. I'm about ready to take you down a peg," he barked.

Jacob stepped back, forgetting about the wine bottle, and held his hands in front of him, palms up, like a traffic cop stopping a car. "Whoa John, what's your problem? I'm not bossing you around. Sometimes people get sick from mixing beer and wine. I just thought you might not want to mix the two." He took another step backward, putting some distance between them. "I don't get it," he said. "You've been itching for a fight all afternoon. Maybe you should just go back to Sara's and we'll forget all this. Get some sleep. If you want, we can talk about it tomorrow."

"Don't be ordering me around, you son of a bitch," John shouted.

Jacob heard footsteps and saw Sara coming into the kitchen. "Sara, maybe you can talk to him. I don't know what his problem is but I'm sick of this," Jacob said, his anger starting to build. Turning back, he said, "John, you need to change your attitude. If you can't do that, then maybe you'd better start thinking about another job."

John stepped toward Jacob, his face bright red, breathing hard, his hands clenched into fists. "You'd better watch yourself, mister. I will cut a man's head off in a minute and think nothing about it," he warned.

Jacob blinked, stunned by what John had said. He could see a vein pulsing on John's forehead, his face was flushed and his breaths were coming in gulps. Jacob didn't understand any of it, it was surreal, but of one thing he was certain. He was becoming afraid of what he was seeing, of John's irrational anger, of his repeated threats. He decided he had to get out of the kitchen, there were too many knives there. Without saying another word, he stepped around John and walked past Sarah into the dining room.

"John, what's the matter? Why are you so upset?" Sara asked, but John wasn't paying attention. His eyes followed Jacob as if he was deciding whether to follow him. Sara put her hand gently on his arm, demanding his attention, "C'mon, John, let's go home," she said softly. "I would really like to get home. I'll get you something to eat and we can talk." She tugged on his arm, nodding her head in the direction of the back door, hoping to leave without going through the living room.

John shrugged off her hand. "I ain't going nowhere, Sara. This has been coming for a long time and now's the time to settle it. That son of a bitch needs to get what's coming to him," he said.

"Settle what?" Sarah asked. "There's nothing to settle. So you had a disagreement. It's over. Let's go home."

Jacob was in his bedroom. He could still hear Sara and John talking in the kitchen. John was angry and he wasn't leaving. He was acting crazy. It was "time to settle it," he said. Jacob was growing more afraid of what he might actually do. Beth and Martha were still in the living room, and Sara was with John in the kitchen. Jacob went to the closet and retrieved the double-barrel shotgun he kept there. He loaded the gun, left the bedroom, and walked back into the living room.

When Beth saw him with the shotgun, she grabbed Martha by the hand and ran out the front door. Jacob watched them go and was glad that she and Martha were safe. Now it was just Sara he had to worry about. There was an archway connecting the living room and the dining room. He walked to one side of it and peeked around the corner. He could see Sara standing with her back toward him in the kitchen doorway some twelve to fourteen feet away, talking to John. Her arms were out in front of her, palms resting on John's chest as if she was trying to block the door. She was pleading with him to go home with her through the back door, but John didn't want to go.

John was clearly angry, and as Jacob watched, he became more afraid for Sara. John repeated his threat to cut off Jacob's head. Jacob thought of all the knives in the kitchen.

"Sara, step away! John, you need to leave now!" Jacob shouted, stepping around the corner into the archway, the shotgun pointing toward the floor. John's head snapped up at the sound of Jacob's voice. He moved to his right to get around Sara, but she stepped in front of him.

"John, please," she begged.

"John, get out of here," Jacob shouted again. This time there was fear in his voice.

John glared back at Jacob. Suddenly he grabbed Sara's arms, stepped to his left, and pulled her behind the kitchen wall where Jacob couldn't see her. He appeared in the door again and looked in Sara's direction, "I'll leave after I've finished what needs to be done," he said. He turned back, locked eyes with Jacob, and started through the kitchen door. He reached his right hand into his pocket. Jacob raised the shotgun and pulled both triggers.

When the police arrived nothing was found in John's pocket. [1]

HOSTILE WORDS AND THREATENING BEHAVIOR

Most confrontations follow a pretty familiar sequence beginning with taunts, insults, and verbal threats, followed by pushing and shoving, followed by punches thrown and weapons used. So it began with John Randall and Jacob Merton. John was rude, insulting, disrespectful of Jacob and his family, unpleasant at the restaurant, verbally threatening during the taxi ride to Christians, taunting at Jacob's house. Yet their confrontation never seemed to move much beyond John's threatening words. There was no pushing, no shoving, no punches thrown, no uplifted knife. There was no evidence that John ever had a weapon or sought to employ one. In fact, although John repeatedly threatened to fight Jacob and to cut off his head, there was no physical contact between the two men until Jacob fired the deadly shots that killed John.

Yet there is still a feel of real hostility about their encounter. John's speech toward Jacob, his use of words, was unquestionably aggressive, intimidating, and threatening. And his behavior seemed odd, unpredictable, and uncharacteristic; the cause of his anger unknown, but the anger itself boiling just below the surface, ready to explode at provocations only he could hear. One thing is certain. Jacob was the target of his hostility.

At his trial for murder, Jacob claimed that he shot John in self-defense, responding to John's deadly threat with deadly force, killing John because there was no alternative. The prosecutor countered that while John may have been abusive verbally, it takes more than just words to trigger the right of self-defense. He argued that there must be some violent act, some behavior, on the part of the victim that threatens the shooter with death or serious bodily injury before deadly force can be used in response. In Jacob's case, he said no such behavior was present, there were only words, and words alone do not justify taking a life.

THE SHOOTER'S WORDS AS PROVOCATION

In some states, but not all, words in self-defense cases have consequences for both parties. Where that is the case, the shooter's language, as well as the victim's must be examined because if by his words the shooter provoked or prolonged the confrontation, or contributed to the circumstances that led to the victim's death, then he or she has misbehaved and cannot claim to have acted in self-defense. States following this approach treat words simply as another way the shooter can misbehave and forfeit his or her right of self-defense.

Other states have a different point of view when it comes to words spoken by the shooter. They say that provocative and insulting words alone, no matter how offensive they might be, can never justify acts of violence by the listener. If, upon hearing such words, the listener attacks and puts the shooter in reasonable fear of death or serious injury, the speaker may use deadly force to avoid being killed or injured and still claim to have acted in self-defense. For example, if A accuses B of dishonesty, and B attacks A with a knife, and in the ensuing melee, B is killed, A may still claim self-defense because his words, although insulting, perhaps libelous even, do not justify B's use of deadly force against him. This is true even if the shooter's words were highly provocative and created the confrontation that led to the victim's death.[2]

There are exceptions in some states where words can never justify a violent response by the listener. One exception recognizes the difference between abusive words and threatening words.[3] It is the difference between words, such as, "You're dishonest," and words such as, "You're dishonest, and I'm going to kill you." The first statement is abusive, the second statement is a threat, and if it provokes a violent response on the part of the listener, the law will not permit the speaker to claim self-defense.

Another exception acknowledges that words can be used as a deliberate provocation to create a response in the listener that justifies violence by the speaker in retaliation. Where deliberate provocation is found, the provocateur may not claim to have acted in self-defense if the listener is subsequently killed.[4] If the shooter's language toward the victim is deliberately insulting and abusive, such that a reasonable person would expect the victim to respond physically, and the victim does in fact respond physically, then the shooter has misbehaved and is at least partially responsible for provoking the confrontation.[5] Shooters cannot provoke fights with an adversary to justify violence against them.

THE VICTIM'S WORDS AS A DEADLY THREAT

Now let's look at the victim's words. The question is whether words alone can justify the use of deadly force to avoid a deadly verbal threat. Here the law is well settled, and there is strong consensus among the states. Words alone are not a basis for people to reasonably believe they face an imminent threat of death or serious bodily injury, and they cannot be used to justify deadly force against the speaker. A common description of the law is: "words alone, however grievous or insulting, cannot justify taking human life with a deadly weapon."[6]

So a person who is taunted, insulted, ridiculed, even verbally threatened with words alone, no matter how egregious or provocative, may not kill the person speaking to them. It is the legal equivalent to "sticks and stones may break my bones but words will never hurt me." It's based on necessity. If words can't kill or injure you physically, then it isn't necessary to kill anyone to avoid hearing them. In short, trash talk doesn't justify homicide.

WORDS AND FURTIVE GESTURES

The fact that a victim's words alone don't justify the use of deadly force against the speaker, doesn't mean the victim's words are unimportant. To the contrary, they are very important because they provide context for behavior that might otherwise be unclear or ambiguous. Such behavior is known as furtive gestures. It is behavior that is itself unclear or the purpose of which is unclear. For example, putting one's hand into a pocket is normal behavior, but the reason for doing so during an argument is very important. It can be an innocent reason or a very dangerous one. It can mean nothing at all or it can mean a very great deal. The person might be reaching for something to show his antagonist, to win the argument, or for a wallet to settle the dispute with money, or for his car keys to leave, or he might be reaching for a knife or a gun. The behavior itself is ambiguous. The intent behind the behavior determines whether the shooter is facing deadly danger.

Furtive gestures must be looked at in context to ascertain their meaning. Take, for example, the driver who reaches under the front seat of his car. There are many reasons a person might do that. He or she might have dropped something and is reaching down to pick it up, or they might be reaching for the lever to slide the seat back or trying to straighten out the floor mat. If the car is sitting in the person's driveway, the reason for such behavior is likely benign. On the other hand, if it is sitting on the side of the highway having just been pulled over by a police officer, the reason for such behavior may be entirely different. The driver might be hiding illegal drugs or, more importantly, reaching for a gun. Words provide context for the behavior. If spoken by the driver contemporaneous with the act of reaching under the seat, they can go a long way in defusing or escalating the possibility of danger.

In the absence of some explanation, furtive gestures remain ambiguous. They may be innocent or they may be dangerous. Either way, they do not justify the use of deadly force. The police officer who stopped the car for a traffic violation can't shoot the driver because he or she reached down under the front seat. The officer can take additional measures to protect himself and to learn what the purpose of the gesture was because within the context of a traffic stop the driver's behavior may portend a deadly confrontation, but deadly force cannot be employed until it becomes clear the gesture presents a deadly threat.

Furtive gestures occur quite frequently in self-defense cases. One way of understanding them and the role words play in clarifying their meaning is to revisit our behavior spectrum, the continuum of possible behaviors, ranging from the most harmless to the most dangerous. Somewhere along the continuum is the crossover point where non-life threatening behavior becomes deadly. Words can have a great impact on where that crossover point falls, in any given situation, moving it toward or away from either end of the spectrum. For example, suppose a driver is cut off by another vehicle, and he becomes enraged. He follows the second driver, catches up with him, and shaking his fist, screams, "If you ever do that again, I'll kill you." His demeanor and his behavior are very threatening, but his words make clear that he is not going to do anyone harm, at least not now, and not until the same driver cuts him off again. He is furious, but he isn't going to attack unless "you ever do that again." The words move the behavior further along the continuum toward the non-deadly end of the spectrum.

Words can also have the opposite effect, making non-threatening behavior very dangerous. Suppose your neighbor walks into your backyard with an ax in his hand. Someone carrying an ax into your backyard is a furtive gesture, its meaning unknown, and isn't a basis to open fire on them. Still, carrying an ax can have different meanings, not all of them good, and words can help to determine what the behavior means. If he says, "Hi neighbor, do you mind if I cut back the bush that's growing through my fence?" carrying the ax suggests one thing. If he says, "I've had enough of your loud music and I'm going to kill you," it suggests something else. Words clarify the meaning of his carrying the ax and his furtive gesture has become clear.

Thus, while words alone can never justify the taking of human life, they can help us to understand if a person's behavior is motivated by malice, hostility, or ill will or by some other reason. If the victim speaks during a confrontation, the question becomes whether the words, when coupled with the behavior, make it reasonable for the shooter to believe that he or she is facing an imminent threat of death or serious injury. If it is reasonable to believe there is deadly danger, it can create reasonable fear in the shooter, turn on the light switch, and permit the shooter to use deadly force, if necessary, to defend himself.[7]

John Randall behaved ambiguously twice just before he was killed. The first time was when he grabbed Sara and pushed her behind the kitchen wall out of Jacob's sight. On the one hand, such behavior could mean that John was getting ready to attack Jacob, clearing his path so he could rush through the door and strike at him. If that was his purpose, then his behavior is evidence of malice, hostility, or ill will toward Jacob, suggesting a mean spirit, and possibly murderous intent.

On the other hand, maybe John was trying to protect Sara from what he saw as a threat to her posed by Jacob holding the shotgun. He pushed her behind the wall because he wanted to get her to a safer place, out of the line of fire. If that was his purpose, then his behavior is evidence of him trying to save a friend, a noble thing, and a very different state of mind from murderous intent. Had he said anything at the time of this furtive gesture, it might have shed light on his intent, on what was motivating his behavior. He didn't speak, however, so the reason he pushed Sara out of the way remains a mystery, part of the case's fact pattern, but still a furtive gesture, insufficient to allow the use of deadly force.

The second time John's behavior was unclear is when he thrust his hand into his pocket as he started through the kitchen door toward Jacob. Immediately before reaching into his pocket, he said to Sara, "I'll leave after I've taken care of what needs to be done." The trial judge told the jury how it should treat this behavior and the words that accompanied it, saying: "Words alone are not an act of aggression which permits the use of deadly force, nor can the placing of a hand in a pocket be considered an act of aggression although, when considered together, such actions may foster an apprehension of danger which would support the use of deadly force in self-defense." The judge's statement sums up nicely the relationship between words and furtive gestures, but makes clear that it is up to the jury to decide whether John's words turned his furtive gesture into a hostile act.

With the threat to cut off his head fresh in Jacob's mind, Jacob believed John was reaching for a knife to attack him. Yet Jacob didn't know what was in John's pocket at the time he pulled both triggers on the shotgun. There was no evidence that John carried a knife routinely, or possessed one that day, or sought to obtain one. The question for the jury then was did John's words to Sara clarify his behavior when he reached into his pocket, turning it from an ambiguous gesture into a deadly threat. The jury found they did not. Why John reached into his pocket was still unknown.

WORDS AND REASONABLE BELIEFS, AND REASONABLE FEARS

The jury in Jacob's case confronted two questions often found in self-defense cases. First, do the facts make it reasonable for Jacob to believe that John threatened him with imminent death or serious bodily injury? Second, was it was reasonable for Jacob to fear that he was in mortal danger.[8] Although the two questions sound alike, they address different issues. The first question focuses on the facts, and whether it is reasonable to believe they indicated the presence of a deadly threat. The second question focuses on the shooter, and whether it is reasonable for him to be afraid of the threat. The two are not always the same.

For example, suppose A is facing B. B has a pistol and is threatening to kill A. Such facts make it reasonable for A to believe that he or she faces an imminent threat of death or serious bodily injury. Suppose, however, that A knows the gun is empty, or that the firing pin is missing, but B does not. Despite facts that depict a deadly threat, is it reasonable for A to fear that he is about to be shot? Is it necessary for him to use deadly force against B to defend himself? Clearly, the answer to both questions is no.

John's furtive gestures remained just that, furtive gestures, the purpose of which was unknown, and in the absence of anything more specific, all the jury was left with are John's verbal threats. They accepted the prosecutor's argument, which was an accurate statement of the law. It takes more than just words to trigger the right of self-defense. There must be some violent act, some behavior, on the part of the victim that threatens the shooter with death or serious bodily injury before deadly force can be used in response. In Jacob's case, the required violent behavior was not there. He had not shot John in self-defense.

That left the jury to ponder whether Jacob was guilty of murder or some other crime. Several facts weighed heavily against him. First, John did not have a reputation for violence, quite the opposite. His reputation was for spouting off, but never engaging in violence. He voiced his grievances, sometimes strongly, but then he moved on, doing what he was told, even if he didn't like it. Jacob had experience with John and he knew that was how John behaved.

A person's reputation for violence, or non-violence, is very important when furtive gestures are involved because, if the reputation is known, as it was in Jacob's case, it signals whether the furtive gesture's purpose is a dangerous one. Simply put, a person known to have a bad temper, to carry and use a knife in the heat of anger, who reaches into his pocket during a hostile encounter, is more likely to be reaching for a weapon than a man known for turning the other cheek. Reputation is so important in furtive gesture cases that some courts have said the meaning of a furtive gesture cannot be determined except in light of the actor's reputation for violence.[9] In Jacob's case, John was known to be mouthy, but not violent.

Second, Jacob was holding a loaded double-barrel shotgun, ready to fire, when John started toward him. Jacob pulled the shotgun's triggers when John reached into his pocket, but at that point he was still some twelve to fourteen feet away from Jacob. Holding the shotgun against a man who appeared to be unarmed, Jacob was in a position of great advantage, and given the distance between them, the jury felt that he had time for the reason behind John's furtive gesture to become more clear before shooting him.

Third, John's behavior conformed to his reputation. He had shot off his mouth, but he didn't follow it up with physical acts. He hadn't pushed, shoved, or punched Jacob. He never threatened anyone with a weapon. All he had done was talk.

Finally, when John and Jacob were arguing in the kitchen, John didn't try to keep Jacob there, and he didn't pursue Jacob when he left. In other words, he showed no interest in pursuing Jacob or prolonging the encounter. When Jacob left the kitchen, and Sara took his place, the confrontation was effectively over. It was Jacob who continued it by going to his bedroom, arming himself with a shotgun, and returning to the living room where he could see and be seen by John. He then proceeded to inflame the situation further by demanding that John get out of the house immediately, provoking a response from John he likely expected, and setting the stage for the final encounter.

The jury decided that there was no factual basis to believe that Jacob was in mortal danger and no reason for him to fear John. They concluded that Jacob had acted out of malice, hostility, and ill will. John was convicted of second-degree murder, and the judge sentenced him to twenty years in the state penitentiary.

6

IMMINENT HARM

WHEN DOES DEADLY DANGER APPEAR?

The drinking began about five years after they were married. So did the beatings. It was always the same. The tensions built between them for reasons she could never understand. Then he would explode, calling her names, hitting her, throwing things at her, until he was exhausted. Later he would say he was sorry for losing control, for what he'd done. He seemed to be okay when he was sober, but he just wouldn't stop drinking. At least that's the way it was in the beginning.

Judy Ann Taylor knew she was in danger when her husband, Floyd Taylor, was in a bad mood. She developed a sixth sense about it, a silent alarm system warning her to be careful. She became watchful, noticed the small things, things that wouldn't matter to most people, and she was constantly on the alert for signs of trouble, but it was very hard because she could never figure out what made him angry. Sometimes she succeeded in avoiding the danger, because after a few cuss words he would turn his attention elsewhere. Sometimes she failed, and when that happened she would pay the price. Then he would hurt her, usually with his hands, sometimes slapping her, sometimes punching her with his fists. Sometimes he did worse.

In the beginning, Floyd was contrite after he sobered up. He apologized. Sometimes he cried. He promised he would never do it again. One time they began counseling at the local mental health center, but it didn't help much because he always went back to the drinking. Finally, he decided it was all her fault, he didn't need the counseling, if she wanted counseling she could go alone. After that, he stopped saying he was sorry after he beat her. She tried harder to please him, to avoid the beatings. It was the only thing she could do.

Judy tried several times to leave Floyd. A couple of times she took some things, left the house, and went to stay with her sister or with friends. No one seemed willing, or able, to help her, to protect her from Floyd. He always found her, came to where she was, took her home, and then beat her for having left. She thought about getting a court order, have a judge tell him to stay away from her, but she was too afraid. She knew Floyd. He was mean, especially when challenged. He wouldn't care about any court order. He told her once that if she got a court order he would use it to "wipe my ass."

She thought a court order might be her death warrant. She knew Floyd would think she had crossed a line, committed an unforgivable sin. It would be something he wouldn't rest easy about, until he'd kill her or hurt her so badly she'd never be the same. The cops would be no help. They couldn't watch her all the time, and he would wait until they weren't there, and then he would come for her. Even if she spotted him and called the police, they wouldn't reach her in time. They never did. He would beat her, most likely to death.

She began to believe the beatings were her fault for having done something wrong, for not understanding Floyd, for not being a good wife. There seemed to be nothing she could do to prevent his anger, so she learned to live in a world she didn't understand, where she didn't know how to escape. She had no power in her world, no ability to control her life, only fear. Danger was always present and serious injury just one mistake away. She had no money, no place to go, no one to help her, no one who could do anything about Floyd. He was above the law, and she knew that sooner or later he would kill her. The only thing certain in her world was the next beating, and all she could do was to be watchful and endure until that time came.

Floyd beat Judy over the next twenty years, slapping her, punching her, kicking her. He threw plates and beer bottles at her. He put cigarettes out on her skin, doused her in hot coffee, slapped her face, and broke her glasses. She didn't go to doctors, and she tried to cover up the bruises, but she was unable to hide the scars that began to appear on her body. The beatings got worse over time, like she'd built up resistance to the pain, so he had to work harder to hurt her.

The psychological abuse was as bad as the physical abuse. Floyd stopped working, having decided she could make money as a prostitute at a nearby truck stop on the interstate. If she resisted, he beat her. If she didn't make enough money at the truck stop, he beat her. He called her "dog," "bitch," and "whore." He joked in front of anyone who would listen about her "profession" as a truck stop prostitute. He made her get down on her knees, bark like a dog, and eat dog food from the dog's dishes. At times, he made her sleep with the dog on the floor beside his bed. He threatened her constantly with beatings and worse if she didn't comply. He did all of this in front of her family, her friends, and her children.

June 10 was much like other days. Floyd told Judy Ann to get into the car, she had to go to work at the truck stop because he needed some money. Their daughter Phyllis and her boyfriend Tom Reed were at the house and offered to take her. Phyllis knew that Floyd was in one of his moods, and that once he got Judy Ann into the car he would beat her. She wanted to spare her mother from the abuse. When Floyd didn't object, the three of them got into Tom's car and left the house. When they arrived at the truck stop, Phyllis and Tom dropped Judy Ann off in the back lot where the long-haul truckers parked. Then they decided to get something to eat, so they parked the car and went inside the restaurant.

About forty-five minutes later Floyd showed up. He parked in the back lot and found Judy Ann standing on the sidewalk near the rear entrance to the building. He'd been drinking.

"How much money you made?" he asked.

"None, Floyd. There ain't many trucks here and I ain't been here long. No business yet," she said.

Floyd's fist flashed, hitting her in the ribs. She staggered back, instinctively bending over and crossing her arms to protect her side. She looked up and Floyd slapped her across the face. She fell onto her leg. "You worthless bitch," he hissed. "What have you been doing all day?"

"Floyd, I just got here" she pleaded, keeping her eyes down, not making eye contact, something he would see as a challenge, provoking him further.

A truck driver by chance was walking out the back door and saw Floyd hit Judy Ann. He turned around, walked back into the building, went to the nearest fast-food counter, and told the waitress to call the cops because there was a man outside beating a woman. Phyllis and Tom, eating at a nearby table, overheard the driver talking and knew it had to be Floyd. They both stopped eating. Phyllis jumped up from the table and rushed for the back door. Tom gulped the last of his soda and ran after her.

They found Floyd and Judy just outside the back door. Judy was on one knee in a small grassy area that ran along the sidewalk, head bent, trying to cover her face with one arm, using the other to protect her stomach. Floyd was kicking at her leg and slapping at her head.

"Get up, goddamn you, you ..."

Phyllis ran up and grabbed her father's arm. "Daddy, stop it," she cried. "What are you doing?"

"I'm sick of this worthless piece of shit," he said, turning toward Phyllis, giving Tom time enough to help Judy Ann to her feet and step away from him. Phyllis knew she was now the one at risk of her father's temper, but she also knew Tom was there, and Tom wasn't afraid of Floyd. He'd made it clear to Floyd that if he ever laid a hand on Phyllis, Tom would beat him to within an inch of his life, and Tom was big enough, tough enough to do it. Floyd didn't mess with Tom.

"Well, somebody in there just called the cops, so you'd better get out of here," Phyllis said, nodding toward the door.

"Who saw me?" he asked.

"How should I know? Some guy," she said. "You'd better go."

Floyd looked around. He didn't hear any sirens or see any flashing police lights. He looked back at his wife, a scowl on his face, and pointed his finger. "You'd better have some money when you get home, bitch," he said, and walked away toward his car.

"C'mon, Mom," Phyllis soothed. "Let's get out of here. Tom's car is parked on the other side of the building."

"I can't, Phyllis. You heard him. I got no money," she said.

"C'mon, Mom. We can't be here when the cops come. It'll just make things worse."

Judy looked at her daughter, then looked at the entrance to the truck stop, thinking about Floyd and the police. If she went home with no money Floyd would be furious, but he might not hit her if she could convince him she'd left to avoid the cops. The cops knew her and they knew Floyd, and if they saw her at the truck stop they would know the man reported for beating a woman was Floyd, and they would find him and arrest him. If that happened she would really be in for it. Floyd would say it was her fault that he got arrested and really beat her until he could no longer lift his arms. She decided that trying to convince Floyd why she left was better than staying and have the cops arrest him, the lesser of two evils so to speak, so she followed her daughter toward Tom's car. It didn't work out the way she had hoped.

When two state troopers arrived at the rest area, the waitress who called in the complaint gave them a description of Floyd's car and the license plate number. A quick registration check returned a name the troopers knew well. Floyd Taylor had beaten Judy Ann in public places before. The two troopers left the rest area and caught up with Floyd before he got home. They arrested him for drunk driving, and he spent the night in jail. The next morning, Judy Ann borrowed the money for his bail and brought it to him at the courthouse.

As soon as he was free, Floyd unleashed a stream of invective and verbal abuse at Judy Ann that lasted throughout the day. She knew he was stoking his anger, sensed great danger in him, danger that was approaching her rapidly. She tried to calm him, stay out of his way, appease him. He was hungry so she made him a sandwich, but when she gave it to him he threw it on the floor. She made him another one, and he threw that one on the floor as well. Then he told her to make a sandwich without touching it, and she did her best to comply. While he stood watching, she used paper towels to remove the bread carefully from its package and place it on a clean plate, paper towels to get the luncheon meat and put it on the bread, paper towels to spread the mustard and mayonnaise, paper towels to put it all together, and cut it diagonally with a knife that she held with yet another paper towel. She was very careful, never touching the food. When she offered it to him, he took the sandwich with one hand, grabbed the back of her head with the other, and pushed it into her face.

Floyd's cruelty continued all day. He screamed at her, called her names, slapped her. He grabbed a lit cigarette from her mouth and put it out on her neck leaving a bright red burn mark. He demanded she wait on him hand and foot and threw things at her while she did it.

About 8 o'clock that evening deputy sheriff John Tate came to the Taylor home, a neighbor had called the sheriff's office about the noise. It wasn't the first time he'd been there. All the deputies knew about the Taylors. Floyd had a bad reputation. He was a known wife beater.

When Tate knocked on the door Judy Ann answered it. Floyd wasn't there. When she saw the deputy sheriff she began to cry. The side of her face was red and swollen, black and blue marks were beginning to show around her left eye. Her lower lip was swollen, a dark purple spot where Floyd had hit her. There was a cigarette burn on her neck.

"He's been hitting me all day," she sobbed. "I can't take it no more."

"Judy Ann, this isn't the first time he's done this," the deputy said.

"I just want him to stop."

"I know you do, Judy Ann, so do I, but there's nothing I can do unless you sign a statement saying what he's done to you. Will you do that?" he asked.

She looked up at him, a crushed Kleenex against her nose. "I can't do that," she said. "If I do that, he'll kill me. I just can't take no more. Just make him stop," she cried desperately.

The deputy pleaded once again. "You shouldn't have to take it anymore Judy Ann, and you don't have to take anymore, but you have to help me. You have to tell the judge what happened. If you do, I can make it stop. Will you help me, Judy? Will you help me tell the judge what he's done to you before this goes too far?"

"I just want you to make him stop," she sobbed.

"Will you give me a statement?"

"He'll kill me if I do."

And so it went, back and forth, until deputy Tate understood that, once again, he'd lost the argument. She was just too afraid. So he suggested that she gather some of her things and go to a friend's house or to a relative's. He said she could come back later if she wanted to. He told her about the county hot-line for battered women and asked her to call them in the morning. He gave her the address for a shelter. He gave her his telephone number and told her to call him if she needed him. Finally, he asked her to be careful. Then he left.

Deputy Tate was back again a few hours later. When he arrived the second time there was an ambulance in the driveway, its red lights flashing in the night, the back doors open, its crew members struggling to lift the gurney, carrying Judy Ann, into the vehicle. Floyd was standing between the gurney and the back of the ambulance, blocking their path, shouting and waving his arms at them. The deputy got out of his car, walked over to the gurney, and looked at Judy Ann. She appeared to be unconscious, but otherwise looked the same as when he'd left her earlier.

"What's going on?" he asked, looking at the attendants.

"Drug overdose," the older one said. "Mr. Taylor here doesn't want us to take her."

"What did she take?"

"Not sure. Looks like pain pills. She was pretty groggy when we got here. We need to get her to a hospital. Mr. Taylor's pretty drunk. He was screaming at her, called her a whore, said he'd make her pay for taking his pills, threatened to kill her, her mother and her grandmother. He's trying to keep us from getting her into the ambulance. Her mom's over there," he said nodding in the direction of an older woman standing nearby on the lawn.

"OK, I'll take care of it. Get her to the hospital," the deputy said and stepped away from the attendant, motioning for Floyd to follow him.

"Come over here Floyd. I want to talk to you a minute." Floyd didn't move.

"C'mon, Floyd. I want to talk to you."

"I ain't going nowhere. This is my house. I'll stand where I want."

"Floyd, Judy's got to go to the hospital. She's taken an overdose. I need you to step away from the ambulance."

"I ain't going nowhere. Let the bitch die."

"Floyd, let me be clear here. Judy's going to the hospital. There's an easy way and a hard way. The easy way is for you to come over here, talk to me, and let these men do their jobs. The hard way is that I arrest you for interfering with them and take you to jail. I understand you spent last night in jail. This time you'll be there longer. You want that, Floyd?"

"She's a worthless piece of shit. A waste of money. Let her die," Floyd screamed.

Floyd's scream seemed to trigger more flashing lights, the yard brightening as two more sheriff's cars arrived, Tate's backup. The two cars stopped and three deputies got out making their way across the lawn. Tate turned and watched their arrival. Floyd also turned and looked at the lawmen. Tate nodded at Floyd, raised his eyebrows, and pointed at the deputies. It was going to be four against one.

"Well, Floyd. It looks like if you don't step away from the ambulance right now you'll be coming with us. You need to understand that will happen. You also need to understand that there's an easy way and a hard way for that to happen, but it will happen. So what's it going to be?"

Floyd didn't answer, and the other deputies started to spread out, encircling him. Suddenly, he bolted for the house. Two deputies moved to intercept him, but it wasn't necessary because he was too drunk to run up the porch steps. He tripped on the second stair and fell on his stomach, half on the steps and half onto the porch. The deputies handcuffed his hands behind his back, rolled him over, and sat him on the steps. He tried to stand up, but one of the deputies pushed him back down. "I wouldn't do that," he said.

Floyd started swearing, but didn't try to get up again. The deputies ignored his yelling and made sure he didn't interfere with the ambulance crew while it loaded Judy Ann for the trip to the hospital. When the ambulance left, they removed Floyd's handcuffs, told him to sleep it off, and let him go. Then they went back on patrol.

Judy Ann went to the hospital, had her stomach pumped, and was released about 2:30 a.m. She spent the rest of the night at her mother's house, and later that morning she went to the county mental health center to see what she could do about Floyd. About noon she went home. Floyd was in the living room sitting in front of the television drinking beer. She tried to talk to him.

"Floyd, this has got to stop. You've got to quit this drinking. We can't go on like this," she said.

Floyd kept watching the television. "I don't drink that much Judy Ann. If you'd just do what you're supposed to, it wouldn't be so bad."

"Floyd, I went to the mental health center this morning to see what we can do. They say you need some help. They say they can help you stop the drinking."

He took another swig from the bottle. "If I want a beer, I want a beer and I ain't going to no shrinks. Half the people who work in that place are drunks and druggies. What do I need them for?"

"Maybe they used to be drinkers Floyd, but they ain't now. They're trying to help people going through the same thing. Floyd, if you don't stop drinking I'm going to ask the judge to make you."

Floyd's head snapped in her direction, his eyes flashing the warning signals she'd seen so many times. "If you do, I'll see them coming and before they get here, I'll cut your throat," he hissed.

Judy Ann froze. She saw hatred in his eyes, heard commitment in his voice. There it was again. Floyd didn't care about judges, about rules. He'd kill her if she went to a judge, before anyone could do anything about it. She shivered involuntarily. She lowered her eyes, looked down at her hands, folded them in her lap, shaking. "Ok, Floyd," she said softly. Then she got up quietly and left the room.

Later on, Billy Whitcomb, one of Floyd's friends, stopped by the house, a case of beer under his arm. He and Floyd sat in the living room drinking beer and watching TV. After a couple of hours of drinking both men were slurring their words. Billie wanted to go pick up his paycheck and Floyd decided Judy Ann should drive them there. The three of them went out to the car. Judy Ann and Floyd got in the front seat and Billy got in the back. Judy Ann started the car and they left the yard. Floyd brought several bottles of beer with them.

Floyd's mood turned ugly in the car. He slapped Judy Ann because she was driving too close to the truck in front of them. Then he filled a paper cup with beer and poured it over her head, laughing as she struggled to drive the car with beer stinging her eyes. He curled up on the front seat, resting his head against the door like he was going to take a nap. When Judy Ann began to relax, thinking he was asleep, he kicked her beside the head, suddenly with his foot, slamming her head into the driver's door window. She jerked the steering wheel, almost losing control of the car, and he screamed at her to pay more attention and chuckled that he'd fooled her. Billy, in the back seat, said nothing, neither did Judy Ann.

By the time they picked up the paycheck and drove back home, Judy Ann was soaked with beer, bruised, and defeated. Phyllis was there and tried to help her mother by at least getting her something to eat. She started fixing her a sandwich.

"I don't want that," her mother said.

"C'mon Mom. You haven't eaten all day. You need something."

"No, no. I can't."

"What do you mean you can't? Grandma sent over a whole bag of groceries for you. There's plenty of food."

"No, Floyd said I'm too fat and I shouldn't eat."

"It's been all day, Mom, and last night you had your stomach pumped, for God's sake. You must be starving."

Judy looked away from her daughter. "I really don't feel very well, what with Floyd being so upset and all. And I don't want to make him any more upset. You know how he is when he's upset. It'll be okay in the morning."

Later that evening, Floyd, feeling the effects of drinking all day, decided to retire early. He got up from his chair in front of the television and
said to Judy Ann, "Let's go to bed." She kept her eyes averted, didn't
respond, but obeyed immediately, standing up from the kitchen table and
following him into the bedroom. There were two twin beds in their bedroom because Floyd didn't want to touch her unless to hit her or when he
wanted sex. Judy Ann sat on her bed and began to unlace her sneakers.

"Get off that bed, whore." Floyd growled. "Dogs don't get on the bed.
They lie on the floor."

"But Floyd, I won't bother you. I promise. And the sheets got to be
washed tomorrow anyway. And I'm really tired."

"Shut up, bitch, and stop your whining. The floor between the beds is
where my dogs sleep and that's good enough for you." Floyd started
toward her, his hands balled into fists.

"Ok, Floyd. Alright, I ..."

Phyllis walked into the bedroom with her and Tom's baby in her arms.
Floyd saw the baby and turned away from Judy Ann. The baby cried
whenever he saw him hit Judy Ann, and Floyd hated the baby crying. He
also knew that if he made the baby cry, Tom Reed would come after him,
and he didn't want that.

"Daddy, I have to go to the store. Can Momma watch the baby while
I'm gone?" she asked.

Floyd looked at the baby in her arms, looked at Judy. "I guess she's
good enough for that," he said. He sat down on his bed and kicked off his
shoes.

Judy took the baby from Phyllis, put him on her bed, built a barricade
of pillows around him, sat down on the floor, and began fussing with him.
Floyd got into his bed and was snoring almost immediately. When the
baby was asleep, Judy lay down on the floor between the beds, covered
herself with a blanket, and tried to get comfortable. She hadn't been there
long before the baby began crying. She feared the noise would wake
Floyd and make him angry, so she picked up the baby as quietly as she
could and went outside onto the porch. Then she decided to walk to her
mother's just down the street.

When she arrived she found her mother watching the television. She
asked her if the baby could spend the night there so Floyd wouldn't be
disturbed and her mother said that would be fine. She also asked if there
were any aspirin in the house because she had a headache. Her mother

told her there was a bottle in her handbag on the kitchen table. Judy Ann located the handbag and began looking for the aspirin. She found it but to her surprise she also found a loaded .38 caliber revolver. She had no idea why her mother had a pistol in her handbag, but she took it, along with the aspirin, and after some idle chatter with her mother until the baby fell asleep she left the house and went home.

She entered the house and went into the bedroom. Floyd was facing the wall, his back toward her, fast asleep. She drew the pistol from her pocket, pointed it at the back of his head, and pulled the trigger. Nothing happened, just a click. She checked the revolver, saw there were bullets in all the cylinders, pointed the gun back at Floyd's head, and pulled the trigger again. This time the pistol fired, the bullet hitting Floyd at the base of his skull. Judy Ann felt her husband's chest. He was making sounds and still breathing so she shot him twice more in the back of the head, checked him again, no more sounds, no more breathing. Two of her three shots to the back of his head were fatal.

Judy Ann was tried for first degree murder and found guilty of voluntary manslaughter. At her trial she testified that she killed her husband "Because I was scared of him and I knowed when he woke up it was going to be the same thing and I was scared when he took me to the truck stop that night it was going to be worse than he had ever been. I just couldn't take it no more. There ain't no way, even if it means going to prison. It's better than living in that. That's worse hell than anything."

Two medical experts, one a forensic psychologist and the other a psychiatrist, testified that Judy Ann suffered from battered wife syndrome, a condition experienced by spouses who have been abused over a long period of time. Both of them told the jury that she honestly believed no one could help her, no one could protect her from Floyd, a man she viewed as being all-powerful, a man the courts couldn't control, and the police couldn't stop. In her mind, she was trapped, they said. She feared for her life and felt she had no choice but to shoot Floyd to save herself and her family.

The trial judge refused her attorney's request to instruct the jury in the law of self-defense. [1]

MUST VIOLENT BEHAVIOR ALWAYS BE PRESENT TO FEAR DEADLY DANGER?

Judges at multiple levels reviewed Judy Ann's case and were of two minds about it. The majority felt that her conviction should stand because it was unreasonable, under the circumstances, for her to believe she faced an imminent threat of death or serious bodily injury. The minority wanted to set aside her conviction because when she shot Floyd she believed reasonably that she was facing death or serious injury. The difference between the two views boiled down to a single question: How soon is imminent?

There are two important questions in every self-defense case: (1) Do the facts support a reasonable belief in the existence of an imminent deadly threat, and (2) did the shooter reasonably fear that he or she was about to be killed or seriously injured?[2] The answer to the second question was never in doubt. There was ample evidence, including the testimony of the two mental health experts, that Judy Ann honestly feared for her life, and that she believed she had to kill Floyd to save herself.

It was the first question that gave the judges trouble; namely, whether the facts showed it was reasonable for Judy Ann to believe Floyd posed an imminent deadly threat. Setting aside, for a moment, his abysmal behavior toward her, how does a sleeping man pose an imminent threat? That question split the judges into two groups: the majority of them unable to accept the idea that a sleeping man poses an imminent threat to anyone, the minority believing a deadly threat could be endemic.

AN IMMINENT THREAT MEANS "RIGHT NOW," IMMEDIATE DEADLY DANGER

The victim's current behavior almost always determines if the threat is imminent. The act of committing some unlawful violent behavior toward another creates a risk of death or serious bodily injury. Normally, it occurs just before the act of self-defense intended to stop it. It is the act that turns on the light switch. The knife poised to stab, the club raised to strike, the gun ready to fire, all require immediate action to avoid the danger.[3] The threat is at hand, its nearness in time apparent, the need to act urgent, making the use of deadly force necessary, unavoidable, a last ditch effort to save oneself.

The majority thought that because Floyd was asleep, no such violent behavior existed. It its mind, Judy Ann had time to respond without using deadly force. She could have stayed at her mother's house, or called the police, or gone to a battered woman's shelter. It wasn't necessary for her to kill Floyd because she didn't need to act immediately to save herself from ongoing unlawful violence. It argued that deadly force may only be used in situations where instant action is required to avoid the danger.

In the majority's view, the meaning of "imminent" is right now, immediate, close in time to the act of self-defense. The threat must be met now, not at some point in the future.[4] "Imminent" means a person is "about to suffer" death or great injury, unless he or she acts immediately to avoid it.[5] It can't "be guarded against by calling for the assistance of others or the protection of the law."[6] If a person has enough time to avoid the danger, there is no need to use deadly force to prevent it from happening. One is not permitted to strike preemptively, kill now to avoid having to kill in the future, because that day may never come.

The majority had four concerns about Judy Ann's behavior. First, the judges were reluctant to admit that there are circumstances where the law is powerless, unable, or unwilling to protect a person from harm. Looking at Judy Ann's case, there is no question, but that the legal system, its police officers, mental health officials, and judges, failed her. Yet the notion of the law's impotence, the idea that people can be put in places where they have to act on their own, because the law fails to recognize the threats they face, or refuses to protect them from deadly danger, doesn't sit well with judges, particularly when the use of deadly force is involved. It is a bias in favor of the legal process with the potential victim carrying the risk.

Second, many judges tend to distrust psychological evidence, believing that testimony about behavior caused by mental disease is unreliable. Unlike physical injuries, mental conditions are intangible, making them harder to judge. A broken bone is easy to see, a broken mind, not so much. Judges are cautious about making sure evidence is not subjective or arbitrary, the product of an expert's bias rather than a true picture of the patient's condition.

Compounding the problem in Judy Ann's case is the legal implication of recognizing battered spouse syndrome in self-defense situations. The diagnosis suggests that individual instances of spouse abuse can accumulate over time, and gradually reach the point where they create a continuous deadly threat, an endemic threat that replaces the single, observable act, threatening a "right now" risk of death or serious bodily injury. If such endemic deadly danger exists, then its victim may use deadly force at any time to protect herself, forcing judges and juries to evaluate a long-term relationship, and what it might lead to. Judges loathe such speculation, believing that what the future might be should never be used as the basis for justifying or excusing a killing. A better approach, in the majority's view, is to follow "an appropriately narrow but firm basis upon which homicide may be justified,"[7] namely, an observable act that triggers the right of self-defense.

The third concern is the fistfight problem. At what point in a confrontation does the physical abuse cross the line from a non-deadly beating to an imminent threat of death or serious bodily injury, requiring an immediate response to avoid it? Put differently, when does physical violence become deadly? Floyd had been physically violent earlier in the day, but he wasn't violent for several hours before Judy Ann shot him. Indeed, he was asleep, enabling her to leave her house and get the gun at her mother's house. Is Floyd's sleep part of Judy Ann's deadly danger? Does a deadly threat continue when its perpetrator is unable to carry it out? The majority was unwilling to engage in that kind of conjecture.

Finally, the majority was concerned about encouraging self-help solutions leading to the preemptive killings of spouses, killings motivated by revenge rather than by self-preservation. It felt that not requiring an observable "right now," a threatening act to trigger self-defense, would place judges in the position of having to decide murder cases based on "subjective speculation that the decedent probably would present a threat to life at a future time and that the defendant would not be able to avoid the predicted threat."[8] Such an approach would produce "opportune killing[s]" of abusive spouses based on subjective beliefs about what the future might hold. "Homicidal self-help would then become a lawful solution, and perhaps the easiest and most effective solution."[9]

AN ENDEMIC DEADLY DANGER WITH POTENTIAL TO EXPLODE AS AN IMMINENT THREAT

The minority had a different view of the case. It argued that there are circumstances in which sustained abuse over time can create a situation where there exists an endemic danger of death or serious bodily injury that at any time without warning, can escalate suddenly into deadly violence. The minority would treat such danger as an imminent threat. In its eyes, what matters most is not how much time passes between the victim's last hostile act and the act of self-defense, but rather whether the facts make it reasonable for the defendant to believe that she was going to be killed or seriously injured if she didn't act to protect herself. The minority argued that, at least in spouse abuse cases, imminent does not necessarily mean "immediate," or "right now," or "about to occur." It is sufficient if the facts make it reasonable for the shooter to believe that she must act immediately to save herself, even if there is no current deadly violence directed against her.

The Model Penal Code, a consensus opinion among legal experts about what the law should be, supports the minority's position. It describes imminent danger as follows: "The actor must believe that his defensive action is immediately necessary and the unlawful force against which he defends must be force that he apprehends will be used on the present occasion, but he need not apprehend that it will be immediately used."

The minority's view does not mean that the amount of time between the threat and the act to prevent it is unimportant in self-defense cases. Quite to the contrary, it is an important factor in determining whether the defendant's belief in the existence of deadly danger is reasonable. For example, it would be unreasonable for one to suggest an endemic deadly danger requiring a deadly response based on a single, isolated confrontation ending with no serious injuries that occurred eight hours before the alleged act of self-defense, and there being no other interactions between the parties during the intervening time.[10] Time is still a factor, but its importance is diminished in favor of more reliance on the victim's reasonable belief.

The minority also supports its view with four arguments. First, it suggests the majority's lack of confidence in mental health testimony is misplaced. In every case that goes to trial there is risk that witnesses will exaggerate or misrepresent the facts or favor one side over the other, but that is why there is a cross-examination to find the truth. If the defendant is the only witness to the events in question, the prosecutor's job becomes more difficult to be sure, but the purpose of the law is not to make the prosecutor's job easy. It's to find the truth and give justice.

Second, Judy Ann was not the only witness to her relationship with Floyd and to what happened on the night she killed him. The testimonies of her daughter Phyllis, her boyfriend Tom Reed, her mother, and deputy Tate all corroborated her story of threats, beatings, cigarette burns, humiliating demands, intimidation, and abuse. The minority felt that there was ample evidence, apart from the psychological evidence, upon which a jury could conclude that Judy Ann suffered from battered wife syndrome, and that she reasonably believed she would be killed or seriously injured unless she acted.

Third, if only concurrent deadly violence triggers the right of self-defense, then how does a person, entrapped in a trend of escalating violence, know when the final act is at hand? Tom Reed testified that on the day Floyd died, he had never seen him so angry. So how could Judy Ann know she would survive Floyd's abuse this time, that when he woke up he wouldn't just start beating her again and keep on beating her, until she died or was seriously injured? How many beatings did she have to suffer? How badly did she have to be injured? How much did she have to endure before she could defend herself?

Finally, the minority dismissed the majority's concern about spouse abuse syndrome becoming an excuse for "homicidal self-help." Perhap, if the mental health testimony had been based on Judy Ann's testimony alone it might have been suspect, but it wasn't. There were multiple eyewitnesses confirming what she said, and their confirmation of the facts minimized the risk of a mental health opinion being the product of a subjective bias or a misunderstanding of Judy Ann's situation. In the minds of the minority, the jury should have been allowed to consider her claim of self-defense.

THE LAW EVOLVES AS NEW THREATS ARE RECOGNIZED

Judy Ann lost her appeal. In the end, the majority view prevailed and her manslaughter conviction was upheld. The law changes, however, as people's attitudes change. Views that were rejected years ago are accepted today. Currently, the great majority of states accept battered wife syndrome as a scientifically recognized psychological condition and admit medical expert testimony about it in court. The debate about how soon is imminent, however, continues, presenting judges and juries alike with difficult questions of guilt or innocence.

7

REASONABLE FEAR

WHAT IS KNOWN, WHAT IS POSSIBLE, AND WHAT IS BELIEF

Stamps is a small town in Lafayette County in the southwest corner of Arkansas, a stone's throw from the Louisiana and Texas borders. It is the only town in the United States named Stamps. About two thousand people live there. The poet Maya Angelou grew up there. Thirty miles north is a town called Hope. Hope produced a president named Bill Clinton and a preacher named Mike Huckabee. Stamps is a peaceful place, for the most part, but in April 1995 Hank Daniels "shot an unarmed man to death on a city street, shooting him fourteen times in the head, neck, chest, abdomen, and buttocks."[1] The man he killed was Mitch Capron.

Hank was convicted of murder and sentenced to life in prison without parole but the verdict didn't sit well with folks in the community, especially among those who knew both men and their history. Hank's lawyer said that when Hank shot Mitch, he was trying to avoid being killed, and he wanted to claim self-defense at Hank's trial. The trial judge said no, he couldn't make that claim because of two reasons. First, Hank shot at Mitch fifteen times with his pistol, hit him fourteen times, and killed him with eleven different shots. Second, the police didn't find a weapon when they arrived and searched Mitch's body.

Hank and Mitch had known each other a long time before the shooting. In many ways they were cut from the same bolt of cloth. Both were in their early thirties, both were about the same size, both had gone to work right out of high school, and both were "kind of rough," as the locals would say. They hung out in the same circles, not exactly outside the law, but maybe a bit too quick to seize upon whatever opportunity might arise, and a bit too slow to recognize the ones that weren't quite right.

Hank worked as a clerk at a local hardware store. His job brought him into contact with many people in the community and, for the most part, they liked him well enough. Mitch was a jack-of-all-trades, a master of anything he could do with his hands or with heavy equipment. If it was mechanical, and it broke, Mitch could fix it. The two men weren't friends. In fact, they didn't like each other at all. There wasn't any particular reason why they didn't get along, no money troubles, no women troubles, no confrontations, neither spoke ill of the other, they just didn't like being in each other's company.

Serious trouble between them began in 1994 about a year before the shooting. There was a fistfight one Friday night between Mitch and a man named Bill McKenzie, predictably, at a bar around closing time. No one really knew what started the fight, what it was all about. Probably it began as such things usually do, a lot of drinking, some perceived slight, a few nasty words, a push, a shove, and then fists flying. Somehow the two combatants pushed their way out of the bar, or got shoved through a door, into the parking lot where they continued to grunt and pound each other, cursing, and swinging their fists. Since it was about closing time, the other bar patrons, sensing a good show to top off the evening, joined them outside to see who would win. A few bets were made, nobody tried to stop it, nobody called the cops, it was just a bar fight after all. Some in the crowd cheered for Mitch, some cheered for Bill McKenzie. Hank was there, watching the match. He wasn't cheering for Mitch.

In Stamps, and almost everywhere else in the United States, a fistfight usually ends when one guy, the winner, gets tired of slugging the other guy, the loser. The winner gets to call the loser a "son of a bitch," strut his stuff a bit, and walk off to a chorus of "attaboys" from his drinking buddies. It's a guy thing. That night it didn't happen that way. The combatants were in full throttle banging away at each other when a gunshot rang out. Mitch screamed, grabbed his leg, and fell to the ground. Bill McKenzie just stood there looking confused, wondering if Mitch was faking it, trying to trick him, maybe set him up for a sucker punch. The spectators weren't confused. They decided as a group, instantly, that it was time to go home, reaching for car keys in their pockets and bolting for their cars. For the next few minutes the parking lot was like the beginning of a stock car race, people shouting, engines starting, motors revving, tires screeching, drivers pushing ahead of the next guy, and a lot of dust flying.

Somebody called the cops, anonymously of course, and said there'd been a shooting at the bar. When the cops arrived all they found was Mitch lying on the ground, screaming, and a lone bartender. The bartender, not wanting to miss the show, had come out to watch the fight along with everybody else, but instead of joining the stampede after the gunshot, he decided to stay and face the music, knowing the cops would get his name eventually and find him anyway. Being a bartender he wasn't very helpful, no, he didn't see anything, no, he didn't hear anything, no, he didn't know what the fight was all about. Gee, he couldn't remember the name of anyone who might have been there. Mitch was just as helpful. He didn't know anyone who was there either and couldn't remember the name of the man he'd been fighting. The police, weary of listening to the nonsense, decided so be it, if Mitch didn't care they didn't care. Mitch was taken to the hospital and patched up, no one was arrested, the cops drove back to the police station and filed a report stating an unknown person shot Mitch while he was fighting with another unknown person, and the only witness, the bartender, didn't know anyone involved. That was pretty much it, case closed.

The incident wasn't forgotten, however. Not much happened in Stamps, and the mysterious shooting was a godsend for those given to gossip, which was just about everybody. People put a lot of creative energy into making it something more than it was, talking of heroes and villains, long standing hatreds, jealousies and love triangles, speculating without much basis for anything they were saying, kind of like talk radio. In Washington, D.C., they call it spin; in Stamps, they call it lies. Still, it couldn't be helped, had to be done, people just couldn't resist, it was such a good story. No one really knew who shot Mitch, but it really didn't matter, and it certainly didn't interfere with the speculation about "who done it." Arguments broke out about this one or that one being the "unknown killer." That Mitch had survived the shooting didn't matter either, there was still a killer "on the loose" in Stamps.

The only opinion that really counted was Mitch's, and he wasn't talking, because truth be told, he had no idea who shot him either. Somehow amidst all the speculation, however, Hank's name surfaced as the villain most likely to have "pulled the trigger." He denied it, but given the absence of any other good candidate, he was good enough for most folks. Groupthink took over and a consensus formed among the few who gave a damn, that Hank was probably the guy who shot Mitch in the leg. After hearing it repeatedly, Mitch himself began to believe it, and Mitch was not a man to take such matters lightly.

About a month after the shooting, Mitch was still on crutches, his leg not completely healed, when he was seen hobbling along the sidewalk on Oak Street near where Hank lived. The neighbors took note because in his right hand, in addition to the crutch handle, was a semi-automatic pistol. When he was about a hundred feet away from Hank's house, Hank and another man came out the front door. They were having a serious conversation and neither of them noticed Mitch on the sidewalk. The two men marched down the cement walkway to the sidewalk, heads bobbing, hands waving, turned left, in front of Mitch, still not seeing him, and continued on their way. Mitch tried to pick up the pace, catch up, but, on crutches, he was too slow.

"Hey, Daniels!" he shouted, causing Hank to stop, turn around, and look in his direction.

"Why'd you shoot me?" Mitch yelled, moving as fast as he could, closing the gap between them.

"I didn't," Hank said.

"You lying bastard. You're dead," Mitch shouted, raising his pistol and firing two quick shots at Hank.

Hank was about forty feet away from Mitch and the shots missed. The man with Hank, seeing the pistol pointed in his direction, dropped to the ground like a cement sack falling off a pickup truck, and covered his head with both hands. Hank turned and started running away from Mitch, down the sidewalk, as fast as he could, ducking and weaving, juking left and right, trying to keep from getting shot. He was almost to the corner when two bullets zipped past his head and clanged into an octagonal stop sign. He juked left and cut across the lawn in front of the house on the corner, trying to put the house between him and Mitch. He ducked behind it just as two more bullets slammed into its clapboard siding. Mitch tried to catch him, hobbling along on his crutches, shooting until he was out of ammunition. He finally reached the end of the block where he could see around the corner of the house, knowing what he would find. Hank was long gone.

Hank didn't stop running at the end of the street, at the Stamps city limits, or at the Arkansas state line. He kept going until he reached Detroit, Michigan, where he stayed with some friends waiting for things to cool down. The Stamps police were called in, and once again were met with silence, nobody saw anything, nobody knew anything. They tried to charge Mitch with reckless endangerment with a firearm, but they couldn't find Hank and no one else was talking. The prosecutor refused to bring the case, and it went into the books as another unsolved crime.

Hank remained in Detroit for several months, returning to Stamps in April 1995. He didn't want to come back, afraid of what Mitch might do, but he had to, he had to get his job back, earn some money, take care of his house on Oak Street. He figured he'd be all right if he was careful, stayed away from Mitch, and got him some protection. So he bought a pistol before he left Detroit and started carrying it in his pocket, everywhere he went. When Hank returned to Stamps, Mitch hadn't changed much, at least not about his feelings toward Hank. He still thought Hank was the one who shot him, and he'd healed up enough to be more effective in doing something about it.

Not long after his return, Hank was in his living room and happened to glance out his front window at the street. He saw Mitch behind the wheel of his car, window down, looking closely at his house as he drove slowly by, as if he was trying to figure out if anyone was at home. A couple of days later it happened again, and this time Hank was standing in front of his house. Mitch drove slowly down the street, stopped the car in front of Hank's house, and stared hard at him. Hank thought his best bet was to act unafraid, so he met Mitch's challenge, locked eyes with him, and stared back. Suddenly Mitch broke eye contact and pulled his car quickly to the curb on the other side of the street. He jumped out, ran to the back of the car, opened the trunk, and reached in.

Hank was certain that Mitch was reaching for a gun in his trunk. He pulled his pistol from his pocket and ran back into his house. He hustled upstairs to a second floor bedroom overlooking the street. Leaning his back against the wall, he peeked around the edge of a window down at the street, but Mitch's car wasn't there, so he waited and watched. He looked across the room at the telephone by the bedside and thought that if Mitch came into view he would call the cops and hope they arrived before the shooting started. After several minutes of nothing, he went to another part of the house where he was able to get a better view of the street. He didn't see Mitch's car anywhere. After a few minutes of more nothing, he decided Mitch had chosen to wait for another time.

It came about a week later. Once again, Hank was outside in the front yard, this time talking to a neighbor. Mitch drove up in his car, pulled over to the curb in front of them, headed in the wrong direction, lowered his window, and asked the neighbor if he'd seen Hank. After he asked the question, he shifted his gaze and stared directly at Hank.

Caught in the byplay, the neighbor was confused, thinking maybe the man in the car didn't know Hank, didn't realize that Hank was standing right next to him. He smiled back at Mitch, nodded his head, and pointed his finger in Hank's direction thinking Mitch would understand the gesture. Mitch said nothing. Hank said nothing. That's when the neighbor realized something was amiss, glancing first at Hank then at Mitch. The two men were glaring at each other, their mutual loathing unmistakable. Mitch again asked the neighbor if he'd seen Hank. Now worried, the neighbor started to speak, but before he could answer Mitch had already started to pull his car away from the curb. Hank stood there, his hand in his pocket, watching the back of Mitch's car until it disappeared around the corner. Then, without saying another word, he turned and walked into his house.

The day Hank killed Mitch was one of those great spring days that only occur in the south, bright and sunny, not too humid, not too hot, with a gentle breeze that makes the flowers dance. Hank was at his mother's house with two of his friends Perry Sanford and Larry Raymond. As usual, his pistol was in his pocket.

The three men were just hanging around, not doing much. They moved a few boxes in his mother's garage, speculated about what it would take to build a workbench, talked a little baseball, and teased Hank's mother about cooking dinner for them. About noon they decided to walk to a nearby dairy bar and have some lunch, after which they planned to go back to Hank's house on Oak Street.

They left his mother's house and walked down the street toward the dairy bar. They hadn't gone far when Hank spotted Mitch and Jamie "Bo" Willis walking toward them on the other side of the street. Even though it was warm, Mitch was wearing a jacket. Hank slowed down.

"Uh-oh, see that?" he asked.

"I see it," Perry Sanford said.

"See what?" Larry Raymond asked, looking around.

"Across the street. You see Mitch Capron and 'Bo' Willis?" Hank asked.

"Capron the one with the jacket?" Larry asked.

"Yup."

"Why's he wearing a jacket on a day like today?" Larry continued.

"Good question."

"You think he's got a gun or something under there?" Perry asked.

"Could be," Hank said. He kept walking, more slowly now, his eyes fixed on Mitch, his right hand in his pants pocket. "The last time I saw him on the street like this he started shooting at me. Emptied his gun."

Larry stopped on the sidewalk. Hank and Perry glanced back at him. "What?" Perry asked.

"What are you talking about? Emptied his gun? I don't like this, man," Larry said. "Let's get the hell out of here."

Hank looked back at Mitch and "Bo" Willis. Both of them were looking in his direction. "He's not after you," he said. "I'm the one he wants to kill."

"What? Kill. But I'm here, man," Larry said. "You know the other guy?"

"Yea, "Bo" Willis. He was there the night Capron got shot at that bar. He's one of the ones who say I did it."

As the three men stood watching, a car entered the intersection down the street, turned left, and headed in their direction. "That car," Hank said, "that's Capron's car. I think…"

Perry interrupted, "Look, he just gave 'Bo' Willis something," he said. "Did you see it, Hank? Mitch took something out of his jacket and gave it to Bo, and Bo put it in his pocket. Maybe that's his gun."

"Did you see a gun?" Hank asked.

"No, but what else could it be?" Perry replied.

"Let's get out of here," Larry said.

The car slowed, crossed over the oncoming lane of travel, and stopped at the curb next to Mitch and "Bo."

"That's Capron's mother," Perry said. "It must be her car."

The car blocked their view of "Bo," but they could still see Mitch talking to his mother, her left arm out the car window, palm up, gesturing in her son's direction, but too far away for them to hear what she was saying. Hank looked over his shoulder back down the street toward his mother's house. He thought maybe he should run for it as fast as he could. If Mitch's mom talked to her son long enough he could make it. He looked back in Mitch's direction. They were still talking, maybe arguing. Mitch's arms were outstretched toward his mother, like he was explaining something. He shook his head no, then opened his jacket, lifted his shirt, and turned around, allowing her to see his waist, front and back.

"What's going on?" Larry asked.

"I don't know. I can't hear them. Maybe they'll get in the car," Hank said, turning and starting toward his mother's house.

Perry shook his head. "Nope. Too late, she's leaving." Hank stopped and the three men watched as Mrs. Capron turned her head, checking for traffic, then drove away from the curb. She cut back across the street into her own lane of travel and drove straight past them. Hank looked back where she'd just left. Mitch and "Bo" Willis had stepped off the sidewalk and were walking diagonally across the street in their direction.

"Did you see Willis give him anything back?" Hank asked hurriedly.

"No," Perry said.

"I wasn't watching," Larry added. "Let's get out of here."

"I can't," Hank said. "If I turn around he'll try to shoot me in the back. I got lucky last time. Man, this is not good." He scanned left, then right, looking for a way to get out of there, but there was no escape. He couldn't outrun a bullet and there was nothing to get behind. All he could do was take his chances. He turned to face Mitch and "Bo," who were already across the street, and tightened the grip on the gun in his pocket.

The three men stood silently as Mitch and "Bo" stepped onto the sidewalk. Hank shifted his feet to square up with Mitch. When Mitch was about five feet from them, he stepped off the sidewalk onto the grass. "Bo" followed and the two men walked on the grass by Hank. Larry glanced at Hank questioning what had just happened, but Hank didn't answer. Instead, he kept his eyes on Mitch.

As if he sensed Hank's stare, Mitch turned around. "You got a problem?" he asked.

"I didn't shoot you, Mitch," Hank said. "I know people have said it, but it isn't true. I didn't do it."

"A lot of people I trust say differently," Mitch said glancing at "Bo." "Bo" moved to his right putting some space between himself and Mitch and Hank.

"Well, they're wrong," Hank said.

"I don't think they're wrong," Mitch said. "I think you're a lying piece of crap. And I think it's about time you paid for it you son-of-a-bitch." Mitch lunged at Hank hitting him with both hands hard on the chest, knocking him back onto the grass. Hank staggered, almost falling, but managing to stay on his feet.

"Son of a bitch," Mitch screamed again, reaching inside his jacket as he came at Hank. Hank drew the pistol from his pocket and pulled the trigger as fast as he could, not stopping until the gun was empty. There were fourteen rounds in the magazine and one in the chamber and Hank shot them all. Mitch was within arm's reach and it was pretty hard to miss at that distance. He fell to the ground at the fifth or sixth shot, but Hank kept pulling the trigger until there was nothing left, until the slide on his gun came back and locked open.

Larry, Perry, and "Bo" all ran into the street when the shooting started. When it stopped, Hank was standing on the grass, trembling, the empty gun in his hand. He was looking at Mitch lying on the sidewalk, blood pooling around his body.

"Jesus Christ," Larry said.

"You alright?" Perry asked, looking at Hank. Hank didn't answer. He stared at Mitch lying at his feet. Blood seemed to be everywhere.

"Bo" knelt down beside Mitch, opened his jacket, felt along the sides of his chest then around his waist. Hank looked away hoping "Bo" could keep Mitch alive, but inside he knew it wasn't going to happen. Mitch was already dead. The police arrived shortly thereafter and searched Mitch's body, but they didn't find any weapon. They arrested Hank, took his gun, but they didn't search anyone else.

FURTIVE GESTURES MAY BE CLARIFIED BY CONTEXT

At the end of Hank's trial the judge refused to let the jury decide whether he had shot Mitch in self-defense. The judge said that Hank had fired fifteen times, and that shooting someone fifteen times was inconsistent with a claim of self-defense. Moreover, the fact that those shots were fired into an unarmed man at close range suggested that Hank had acted out of malice, hostility, and ill will and not out of a desire to protect himself from harm. The jury convicted Hank of murder and the judge sentenced him to life in prison without parole.

Hank's lawyer appealed the conviction arguing that the jury should have been allowed to determine if Hank reasonably feared he was about to be killed or seriously injured at the time of the shooting. If the jury thought such was the case, then Hank couldn't be convicted of murder because he didn't possess the requisite murderous intent. The attorney asked the appeals court to give Hank a new trial and to allow him to tell the jury his side of the story. The appellate court spent a lot of time looking at the facts because the case was difficult to untangle.

The pivotal question was whether it was reasonable for Hank to believe that when Mitch reached into his jacket as the fight began on the sidewalk, he was reaching for a gun to shoot Hank. If it was reasonable for Hank to believe that Mitch had a gun then it was reasonable for him to fear for his life, and if it was reasonable for Hank to fear for his life, then he was permitted to use deadly force to avoid being killed. The facts of the case fell into three categories: what was known to be true, what might be true, and what Hank believed to be true. That there was no gun on Mitch's body when the police arrived was known to be true. That fact, however, given the circumstances surrounding the shooting, doesn't negate the possibility that Mitch may have had a gun on him when he was shot, and it doesn't change Hank's response to Mitch's behavior.

Mitch's act of reaching for something inside his jacket as he charged at Hank the second time is a furtive gesture, behavior that is ambiguous, unclear, its purpose unknown. There's no question about who started the fight. Mitch attacked Hank suddenly, violently, and without provocation. He failed to knock Hank to the ground with his first assault and moved to attack him again, this time reaching inside his coat as he did so. If his behavior is looked at only in the context of the fistfight that unfolded on the sidewalk, then it is a part of just a fistfight. It remains a furtive gesture, its purpose unknown, and does not warrant the use of deadly force in response.

Hank is entitled, however, to assess Mitch's behavior, and his intent, not only by his behavior on the sidewalk, but also by his behavior toward Hank in the past. He may also take into account Mitch's reputation for violence and rely on his own prior experiences with Mitch. That additional information provides a very different context around Mitch's furtive gesture.

On three previous occasions when they met, Mitch either had a gun on him or was suspected of having a gun on him. Hank believed he had a gun. The first time, Mitch shot at Hank with a pistol as Hank ran down the street. Not only did he possess a gun on that occasion, but he also demonstrated the willingness to use it against Hank. The second time, Mitch pulled his car quickly to the curb after a confrontation with Hank in front of his house, opened the trunk, and reached for something inside. Given his threat to kill Hank, his prior attempt to shoot him, and it being hard to think of any other reason why he might be reaching into the trunk at that time, it is highly likely that he was reaching for a gun. The third occasion occurred just prior to Mitch being killed, when he passed something to "Bo," for "Bo" to hide from his mother. Mitch's behavior, the gestures of inquiry and denial between him and his mother, his lifting his shirt and turning around so his mother could see the front and back of his waist, implies that he was concealing something from her, and that whatever it was, it could be hidden in his waistband. It is but a short step to believe that the object he was hiding from his mother was a gun. "Bo" gave whatever he was hiding back to Mitch after his mother left. Watching this behavior from across the street, Hank believed that what they were hiding was a gun.

JUDGING REASONABLENESS

At the heart of every valid self-defense claim is a reasonable fear, held in good faith, that imminent death or serious bodily injury is about to befall a person if he or she doesn't act immediately to avoid it. It isn't about the number of shots fired or the presence of a weapon, it is about the reasonableness of the shooter's belief that he or she is about to be killed or injured. The question is what would a reasonable person, or a person of reasonable courage, believe if faced with the same fact pattern as the shooter? If a reasonable person would believe there exists an imminent threat of death or serious bodily injury, then the shooter may claim self-defense. If a reasonable person wouldn't believe such is the case, then the shooter may not claim self-defense.

As we have said repeatedly, there are two important questions that focus on determining reasonableness: (1) do the facts make it reasonable for the shooter to believe that there exists an imminent threat of death or serious injury, and (2) was it reasonable for the shooter to be afraid of that threat. Reasonable fear is based on a reasonable belief in the existence of a deadly threat. If the facts are such that it is not reasonable to believe a deadly threat exists, then it is not reasonable to kill anyone based on fear of being killed or injured.

Let's look at the first question, whether the facts support a reasonable belief in the existence of a deadly threat. The majority of states say that reasonableness is what a reasonable person, or a person of reasonable courage, would believe if faced with the same set of facts as the shooter.[2] Under this approach the jury acts as a hypothetical reasonable person, looks at the facts, and decides what a reasonable person would believe in the same situation. If the jury thinks a reasonable person would believe the facts show the shooter was in deadly danger, then it's reasonable for the shooter to hold such a belief. If the jury thinks a reasonable person wouldn't believe such danger existed, then the shooter's belief is unreasonable.

A minority of states follows a different approach. They say that reasonableness is determined not by what a third party reasonable person might believe, but rather by what was reasonable for the defendant to believe, in good faith, based on the situation as he or she perceived it at the time of the killing. In these states, juries look at the facts through the eyes of the shooter to determine, based on what he or she perceived, whether it is reasonable to believe that deadly danger was present.[3] Again, if the jury decides it was reasonable for the shooter to believe a deadly threat existed, then there was a right to use deadly force to avoid it. If the jury decides it wasn't reasonable for the shooter to hold such a belief, then the defendant may not use deadly force.

PERCEPTIONS AS WELL AS REALITY CAN TRIGGER SELF-DEFENSE

Notice that nowhere do we say that reasonableness must be based on actual fact, that the facts must accurately or realistically portray an actual, real imminent threat of death or serious injury. That's because the threat doesn't have to be real. It only has to appear to be real, such that a person encountering it would reasonably believe it was real. Put differently, the shooter's perception of the threat doesn't have to be accurate. It has to be reasonable. If it's reasonable, then the shooter may respond with deadly force even though a real threat doesn't actually exist.

That means the issue in self-defense cases is not whether the victim is actually endangering the shooter, but whether he or she appears to be endangering the shooter such that a reasonable person would be afraid under the circumstances. Neither the majority nor the minority approach for determining reasonableness requires that the deadly threat actually exist only that it seemed to exist, such that a reasonable person would believe in its presence.

For example, suppose a stranger pulls a gun and points it at you and threatens to shoot you, causing you to draw your own pistol and kill him. The facts certainly make it reasonable for you to believe that you are facing an imminent threat of death or serious bodily injury. It is also reasonable for you to fear that threat and take measures to save your life. In short, the circumstances indicate deadly danger, and the deadly danger warrants your fear. But what if the stranger's gun is unloaded? It can't hurt you because it has no bullets in it. The threat is not real and you were never in any real danger. Unless you knew that beforehand, it doesn't matter that the gun is empty because reasonableness is based on the facts as they were thought to exist at the time of the shooting. A reasonable person presented the facts without knowing the gun was unloaded would still believe that he or she faced an imminent deadly threat and would still be fearful of losing his or her life because of that threat. If the threat appears to be real, even though it isn't, a person may still react to it and take necessary measures to avoid it. Every police officer who has faced a person with a gun, believing it was loaded when it was not, a person who wants to commit "suicide by cop" understands the issue of reasonableness in the presence of a threat that isn't real.

Perceptions can also work against a claim of self-defense. For example, when the police arrived they didn't find a gun on Mitch's body, and that fact worked against Hank. So what was the item "Bo" concealed from Mitch's mother and then gave back to him after she left? Mitch and "Bo's" secretive behavior, passing the item back and forth, creates a question of whether Mitch had a gun on him at the time he was shot, and "Bo" removed it as he lay dying on the sidewalk. "Bo's" behavior after the shooting suggests Mitch may have been armed. "Bo" knelt down beside his friend, opened his jacket, and moved his hands over Mitch's sides and waist. In police parlance he contaminated the body creating a possibility that a gun was removed from it before they arrived. The perception that Mitch was unarmed, while true when the police arrived, may not have been true when Hank fired the shots that killed him. Unfortunately, the police failed to search anyone at the scene other than Hank, meaning that "Bo," the man who had already hidden something on Mitch's behalf that day, is the only person who knows if Mitch was armed.

REALITY, PERCEPTION, AND MISTAKES

If the appearance of deadly danger, rather than its reality, supports a claim of self-defense, then logically, in certain situations, a person may still employ deadly force even though he or she has misjudged the danger, mistaken the threat, or been misled by the facts, the stranger pointing an unloaded gun at you being a case in point. The law allows for this kind of case, recognizing there is not always enough time in self-defense situations for a careful examination of all the facts before action must be taken or forfeited. Sometimes life and death decisions must be made in a split second, and human beings, in fast moving situations, cannot always determine, with complete accuracy, if the threat is real.

The law judges these kinds of cases by assuming the shooter would have had the right to use deadly force had his or her assessment of the threat been accurate. A caveat is that it looks at the reasonableness of the mistake. If the shooter's mistake is reasonable, because under the circumstances a reasonable person would have made the same mistake, then the shooter properly exercised his right of self-defense. If the shooter's mistake is unreasonable, then he or she will be held accountable for the victim's unlawful death.[4] Once again, the states use the same approaches for deciding what is reasonable. As long as the shooter has a reasonable fear, honestly held, of a deadly threat, and the facts as they appear to a reasonable person support the perception of such a threat, then the shooter may exercise his or her right of self-defense, even if he or she is mistaken about the nature of the threat.[5]

WHAT IS A REASONABLE FEAR?

Now the question is: was it reasonable for Hank to fear for his life when he encountered Mitch on the sidewalk? If there is imminent deadly danger, or at least the appearance of imminent deadly danger, then the jury must decide if the shooter's fear of the danger was reasonable and honestly held. There are two parts to this question. Was it reasonable and was it honestly held? The standard approaches for determining reasonableness apply. At the same time, it is worth looking a little bit more closely at what constitutes a reasonable fear.

A reasonable fear is more than a mere declaration of fear, a naked expression of the shooter's fright or terror. The evidence must show that the shooter was the target of an unlawful, deadly threat, and not just fearful of his or her circumstances. For example, suppose you're in a garage late at night on your way to your car when a stranger approaches. Alarm bells sound inside your head, your senses alert, your instincts shout at you, beware, pay attention. The stranger isn't doing anything threatening, just walking toward you, but you're uncomfortable about the parking garage, about the time of night, about no one else being around, about what is happening. It just doesn't feel right.

Your fear is quite genuine, but it's said to be undifferentiated because the stranger's behavior is not directed specifically at you, and there's nothing you can point to that suggests you specifically are the intended target of some unlawful violent behavior. You can't pull a handgun out of your waistband or your pocketbook and shoot the stranger and then claim self-defense because the facts don't support a reasonable belief that the stranger presents an imminent deadly threat. He has done nothing threatening, and the most likely outcome of your encounter is that the stranger walks past you, gets into a car, and drives away.

Change the circumstances a bit and you have a much different result. Suppose the stranger pulls a knife and picks up the pace staring intently in your direction, walking rapidly and directly at you. Your fear is no longer undifferentiated. Indeed, it is likely to be quite focused. The facts now show that you specifically are the target, and that the threat is potentially a deadly one. The stranger has behaved in a hostile manner, observable, threatening, imminent, fixated on you. A "danger-danger-danger" warning bell is now clanging inside your head, signaling that you must act immediately if you wish to avoid being killed or hurt. The facts now support your belief in the existence of a deadly threat against you, and your fear of that threat, of being killed or injured, is entirely reasonable. Indeed, given the situation, it is hard to fathom how it wouldn't be.

Next is the second part of the question: is the reasonable fear honestly held? The shooter's reputation and credibility are important in deciding this question. If he or she testifies is the testimony believable? If he or she doesn't testify, is there other testimony or are there other facts in the case that corroborate what the shooter says happened? Does the shooter have a reputation for violence or nonviolence? Does the shooter have a reputation for honesty and truthfulness? Did he or she behave in a way that suggests fear of being killed or seriously hurt? Do the shooter's lifestyle and habits suggest stability and reliability? These are some of the questions a jury might ask in thinking about whether the shooter honestly feared for his or her life.

FURTIVE GESTURES AS PART OF A KNOWN RELATIONSHIP

Hank's attorney argued to the appellate court that Hank shot Mitch because he feared Mitch was about to pull a gun and shoot him, and that given the circumstances of their prior relationship, his fear of death or injury was warranted and reasonable even if his assessment of the threat was mistaken. The trial judge, he claimed, focused too narrowly on the circumstances of just the final encounter and should have expanded the context of Mitch's furtive gesture to include other prior encounters.

The appellate court agreed with him concluding that the jury should have been allowed to consider Hank's assessment of Mitch's furtive gesture within the context of their entire relationship. Hank was entitled to use his knowledge of Mitch's reputation and his past behavior toward Hank in assessing the reason why Mitch was reaching inside his coat. The appellate court set aside Hank's conviction and sent the case back to the lower court for a new trial at which Hank would be allowed to tell the jury his side of the story.

8

DUTY TO RETREAT

INVESTIGATING POSSIBLE DANGER

Michael Smith was a twenty-eight-year-old hospital staff nurse from Wilmington, Delaware, a friendly young man, with a ready smile, well liked by his co-workers and by the patients he cared for. He was average-sized with Caribbean dark features and an athlete's build. Quick and strong, he was competitive, loved sports, and was pretty good at most of them. If you needed another player, even at the last minute, Michael was usually a good bet regardless of what game you were playing, unless he was with Rebecca Cohen.

Rebecca was a bright and spunky twenty-five-year-old staff nurse at the hospital. Michael thought she made the sun rise every morning. She loved sports, too, but without the testosterone. She was a runner, chalking up four miles a day, more on the weekend if she was feeling ambitious. She met Michael at a hospital staff meeting. Later he had spotted her working out, had been smart enough to buy some running shoes, and the rest, as they say, was history. Michael was more than smitten. He thought himself the luckiest guy in the world. He counted days until the weekends when he would be with Rebecca, and he told his friends he couldn't believe she was his.

The two made a great couple. They were fun to be with. After they moved in together, Michael's sports time took a serious hit. Rebecca worried he'd get hurt playing some of the more physical games, especially football. The guys he played with couldn't seem to understand it was just touch football, not the NFL, and Michael invariably was the oldest guy in the game. She urged him to give it up, stick with running and tennis, act his age. His buddies teased him. They accused him of becoming a wimp. He was henpecked, "Becky's boy," they said. Michael didn't care. He was just too happy.

It was Rebecca's concern about pickup football that made her think of spending a day with Michael at the shore on one of her off weekends. She told him she wanted to get away from the city and asked if he would take her to Rehoboth, maybe find an empty spot on the beach, have a picnic, just sit and watch the waves roll in. Michael wasn't hard to convince. For Rebecca, he was never hard to convince.

So one Saturday morning late in September they packed a cooler, grabbed an old blanket, picked out a bottle of wine, and threw it all into Michael's Mustang. Michael took his .38 caliber revolver and locked it in the glove compartment of his car. He sometimes took the pistol with him, particularly when he expected to be driving at night, just in case. Their packing done, they both grabbed a cup of coffee for the road and headed south on Route 9 for Dover.

It was a perfect fall day, cool but not cold, the sky was bright blue, dotted here and there with puffy white clouds, even the traffic was light. About an hour out they stopped at a general store for some ice cream, and Rebecca happened to pick up a brochure about the Prime Hook National Wildlife Refuge.

"Hey Michael, look at this, this is kind of interesting," she said. "It says this time of the year, 100,000 snow geese and about 80,000 ducks stop over at this wildlife refuge on their way south."

Michael was pulling a twenty dollar bill from his wallet to pay for the ice cream. "Yea, I guess it's that time of year, isn't it," he said, handing the money to the woman at the cash register.

"Wow, look at these pictures. Amazing. Let's go, Michael."

"Go where?"

"To the Prime Hook National Wildlife Refuge, it's not far."

"This is Delaware babe, nothing's far."

Rebecca raised her eyes and gave him "the look." "Alright, wise guy," she said. "Seriously, it's down by Milford. Let's go. I'd like to see it. I've got the camera and we can take some pictures. OK?"

"How about we eat the ice cream first," he said, smiling. She squinted one eye at him, mumbled something under her breath, and went back to reading the brochure. Typical Rebecca, he thought, loves animals.

Back in the car, they continued south to Dover, got on Route 1, and drove toward Milford. They found the wildlife refuge easy enough, stopped at the visitor's center, picked up a map of the place, and set out to explore it. Remarkably, the day worked out just as Rebecca had hoped. They found a deserted spot on the beach, spread out their blanket, and spent a few hours just sitting, eating, watching the waves and the migrating birds. About 5 o'clock, when the sky was signaling the day's end they left the park and began making their way back to Wilmington, driving generally north, in no particular hurry, having no particular route in mind.

About an hour and a half later they were parked in a pullover area on an elevated portion of a secondary road looking west toward what was going to be a spectacular sunset. The pullover area wasn't big, maybe able to handle three or four cars if people were careful, but that didn't matter because nobody else was there, they had the place to themselves.

They hadn't been there long when another car came up the road, traveling in their direction. When it got close enough to see into the pullover area, it slowed down and put on its turn signal, indicating its intent to pull in. Michael noticed the car's flashing light in his rear-view mirror.

"Looks like we've got company," he said.

Rebecca leaned forward in her seat and looked into the passenger door mirror. "There's enough room for two, he can park up there," she said, pointing to the space in front of them.

The car, an older Chevrolet, had seen better days and probably better owners. The paint on is hood was marred by a combination of sun damage and grime. The driver appeared to be a middle-aged man, somewhat overweight from what they could see, unshaven, with long stringy hair, wearing a camouflage shirt and a New York Yankees baseball cap. He was alone.

"I wonder what he's coming in here for," Michael said.

"Maybe he wants to see the sunset too," Rebecca said.

"Doesn't look like the sunset type."

"Stop being cynical."

"I'm not being cynical."

The Chevrolet started to pass on the right side of their car, but moved very slowly. Michael thought maybe the driver was checking out his Mustang. He turned in his seat to get a better look and saw that the driver wasn't interested in his car at all. He was fixated on Rebecca, staring intently at her, turning his head as he inched along her side of the car.

Rebecca seemed to feel the intensity of his gaze, glanced in the man's direction, met his stare, and turned quickly away. She shrugged her shoulders, uncomfortable, and ignored the car as it passed. Just another example of what women had to put up with every day, she thought.

The man continued turning his head to look at Rebecca, paying no attention to where he was going until he was looking back over his left shoulder. He stopped the car, lifted his eyes, and looked at Michael. He sat there a minute, apparently thinking, and then he sped up, moved in front of them, and parked.

"Well, that was awkward," Rebecca said, looking at Michael.

"Creepy," he replied. "I wonder what he's doing now."

They looked through the windshield at the car in front of them. The man was moving around inside the car, leaning across the front seat, getting something from the glove compartment, straightening himself, as if he was putting whatever it was into his front pocket, or maybe tucking it inside his belt. He opened the door, got out of his car, glanced back at Michael and Rebecca, and walked into the woods.

"I wonder where he's going now," Rebecca said.

"Probably to take a leak," Michael said.

"You think so?"

"What else. That's probably why he was checking us out."

"Yea, maybe. Still pretty weird though."

"Hey, what are you going to do? The world's full of weird people," Michael said, reaching down, hitting the lock switch securing the car's doors. The sound of snapping door locks caught Rebecca's attention.

"Maybe we just ought to go," she said.

"Let's wait a minute. It's a pretty sunset, it'll be gone soon enough."

"It is," she said, looking west at the horizon. The fading sun was shooting orange rays across the sky and creating a reddish glow near the horizon.

"We don't see many of these from the apartmen," she said.

"We surely don't," he replied.

Michael thought he caught a glimpse of movement in the outside rearview mirror attached to the driver's door. He turned his head and looked more carefully. There was nothing there, just a bunch of trees on a small knoll behind them near the entrance to the pullover area. Rebecca saw him looking in the mirror.

"What's the matter?" she asked.

"Oh, I thought I saw something in the mirror, maybe not. It was in the trees back there, maybe a raccoon or something looking for food," he said.

Then Michael saw the movement again in the mirror. This time he was sure what it was. The man from the car was watching them from the trees on the knoll behind them. He must have gone into the woods far enough not to be seen then circled back around until he came out in back of them. He was just standing there, very close, maybe twenty-five yards away, looking in their direction. His camouflage shirt made it hard to see him unless he moved, probably why Michael missed him the first time. Michael reached over, unlocked the glove compartment, and took out his revolver.

Rebecca's eyes grew wide when she saw Michael put the gun in his lap. "What are you doing?"

"Our friend from the car up front is standing in the trees back there watching us."

Rebecca turned in her seat and looked out the back window. "What's he doing? I don't see him."

"He's just standing there. See the bank, then the pine trees. He's right in the middle of those pine trees. Hard to see when he doesn't move."

"I don't see him, but I don't care. Let's get out of here."

Michael kept his eyes glued to the rearview mirror on his door. The man was still standing there, not moving. "I don't know," he said. "I don't like the way he was moving around before he got out of his car. He put something in his belt. I think he's got a gun."

"You don't know that, Michael. Let's just go."

"What happens if he does and I start the car? What happens if he comes running out of the woods shooting at us? We won't make it out of here before he gets to us."

"I don't know. I think we can get away before he gets too close. Let's go."

"Look, you got something to write with?"

"Yes."

"Write down his license plate number while I watch him."

Rebecca reached into the back seat and grabbed her pocketbook. She produced a piece of paper and a pen and wrote down the car's plate number and its color.

"What kind of car is it?" she asked.

Michael's eyes slid from the mirror to the man's car and back again. "Looks like an old Chevy Impala, maybe 1990s, I don't know," he said. Rebecca wrote some more.

"OK, got it," she said. "Let's go."

Michael didn't move. "This is what I want to do," he said. "I'm going to get out and go talk to him. I want you to take the car and drive up the road, keep going until you're out of sight. I've got my cell and I'll call you if everything is OK. Then you can come back and get me. If I don't call in five minutes, or you hear anything that doesn't sound right, call the cops."

"You mean doesn't sound right like gunshots. Michael, I'm not going to do that."

"Becky, you are going to do that. I think he's got a gun and I don't want you around if he does. I don't know if he wants anything from us, but I think so. I'm driving, and he's too close. If we try to leave, and he decides to come after us, there's nothing I can do to stop him and we won't make it before he's on us. I'm afraid one of us is going to get hurt and I don't want it to be you. I'll go talk to him, keep him occupied until you get out of here. If everything's OK you can come back and get me. If not, you can call the police, but at least you'll be out of here."

"Why don't we just call the cops now."

"Because he's watching us and maybe that'll set him off. Besides, if he doesn't have a gun we're going to look pretty stupid calling the cops saying there's a bogeyman in the woods with a gun."

Michael turned and looked at Rebecca, pleading. "Look Becky, please just do this. This guy doesn't care about me. This is about you. You saw the way he looked at you when he pulled in. You need to get out of here as fast as you can. If you're gone it's over, there's nothing he can do. I can stop him if he tries to follow you. So please, when I get out of the car just slide over, start it up, and get out of here. I'll call you."

Rebecca looked at Michael's face and saw the concern there, a reflection of her own growing fear. Michael turned back toward the mirror, put his hand around the pistol in his lap, and continued watching.

"Alright," she said. "I'll go, but if I don't hear from you in five minutes I'm calling the cops."

Michael nodded but he knew it wouldn't matter. If the guy had a gun and came after him it would all be over before the cops got there. He was afraid, afraid for himself, and for Rebecca. First and foremost he wanted to see her away from there.

Michael looked down at the ignition. The keys were in it. He was wearing a light jacket and put the revolver in its pocket, took a deep breath, looked at Rebecca. "OK," he said. "Here I go."

He got out of the car, closed the door, and turned toward the rear of the Mustang. Rebecca was already sliding across the console into the driver's seat. His eyes picked up the man in the woods. He was moving but Michael couldn't see what he was doing. He heard Rebecca start the engine, put the car in gear, and the car start moving. The Mustang's tires popped on the gravel as Rebecca drove toward the exit. Michael kept his eyes on the man in the trees, his hands in his jacket pockets.

If the man is going to attack he'll do it now, he thought. He found himself thinking like a linebacker, calculating where the man might go and how he would intercept him before he reached Rebecca. Then he heard the Mustang accelerate; Rebecca was on the highway moving rapidly down the road away from the rest stop, away from the danger. He glanced quickly over his shoulder and let out his breath. The Mustang was gone and she was safe.

He turned back to the man in the woods suddenly aware that he was standing in the middle of nowhere Delaware with a gun in his pocket confronting a strange man who was intensely interested in Rebecca. He felt very alone, very afraid, and he didn't know what to do.

The man stepped out of the trees, his camouflage shirt untucked and his black chino pants dirty around the knees. He was heavyset, bigger than Michael but out of shape, a beer belly stretching the buttons on his shirt. There was something heavy in the right pocket of his pants causing them to sag on that side. Michael thought the bulge looked like the outline of a semiautomatic pistol. The man said nothing. He just stood on the edge of the knoll looking down at Michael.

"What were you doing up there? Watching us?" Michael asked, but the man didn't answer.

"What were you doing up there?" he repeated.

"Nothing," the man said.

"What have you got in your pocket?"

"Nothing."

"Come on down," Michael said. "Let's talk,"

Michael's nursing skills kicked in and he began to assess the man. Apart from being slow to answer and his unusual behavior, he appeared to understand Michael's questions, know where he was, and what he was doing. That was a beginning, Michael thought. He would talk to the man, figure out what was going on, maybe it would all be OK.

"C'mon down. Let's talk," Michael said again.

The knoll where the man was standing came from the dirt, scraped from the side of the road when the pullover area was built. It wasn't very high but it was steep, the work of a bulldozer pushing earth. The man started down the bank, but half way down he slipped and started to fall. He reached out to steady himself, one hand grabbing for the bank the other reaching for the bulge in his pants pocket, his fingers spread like he was reaching for a pistol in its holster.

Instinctively, Michael stepped back creating some distance between himself and the stranger, his senses screaming danger. Now he was certain the man had a gun. Michael watched the man right himself, shifted the weight in his pocket, and stepped toward him. Once again, he stepped backward maintaining his distance.

"Wait, just stay there a minute," Michael said firmly, signaling with his hand for the man to stop, trying to control his movements.

"I don't know you. Who are you? What do you want?"

"I wanted to talk to the woman," the man said.

As soon as he spoke Michael realized the man was very angry. What he wanted was Rebecca, and Michael had prevented that by sending her away. The question now was, what was he going to do about it. Michael's first thought was to run, get away as fast as he could.

The stranger seemed to read his mind. He hooked his left thumb behind his belt buckle and his right thumb on the edge of his bulging pants pocket. He smiled at Michael, smug, dismissive. Michael stepped backward again. The stranger let his hands fall to his side and moved forward, still smiling.

"Wait, look, she's not here. She's gone. There's nothing I can do about…." Before Michael could finish the sentence the man charged, wrapping his arms around Michael's waist, hitting him in the midsection with his shoulder, tackling him to the pavement. Michael tried to avoid landing on his back, turning as he fell, landing hard on his left shoulder but with his right arm free. He twisted some more and punched the man in the face, twice, as fast as he could. The man let go and Michael scrambled to his feet. The man jumped up almost as fast, unhurt by Michael's blows. Michael backed up the road, his left arm in front of him, palm out, pumping the air motioning for the man to stop.

"Jesus, man, what are you doing? She's gone. Let's talk about it. It's not my fault. There's no need for this," Michael babbled, backing away, looking for words that might make a connection, ease the man's anger, calm him down.

The man continued toward him. "You sent her away," he accused, his voice flat, determined, angry, and dangerous.

"Let's call her. I've got my cell phone," Michael offered quickly. He moved his left hand toward his pocket.

"Don't do that," the man screamed, and charged him again, the same move, head down, shoulder lowered, hitting Michael squarely in the mid-section, this time knocking him flat on his back in the middle of the road. Michael's head hit the pavement with an audible thud, stunning him and almost knocking him unconscious. His attacker landed on top of Michael's chest. The man got quickly to his knees, hit Michael in the face with his fist.

"You son of a bitch, I'll kill you for that," he screamed. He leaned back toward Michael's knees and reached into his pocket, the one Michael knew held the pistol, and tried to pull it out, but he seemed to be having trouble.

Michael realized instinctively that if the man succeeded in getting the pistol out of his pocket he would die. He drew his own pistol from his jacket pocket and fired. A quarter of a mile away Rebecca heard three shots. She dialed 911.

The stranger's name was Ryan Chesney and he died before reaching the hospital. He was mentally disturbed, under the care of a psychiatrist, and had stopped taking his medicine. There was a .45 caliber pistol in his pocket. No one knew how or where he got it. When the police removed it the safety was off and the hammer was cocked, but it was caught in the lining of his pants pocket. The snag probably saved Michael's life. Michael Smith was tried in a Delaware state court, convicted of manslaughter, and sent to prison. He appealed the conviction. [1]

THE DUTY TO RETREAT AT THE CENTER OF CONTROVERSY

The duty to retreat is one of the most controversial areas of American self-defense law. Some people see it as part of a never-ending political struggle between liberals and conservatives, between those who tend to favor collective responsibility and those who tend to favor individual responsibility, those who believe government should protect us versus those who believe we should protect ourselves. Others see it in economic terms: rich versus poor, people who can afford to hire bodyguards to protect them versus people who can't. Still others see the duty as having racial overtones, an unfortunate truth, because some of the nation's early gun laws were passed to limit African Americans from possessing firearms. Regardless of the political overtones, the duty to retreat is controversial because it requires behavior that many Americans find distasteful. Understanding it requires a short trip through a bit of English and U.S. legal history.

THE DUTY'S ORIGIN IS IN ENGLISH COMMON LAW

The duty to retreat comes from English common law, law made by early English judges, not the king or the Parliament. It began during the Middle Ages, a product of English courts trying to be fair, looking to ensure that people in similar circumstances received similar treatment. Judges, faced with a particular fact pattern, began to seek out other judges who had handled similar cases to learn what they had decided, and more importantly, why they'd decided the way they did. The practice of consulting other judges with similar cases gave rise to the written decision, a way for judges to explain their opinions to a wider audience. Over time, these written decisions produced a common understanding, a common law, of how to handle a particular type of case. Self-defense was one of them.

In early England, indeed in modern England, the government doesn't approve of people defending themselves with deadly force, even when faced with mortal danger. Through much of English history only government officials, or agents of the king, could take a life and then claim the killing was justified. Anyone else involved in such an act was guilty of "homicide by misadventure," forfeited his assets to the crown, and might avoid further punishment by seeking the king's pardon.[2] The king might or might not grant a pardon, and the fact the person seeking it was trying to avoid his own death or serious injury played no part in his decision. The king could grant or withhold his forgiveness as he pleased. It was a good time and place to be a friend of the king.

The king's preferences notwithstanding, people opted to defend themselves against deadly threats, some of them in situations where they were clearly justified in doing so. English judges, faced with such cases, gradually, begrudgingly, began to recognize an individual right of self-defense. They didn't like the concept, however, perhaps they even feared it because they believed the ability to use force to protect oneself from deadly danger, in the hands of common people, would become a subterfuge to justify murder.

To prevent such abuse they tightly controlled the circumstances under which a person could claim self-defense. One of the controls they devised was that before a person could fight back, he had to show he had retreated "to the wall,"[3] a legal term of art used to describe a point in time at which the person, at least figuratively speaking, was trapped with his back against a wall and no way to escape, his only option being either to protect himself with deadly force or forfeit his life. The judges saw it as a way to guard against murder, but in practical terms, on the English street, it meant that a person facing death or serious injury had to either run away or accept a position of disadvantage, waiting until his attacker had complete control of the situation before using deadly force in response.

THE SPIRIT OF THE AMERICAN "WEST"

Common law notions of self-defense followed English colonists to America, and with them came the duty to retreat. America was not jolly old England, however. The new world had more than its fair share of thieves, murderers, and other scofflaws. It was also home to hostile native peoples who interpreted retreat in the face of one's enemy as a sign of weakness to be exploited. Moreover, European governments were not a benign presence in the new world. They recruited Native American tribes to serve as their proxies, and launched attacks against settlements belonging to other countries. It was hard for people on the frontier to know, at any given moment, which European conspiracy, in which European court, might bring them suddenly face-to-face with people who wanted to kill them. In addition to outsider threats, America's colonies had their own ruling elites who were inclined to impose their particular brand of politics or religious beliefs on others. It was not uncommon for local governments to enforce the wants of one group over another, all in service of the greater good, of course. Americans learned the hard way and quickly that money, status, and political elitism could be hard taskmasters on common folk.

Left to figure out how to deal with the new world's violence on their own, Americans first resisted, then rejected, English notions of self-defense. Running away in the face of sudden danger, or waiting until one was at a disadvantage that was likely to get him killed, didn't seem like such a good idea on the American frontier. There wasn't much sense in retreating "to the wall," in a world where, if you were lucky enough to get your back covered by a wall, there was no one else there to help you. In the "untamed West," places like Ohio, people thought it shear madness to rely on others, particularly on government officials, to guarantee their personal safety. So they began to discard the common law notion of retreat in the face of deadly danger, and in its stead created a new, less restrictive approach to self-defense, one that did not require retreat in the face of danger. They took the new approach with them as they marched westward toward the Pacific. Courts in the newly formed territories adopted and refined it as judges made law and legislatures followed up by formally writing it into the statutes.

THE "TRUE MAN" DOCTRINE

In 1876, an Ohio court convicted a man named James W. Erwin of second degree murder for killing his son-in-law over a dispute involving possession of a shed. The son-in-law confronted Erwin threatening him with an ax. Erwin warned his son-in-law to stay away from him with the ax, but his son-in-law ignored the warning and Erwin shot and killed him. In an appeal of his conviction for murder, Erwin challenged directly the common law notion of a duty to retreat, arguing that people under sudden attack should not be required to run from their attackers. The Ohio Supreme Court agreed with him, writing in its opinion: "[a] true man, who is without fault, is not obliged to fly from an assailant, who, by violence or surprise, maliciously seeks to take his life or do him enormous bodily harm."[4] Thus was born the "true man" doctrine, a view that holds an innocent person, who is suddenly attacked and threatened with death or great bodily injury, is not required to retreat "to the wall" before defending himself with deadly force.

The next year, the Indiana Supreme Court followed Ohio's lead in a case involving one of its citizens named John Runyan. Runyan killed a man who attacked him as he was leaning against the side of a building waiting for the results of an election. Runyan had done nothing to provoke the attack. One of the issues at his trial was whether he should have retreated when the threat became clear. He was convicted of murder and appealed his case to the Indiana Supreme Court, which concluded that he had no duty to retreat under the circumstances. The court described what it called the "American mind" observing that "when a person, being without fault and in a place where he has a right to be, is violently assaulted, he may, without retreating, repel force with force, and if, in the reasonable exercise of his right of self-defense, his assailant is killed, he is justifiable."[5] This language addresses a concern that lies at the heart of the duty to retreat, and one that troubles many Americans, namely, if I'm peacefully in a place where I have a right to be and I have done nothing wrong and I'm not bothering anyone, and I am suddenly attacked or threatened by another person who may not like me, or who may not want me there, why do I have to run away so someone else by threat of force can take my place? According to the Runyan case, you don't have to, at least not if the threat appears suddenly and without warning.

In 1905, the Minnesota Supreme Court continued the willingness of "Western" courts to limit the common law duty to retreat by expanding the "true man" doctrine to situations in which the person attacked, if required to retreat, would be exposed to great danger. The case involved an armed confrontation between two men with guns, and the gunfight's survivor claimed that he shot his adversary in self-defense. The Minnesota Supreme Court noted the common law duty to retreat was conceived before the general introduction of firearms and observed that "what might be a reasonable chance for escape in one situation might in the other be certain death. Self-defense has not, by statute nor by judicial opinion, been distorted, by an unreasonable requirement of the duty to retreat, into self-destruction."[6] The court concluded that imposing a duty to retreat in situations where there is no safe way to escape, is unreasonable and dangerous because it exposes the person being attacked to death or serious injury. Trite but true, the man or woman who can outrun a bullet has yet to be born. Thus the "true man" doctrine was expanded to eliminate the duty to retreat in situations where the person under attack is unable to escape safely, that is, unable to leave without being exposed to danger.

Today, all states follow the "true man" doctrine, as described in John Runyan's case, in one form or another. The settled law is that a person who is innocent of any wrongdoing, and in a place where he or she has a right to be, if confronted suddenly with imminent deadly danger may use deadly force if necessary to avoid the danger without first trying to escape. The reason is because there's no time to do anything else. U.S. Supreme Court justice Oliver Wendell Holmes Jr. described the doctrine's justification succinctly in 1921 in the case of *Brown v. United States*. He wrote "Detached reflection cannot be demanded in the presence of an uplifted knife."[7] Put another way, the need to act quickly or perish in the face of a sudden attack trumps the duty to retreat.

THE DUTY TO RETREAT AND THREATS THAT ESCALATE GRADUALLY

The need to act quickly does not eliminate the duty to retreat altogether. There is still the question of how the duty applies in situations that do not involve a sudden unprovoked attack, where there is some amount of time to consider alternatives to the use of deadly force, some amount of time to escape. Such cases often arise in the context of an escalating physical confrontation or a long simmering personal dislike. During these encounters there is usually a point in time where there are different pathways forward, a fork in the road so to speak, one path leading to further confrontation, the other to de-escalation. The issue often boils down to whether the defendant had sufficient time to take safely the path that would have avoided the confrontation. Questions about the duty to retreat in these types of cases continue to generate significant legal and political controversy.

The duty to retreat continues to be a factor in many self-defense claims. In some states it is part of the formal written law, in others it exists as a part of necessity, the question being whether at the time of the killing there was a reasonable alternative to the use of deadly force. The circumstances in which Michael Smith found himself in the pullover area on that late September evening in Delaware are a good example of how the duty to retreat often works, and why it is so controversial.

Delaware is a state that still formally recognizes a duty to retreat as part of its self-defense law. The judge's instructions to the jury in Michael's case describe the duty nicely.

"If the deceased first attacked the defendant, even though the attack was of such a character as to create in the defendant's mind a reasonable belief that he was in danger of death or great bodily harm, it was the defendant's duty to retreat, if he could safely do so, or to use such other reasonable means as were within his power to avoid the killing of the assailant."[8]

There is no question that Michael was in a place where he had a right to be or that Ryan Chesney was the aggressor who started the fight that led to his own death, a man intent on using unlawful violence to achieve unlawful aims toward Michael and toward Rebecca. When Chesney tried to pull the pistol from his pocket, Michael's back, as he lay in the middle of the road after being knocked down, was literarily and figuratively "against the wall." Chesney was on top of him and he had nowhere to go and no option available but to fight back or die. Yet in duty to retreat states that does not resolve the issue of Michael's innocence or guilt.

If one goes back in time, before Rebecca drove away in Michael's car, there were moments as the confrontation was escalating when danger seemed to be present and non-deadly alternatives available to avoid it. Michael became uncomfortable when Chesney entered the pullover area, and his discomfort increased when he watched as Chesney retrieved what Michael thought was a gun and put it into his pocket. When Michael locked the car doors in response to Chesney walking into the woods, it suggested that he sensed the possibility of danger, and if he didn't realize it then, he clearly did when he retrieved his own pistol after seeing Chesney watching them from the tree line. At any point during this period

Michael could have tried to avoid what he knew or thought might be danger by simply driving away.

He didn't because he thought there was a serious risk in doing so, one that would expose both him and Rebecca to the possibility of being shot. Chesney was not very far away, and if his intent was to take Rebecca, as Michael feared it was, he could be on them with his pistol before Michael could start the car and leave the area. Moreover, if Chesney attacked while Michael was trying to drive away, it would prevent him from protecting Rebecca. Michael believed Rebecca was the target and his first priority was to see her away safely. He thought the best way to achieve that was for him to distract Chesney while she escaped.

The Delaware jury didn't see it that way. It decided that Michael, as he sat in the car, his pistol in his lap, knew there was danger, and at that point in time he could have avoided the use of deadly force by driving away. His failure to retreat set the stage for the subsequent encounter in which Chesney was killed. Although the jury was not there and did not face the danger, it chose to substitute its judgment for Michael's about the danger associated with driving away and the risk it posed to both Michael and Rebecca. The jury convicted him of manslaughter, and upon appeal the Delaware Supreme Court upheld his conviction.

In duty to retreat states, as a matter of public policy, a person's first obligation, if confronted with danger, is to escape if possible. The fact that he or she did nothing wrong, or is in a place where they have a lawful right to be, or are acting peacefully, is irrelevant. The first duty is to flee. In practical terms it places defendants in the same position as people in early England. They must either run or wait until they are trapped with their backs "to the wall" with no possibility of escape before using deadly force to protect themselves. That idea, the notion that an innocent person who has done nothing wrong must give ground and run in the face of threats and intimidation doesn't sit well with the "American mind," and it is a driving force behind "stand-your-ground" laws.

9

STAND YOUR GROUND

TRYING TO AVOID TROUBLE

John Dempsey was twenty-two years old, lived in West Palm Beach, Florida, and worked road construction. He was a clean-cut, muscular young man of medium height with blond hair and blue eyes, a classic southern California beach boy, only on the wrong coast. He'd been accepted to several colleges out of high school, but decided to take a year off and work. He landed a job on a road crew and soon was sweating in the hot sun up and down Florida's east coast. He loved the job, the money was good, and somehow he just never showed up to register for college classes.

He was easy going, and fit in well with the roustabouts on his road crew. They were a hard working, hard playing bunch, sometimes playing a little too hard. A year before the shooting, the crew was celebrating John's twenty-first birthday in a Boynton Beach bar when a fistfight broke out between one of the crewmembers and a regular patron of the bar. The patron apparently took umbrage at some of the crew's language.

Before he knew what was happening, John found himself in the midst of a full-fledged bar brawl, something reminiscent of Dodge City in the 1880s. People were smacking each other around, smashing glasses and dishes, breaking up the furniture. In true Wild West fashion somebody threw a chair that scored a direct hit on the mirror behind the bar and broke a whole bunch of whisky bottles below it sending booze and broken glass flying in all directions. No one ever really figured out who threw the chair. When the fight was over, a slow cooker full of meatballs came up missing. No one ever figured out that one either.

The fight finally ended as most such things usually do. A couple of guys were taken to the emergency room with cuts and bruises, but nobody was seriously hurt. The bar suffered quite a bit of damage, but nobody got too excited about a bunch of broken furniture. The whole thing was just bad enough, or depending on your point of view, just good enough to qualify as a local legend. Most people thought it interesting, a story on other "historic" brawls ran in the local paper, and on the whole all the participants were quite proud of having been there.

Money for the damage came flooding into the bar's owners, most of it from people who weren't there during the fight, making the brawl very profitable, and the owners very happy. They put a sign up in the window for about a month after the incident, "This is where it happened!" and the number of patrons shot up, making them some more money. The cash, not to mention the notoriety, soothed everyone's hard feelings, and the general attitude became "hey nobody got hurt," "boys will be boys," and "you've got to admit, it was one helluva bar fight."

Unfortunately, cops everywhere hate bar fights, too much work, bad for the uniforms, and the Boynton Beach cops were no different. The fight was unseemly, offended their sense of good order, particularly the smashed mirror and broken whiskey bottles. Pleas for mercy were ignored, self-righteousness prevailed, and the legal charges flew. The prosecutor charged John and several others with participating in a riot. That seemed a bit excessive, but there was an upside. The charge, being somewhat unusual, caught the imagination of the local, then the national, media. The reporters picked up on the "boys will be boys" theme and portrayed the incident as a rockem-sockem, pie in the face, John Wayne worthy, fisticuffs, which, of course, made being part of it very valuable.

John hired a lawyer who cut him a quick deal. He pled guilty to the charge in exchange for paying a fine and six months probation. It seemed the quickest and cheapest way to make the problem go away. Then he went back to work, a little poorer and a little wiser.

It was during the fall of 2004, on a Friday evening, when the summer heat was leaving and the tourists were arriving, that John decided to meet Pete Suarez after work at a keg party. Pete was a member of his road crew. He was nineteen and popular with the crew, a hard worker with an easy smile. John arrived at the address Pete gave him around 8 p.m. He parked his pickup truck among dozens of others on the front lawn of a one-story, white stucco house and walked to the patio in back where there were maybe fifty or sixty people drinking beer and talking. In the background music blared through speakers set at one end of the patio.

The place was what you'd expect to find in one of Florida's working class neighborhoods. The house was a single story, cement block ranch, a standard flag stone patio in the back. There were tables and chairs strewn about. In one corner of the patio was a large, round plastic table with a small hole in the middle and an umbrella sticking out. People were sitting around the table talking and laughing. John didn't know any of them. A wooden table, obviously from inside the house, stood in another corner of the patio. On it was a large metal tub filled with ice and the beer keg. Another small table next to it contained stacks of clear plastic cups, and beside that the obligatory large, plastic trash can, half full of empty cups, dirty plates, soda cans, plastic water bottles, and bees, the refuse of what appeared to be a good time.

John searched faces in the crowd looking for Pete but didn't see him. The search was revealing in other ways though. The crowd seemed young to John, borderline high school. Not everyone looked that way, but enough to notice. He thought some of the younger looking ones were a little too boisterous, a little too animated, talked too much, laughed too loud, giggled too often. John looked for someone older, someone who maybe owned the place, an adult. Nobody seemed to fit the bill and he began to wonder if maybe they were inside the house, or if maybe he was at an underage drinking party at the home of some kid whose parents were away. It had been known to happen. He decided to make a quick search for Pete and then leave.

He spied a couple of attractive young women in their early twenties dressed in blue jeans and T-shirts standing by themselves with cups of beer in their hands. They looked like people Pete might know, so he walked over to them. Sensing his approach, they turned and smiled. When they did, John thought they were twins.

"Hi, I'm John," he said. "I'm looking for a friend of mine named Pete Suarez. You guys know him by any chance?"

"I do," the shorter one said. She was shorter by maybe a half-inch. "I think he's around here somewhere. I saw him earlier."

"You guys twins?" John asked.

"No, us guys are just sisters," the taller one said laughing. "A lot of people think we're twins, but we're not."

"You think it's OK if I get a beer and see if I can find Pete?" John asked.

"Oh, sure. No problem. Help yourself," the taller one said, nodding toward the keg. "You from around here?"

"Yea, I live in Wellington. You?"

"Hey, nice. We live in West Palm," the taller one said. "I'm Erin. This is my sister, Shana."

"Nice to meet you. My friend Pete asked me to meet him here. I'm afraid he's the only one I know."

"No worries," Erin said. "Everybody here's pretty laid back. Get yourself a beer and come on back."

"Thanks, I will. Let me see if I can find Pete first and I'll catch up with you later."

"Great. Tell Pete Shana is asking about him," Erin said, with eyes twinkling, waiting for her sister's reaction. Shana turned a bit red, shook her head, grinned, and rolled her eyes.

"I will," John said smiling. "See you in a bit."

John left the two laughing, Erin teasing Shana about Pete Suarez. He threaded his way through the crowd to where several people were gathered around the beer keg. He stood there a minute before realizing that nobody was actually getting any beer. They were just standing there talking and blocking the way. He excused himself, slid sideways between two guys, picked up a plastic cup, and filled it with beer, misjudging it as usual, causing the beer to foam over the cup, onto his hand, and down onto the ground. Excusing himself again, he moved back through the talkers, away from the table.

He worked his way through the partygoers, across the patio, to the back door of the house. He decided to go in and look for Pete. He turned the doorknob and pushed open the door, or at least he tried to. The door moved, but then hit something and stopped. Swearing came from inside the house and John heard the slosh of a beer cup hitting the floor.

"Jesus, man. What the hell are you doing?" someone cried from inside.

John stepped back and the door opened. Standing there was a young man in shorts and a sleeveless T-shirt. He was in his late teens or early twenties, muscular, and heavily tattooed with dark blue patterns and pictures on his arms, neck, and chest. He was bigger than John by about thirty pounds. He had a scraggly beard and wore a dirty baseball cap with a Bass Pro Shops logo on it. He looked like he might have spent the day out in a boat on the water. His low cut sneakers and his legs were drenched in beer. An empty plastic beer cup lay on its side at his feet. A second young man similarly dressed but minus the tattoos, and the beer on his legs, was right behind him.

"Ah damn. I'm sorry," John said. "I didn't see you there. Let me get something and I'll clean up this mess." John took a handkerchief from his back pocket and offered it to the young man. "Here, this will get it off your legs. I'll go get some paper towels."

The young man made no move to take the handkerchief. He just stood there staring at John, obviously angry. "Look, I'm really sorry," John tried again. "I certainly didn't mean to do it. Let me help get it cleaned up and then I'll get you another beer."

"I don't need your help, man. I just want you out of my face."

"You ought to kick his ass, Sean," said the young man behind him.

"Shut up, Garrett. I don't need you mouthing off," Sean said.

"OK, I got it," John said. "I'm gone, but I just want you to know I didn't mean it, and I'm sorry. Sure you don't want the handkerchief to wipe off your legs?" John held out the handkerchief again.

"Bug off, man."

John held his hands up in front of him, palms out, the handkerchief dangling from one of them. "OK, OK. I'm out of here." He turned around and walked away from the door. "What an asshole," he heard Garrett say before sounds of other conversations drowned him out. John couldn't blame Sean for being angry. The beer cup must have been almost full when the door knocked it out of Sean's hand. Still, it was an accident, and he'd apologized and done what he could to make it right.

He maneuvered once more around the patio looking for Pete, but didn't see him. He stopped looking when he met Erin and Shana again.

"Well, no luck," he said. "I don't know where he is."

"That's funny. I know I saw him earlier," Shana said. "You saw him, didn't you?" she asked, looking at her sister.

"Yea, I saw him. He was with B2. They were getting beer."

John raised his eyebrows. "B2?"

"Bobby Bell," Erin said. He drives a Vette. The guys think it's great. I think it sucks. Did you see a red Vette out front when you came in? That's B2's."

"I don't know. I didn't pay much attention. I'll have to go look. By the way, do you know a couple of guys named Sean and Garrett?"

Shana looked at Erin. "Yes, we know them," she said. "Why do you ask?"

"Well, I just tried to go into the house and when I pushed the door open I knocked a beer out of Sean's hand accidently. He got pretty riled about it. I thought he was going to take a swing at me."

"That sounds about right," Erin said. "Sean Riley and Garrett Cray. They're a couple of assholes and ..."

"Erin!" Shana interrupted.

"Well, they are," Erin persisted. "They think they're pretty special, and they like getting in fights. Remember what they did to Walter?" She turned to John. "Be careful around them. They're mean, and they gang up on people."

"Who's Walter?"

"He's a guy we know," Shana said. "Garrett got mad at him for something. He and Sean came up behind him and Garrett put a rope around his neck and started choking him while Sean started punching him. They really beat him up."

"What happened?"

"Nothing really. A bunch of guys jumped in and stopped it. If they hadn't Walter would have really been messed up. Somebody called the cops, but by the time they got there everybody was gone. Walter went around for a week with a rope burn on his neck, poor guy."

"Walter's not the first one," Erin said. "They've done that before. Someday they're really going to hurt somebody. Like I said, a couple of real assholes."

"Thanks for the tip ladies. Erin, I have to say, you really need to come out of your shell more. Say what you really think," John smiled. Erin laughed.

"Yea, my sister's really shy, isn't she?" Shana added. "But seriously John, she's right. Be careful of those guys. They're bad news."

"I will. I just came here to meet Pete. Maybe I'll get a refill and then go out front and see if his car is parked out there. Either of you want another beer?"

"No thanks."

"I'll have one, thanks," Erin said.

"OK, be right back." John left the two women, made his way to the beer keg and filled two cups. He turned to go back the way he'd come and almost bumped into Sean Riley again.

"You spill another beer on me and I will kick your ass," Sean growled.

John just stood there. He couldn't believe it, the same guy twice at one party. He shook his head. "Look, I'm sorry. I …"

"You're about to be more than sorry."

"Why don't we just kick his ass and get it over with," Garrett said.

"Who the hell are you and what are you doing here anyway?" Sean asked.

"My name's John Dempsey. I'm looking for my friend, Pete Suarez. I don't think he's here so I'm taking this beer to someone and then I'm leaving. I'm not looking for a fight. I'm on my way out of here." Seeing a pathway to his right, John moved in that direction, away from Sean and Garrett. He half expected one of them to grab his arm and spin him around, but nothing happened. He made his way back to Erin and Shana who were watching the encounter with Sean.

"Erin, here's your beer," he said.

"I see you met Sean Riley again."

"I can't believe it. I almost dropped another beer on him. Unreal."

"Like I said, he's an asshole," she said as if that explained everything.

"I think I'll go out front, finish my beer, and if Pete doesn't show up I'll just leave. I hang around here long enough and sooner or later I'm going to drop another beer on that guy. It's not worth it."

"Yea, we're going to leave too, pretty soon. The crowd's a little young. It wouldn't surprise me to see the cops show up," Erin said.

"Too bad you couldn't find Pete," Shana said. "Give me your cell phone number and if I see him later I'll tell him to call you." She rummaged around in her pocketbook and pulled out paper and a pencil.

"Hey, thanks." John took the paper and pencil, wrote down his e-mail and telephone number, and handed it back. "I appreciate it. I'll see you guys later."

Erin looked at John, then at Shana. "That was pretty slick, Shay. Nice number pickup there. Good job. I'm sure we'll see you around, John," she said, the beginnings of a grin at the corners of her mouth. Shana started to blush.

"Ah, right," John said laughing. "Please do. Give me a call. We can grab a beer. Take care. See ya." He turned and walked toward the front of the house, a smile on his face. He could hear Erin laughing as Shana scolded her about his telephone number. Ahh, sisterly love, he thought. He looked back once and Erin winked at him, thoroughly enjoying herself.

He went to the front of the house and spotted B2's red Corvette parked there. At least the two women had been right about that, he thought. He walked over to his truck, placed his beer on the hood, and leaned against the grill. Then he realized he hadn't even thought about calling Pete. He took out his cell phone, dialed Pete's number, was sent to his voicemail, left a message, and hung up. He thought about leaving. He wanted to see Pete, but he didn't want to hang around and run the risk of bumping into Sean Riley again. That wouldn't end well. He decided he would wait a few minutes longer and if Pete didn't show up he would leave.

He poured what was left of his beer onto the grass, walked to the driver's side of the truck, opened the door, and put the empty cup into a plastic trash bag he kept behind the seat. Next to the trash bag was his 9 mm pistol in a heavy plastic carrying case. John liked the pistol because it was compact and easily concealed. He thought of Erin and Shana's warnings about Sean Riley and decided he should heed hem. He took the gun from its case, loaded it, and put it into his pants pocket. He walked back to the front of the truck, leaned against the grill, and folded his arms. He decided fifteen minutes was it, if Pete didn't show up by then, he was gone.

He'd been leaning there about ten minutes when Garrett Cray walked around the corner of the house, spotted him, stopped, then turned around and went back the way he had come. He reappeared a moment later and simply stood there looking in John's direction. Shortly after that Sean Riley and two other young men walked around the corner. The strangers with Sean looked to be high schoolers. Each of them was carrying a cup of beer. So was Sean.

They spread out, four abreast, and started walking toward John, Sean slightly in the lead. An image of Wyatt Earp, Doc Holliday, and the Earp brothers walking up a dusty street to the O.K. Corral in Tombstone popped into John's head. All it needed was the music. He unfolded his arms and pushed himself away from the grill of his truck. When the four men reached John, the two high schoolers took up positions near the truck's headlights on either side of him blocking his escape in those directions. Sean stood in the middle and Garrett stood to his left.

"I thought I told you to get out of here," Sean said.

"I'm not sure that's quite the way I heard it. I said I was going to take a beer to a friend and then leave," John said.

"Well, asshole, I don't see any beers in your hands so you should be gone." There was snickering from the two youngsters near the headlights. Garratt glanced toward Sean. "Let's take this son of a bitch out," he said.

"What do you think asshole? Should we take you out?" Sean glared at John. His chest stuck out. His right hand still held the cup of beer. His left was curled into a fist. He threw the cup of beer at John's legs, its contents striking him near the knees. John could feel the beer running down his pant legs and into his sneakers. "Oh, sorry. I didn't mean it. Want my handkerchief?' Sean said, flipping the cup, hitting John near his belt buckle. More snickers from the high schoolers.

John put his hand into his pocket and grasped the handgun. "I understand you're Sean Riley and you like to fight. I'm not interested in fighting you, Sean, and I didn't mean to spill your beer. Now my shoes are wet, just like yours, so we're even. Let's be done with it. You go your way and I'll go mine."

"Oh, you're going on your way asshole." Sean reached his right hand into his pocket and brought out what appeared to be a small black dowel. He rapped his hand tightly around it.

John had been working on the road crew long enough to know what it was a role of quarters wrapped in electric tape to harden his fist. Sean was psyching himself up for a fight and it was just a matter of time before the first punch was thrown. John decided he had nothing to lose. Maybe he could throw him off with a little bravado.

"OK, dipshit. I've had enough. You may be big and tough, but if something starts here, one thing I can promise you is that you're going to get hurt. I may get hurt but you, fat boy, are going to get hurt. Count on it." John let his anger show, locking eyes with Sean, glaring at him, unafraid, prepared to accept the challenge, come what may. He thought he saw hesitation in Sean's face. Perhaps he wasn't so sure now.

"You going to let this asshole talk to you like that?" Garrett almost shouted.

"Eat shit mister," the youngster on John's right said. John glanced in his direction. A kid, he thought, too young to end an insult without the "mister." That was John's mistake.

Seeing him distracted by the kid's comment, Sean struck his right fist with the roll of quarters in it, shooting out, and hitting John in the face just under his left eye. The blow was a powerful one knocking John back against the hood of his truck. He bounced against the vehicle, but kept his footing, and looked up to see Sean and Garrett moving toward him. Sean grabbed the front of his shirt. John could see the youngster on his left, out of the corner of his eye, coming at him with something in his hand. Time slowed down as he pulled the pistol from his pocket, jammed it into Sean's side, and pulled the trigger twice, as fast as he could. Then he pointed it at Garrett and pulled the trigger again. Sean stood still in front of him. Garrett turned and staggered back toward the corner of the house, the two high schoolers scattered among the cars. Sean's eyes rolled into the back of his head and he dropped to the ground. Garrett took about a dozen steps holding onto his stomach, and then he too fell to the ground.

John Dempsey was convicted in the Circuit Court for Palm Beach County, Florida, on two counts of second degree murder. He appealed his conviction.[1]

MOVING FROM THE COMMON LAW TO THE "TRUE MAN" DOCTRINE

John Dempsey's case is a little difficult to unpack because it came right at the time Florida was transitioning from the common law to a statutory "true man" standard of self-defense. Nevertheless, it illustrates nicely the difference between the two approaches. So let's take it apart and look at it.

The duty to retreat grew from the fear of common law judges that the use of deadly force to protect oneself against deadly danger would become a subterfuge for murder. To keep people from using it as an excuse to kill each other, they embraced the idea that before resorting to deadly force, the person who was threatened had to first show that he or she had done everything possible to avoid the killing. A person in danger of unlawful violence had to retreat "to the wall."[2] In other words, he or she had to be trapped, with no escape, and no alternative, but to use deadly force to avoid his or her own death or serious bodily injury.

The "true man" doctrine evolved to cover situations where a deadly threat appeared suddenly, without warning, and there was no time to consider what the available alternatives might be, or how to avoid the use of deadly force. There was no requirement to retreat if there were no avenues of escape available, or no time to take them. The "true man" doctrine did not extend to those situations where the threat appeared more gradually, providing time to assess possible avenues of escape, time to avoid the use of deadly force. In those situations the common law duty to retreat still applied, and people were required to flee in the face of deadly danger. Stand-your-ground laws operate to extend the "true man" approach more broadly to other encounters, provided the person threatened with unlawful violence is behaving lawfully and is in a place where he or she has a lawful right to be. The "true man" standard descends from the "American mind" line of cases that began with John Runyan's trial in Indiana in 1877.

The state of the law in Florida, before October 1, 2005, was that the "true man" doctrine governed situations where the deadly threat appeared suddenly and without warning, and the common law, with its duty to retreat, governed situations where the threat appeared more gradually over time. There was also a Castle Doctrine exception to the common law that provided that there is no duty to retreat in one's own home.[3] In situations where the common law applied, a person claiming self-defense had to show that no avenue of escape existed, or that there was no time to take it, or that taking it would have been futile or too dangerous.[4]

On October 1, 2005, Florida's new self-defense statute went into effect modifying the common law. It said, "A person who is not engaged in an unlawful activity and who is attacked in any other place where he or she has a right to be has no duty to retreat and has the right to stand his or her ground and meet force with force, including deadly force if he or she reasonably believes it is necessary to do so to prevent death or great bodily harm to himself or herself or another or to prevent the commission of a forcible felony."[5] In short, under the new statute, if an innocent person who is behaving lawfully is threatened with deadly danger, he or she doesn't have to back down or look for avenues of escape or flee before resorting to deadly force. He or she can use all reasonable means to avoid death or injury, including deadly force if necessary.

THE CASE OF GEORGE ZIMMERMAN AND TRAYVON MARTIN

Florida's new statute became known as the stand-your-ground law, and it has been the subject of much debate between gun control and gun rights advocates. The debate intensified after an incident in Sanford, Florida, on February 26, 2012, involving George Zimmerman, a neighborhood watch volunteer, and Trayvon Martin, an unarmed teenager. The two men got into a fistfight that escalated to where they were rolling around on the ground, struggling with each other, and Zimmerman, fearing for his life, killed Martin with a handgun. The shooting brought a wave of national media attention to Florida's stand-your-ground law, some of which was misleading unfortunately.

As sometimes happens, the media's coverage produced more heat than light, and sensationalism trumped the truth. Almost immediately, the preferred story line became that Zimmerman, a "'wannabe cop,' racially profiled, and ultimately killed Martin, because he was a black, hoodie-clad teenager, in a gated community, who simply wanted some Skittles."[6] Media outlets competed with each other, at times recklessly, for new details of the shooting. Some of the reporting was grossly irresponsible as well as grossly inaccurate.

For example, NBC News edited and then broadcast a tape recording of Zimmerman's phone call to the police to make the recording sound inaccurate, as if Zimmerman was suspicious of Martin because of his race, when in fact the tape's unedited version showed the police dispatcher had asked Zimmerman to describe Martin, and Zimmerman had replied by saying, among other things, that Martin was black. NBC later apologized for its reporting, but the damage was done. The retraction didn't get the same level of coverage as the initial report, and Zimmerman's alleged racism became part of the public narrative.

Not to be outdone, ABC News reported that a police surveillance video showed Zimmerman had come through the fight unharmed, no bleeding, no cuts, no abrasions. That story also proved to be false, but once again it became part of the media's narrative, at least until the time of trial when medical and photographic evidence demonstrated that Zimmerman, without question, had received significant injuries, both to his face and to the back of his head during the fight.

Perhaps the most biased coverage occurred after the media learned Zimmerman's mother was Peruvian. Having called him a racist, some media outlets began referring to him as a "white Hispanic."[7] Nevertheless, when Zimmerman's trial was over, the jury found him not guilty of murdering Trayvon Martin.

Suffice it to say, the media's coverage of Trayvon Martin's death was not the finest example of facts based reporting and left misimpressions of Florida's stand-your-ground statute, what happened to George Zimmerman and Trayvon Martin, and why. For example, Florida's statute was depicted as controversial, extreme, and outside the mainstream when in fact it was based on the "true man" line of cases that by 2012 was a well-known precedent followed by virtually every state in the union in situations where the threat appeared suddenly. An accurate explanation of the law and its historic basis when there was so much money to be made from sensational headlines was perhaps too much to expect. Nevertheless, despite the poor reporting, or perhaps because of it, more people began to look at the "true man" line of cases and to make up their own minds. Stand-your-ground statutes have been growing in popularity. Between 2005 and 2014, at least twenty-four states followed Florida's lead and enacted them.[8] Today, a majority of the states, whether by statute or by judge, follow some form of the stand-your-ground approach to self-defense.[9]

TRANSITION POINTS AND STAND-YOUR-GROUND LAWS

The effect of stand-your-ground laws is to make the prosecutor's job more difficult in murder cases where self-defense is an issue because the government can no longer use the duty to retreat to suggest there were opportunities, at times remote, before the actual killing when the shooter could have avoided the use of deadly force and simply chose not to do so. Getting the jury to focus on the shooter's behavior before the threat has fully formed to argue the duty to retreat was ignored is a common prosecutorial tactic in states where the duty still exists and the deadly danger emerges gradually over time.

It is a fairly easy thing to do. Prosecutors trace the chain of events back in time to a point to before the threat is undeniably clear, and then argue the shooter should have recognized the impending danger, should have done something to avoid it, and by failing to do so breached their duty to retreat. That is what happened to Michael Smith in Delaware. He was convicted of manslaughter for failing to retreat at a point when arguably the presence of deadly danger was not clear, or at least not clearly understood.

Indeed, it is the tendency of juries, in the comfort of their jury rooms, to seize upon these transition points before the threat is fully known and use them to deny what otherwise appear to be valid claims of self-defense that has propelled state legislatures to enact stand-your-ground laws. It is important to remember that the purpose of these laws is to protect innocent people from unlawful violence and intimidation in situations where the threat emerges gradually. As long as the person behaves lawfully, such laws permit people to go about their business without being forced to flee in the face of unlawful dangers created by others.

STAND-YOUR-GROUND LAWS AND DISQUALIFYING BEHAVIOR

When John Dempsey went to trial for second degree murder, Florida's stand-your-ground law had just been enacted, and there was a question about whether the new statute or the common law applied to his case. The timing of his trial produced a unique interplay between the two approaches.

Normally, one would expect John Dempsey's lawyer to argue that Florida's new stand-your-ground statute applied to the case, and therefore John had no duty to retreat. The facts of his case seemed to be very much in line with the new statute's definition of self-defense. John had a right to be where he was. There was no evidence that he misbehaved while there. He didn't crash the party, or was otherwise a trespasser. No one asked him to leave. He was clearly not the aggressor. He had walked away from two prior encounters with Sean to avoid a confrontation. Two of the four men who surrounded him had reputations for violence that he was aware of, one of them was holding a roll of quarters in his hand to make his fist harder, and he was attacked suddenly, without warning, sucker punched really. His case seemed tailor-made to fit the new law.

For that reason, the prosecutor would have been expected to argue just the opposite, namely that the new law didn't apply and therefore the common law, with its duty to retreat required John to show that before he responded with deadly force, he had tried to avoid the confrontation. The common law imposes a greater burden on the defendant.

It didn't happen that way. In fact, it was just the opposite. John's attorney argued in favor of the common law, and the prosecutor argued in favor of the new statute. The reason is because John pled guilty to the charge of rioting for his participation in the Boynton Beach bar brawl.

Under Florida law rioting is a third degree felony, punishable by imprisonment for up to five years.[10] That John paid his fine and completed his probation didn't change the character of the offense, it was still a felony. People convicted of felonies in Florida are barred from possessing firearms. In fact, a convicted felon's possession of a handgun in Florida is itself a felony.[11]

Florida's new stand-your-ground statute begins by stating specifically, "A person who is not engaged in an unlawful activity, and who is attacked in any other place where he or she has a right to be has no duty to retreat … etc." It doesn't speak of an innocent person in a place he or she has a right to be, or a person who doesn't provoke, prolong, or contribute to the danger being in a place he or she has a right to be. It speaks of a person who is not engaged in unlawful activity. The prosecutor argued that Florida's stand-your-ground law governed John's case and that it disqualified him from claiming self-defense because as a convicted felon in possession of a handgun, he was in violation of state law at the time of the shooting.

The trial judge agreed with the prosecutor, ruled that John's possession of the pistol was unlawful conduct that prevented him from claiming self-defense, and the jury convicted him of murder.

WHAT HAPPENS WHEN STAND-YOUR-GROUND LAWS DON'T APPLY

Florida's District Court of Appeals for the Fourth Circuit saw the case differently. It said the wording of the statute did not defeat John's self-defense claim because the language wasn't intended to define the meaning of self-defense, but rather what cases the new law covered. In other words, it didn't mean that John had no claim of self-defense, but only that the new statute did not apply to his case. The trial judge misconstrued the new statute, it said, when it ruled that John's unlawful act prevented him from claiming self-defense. He could still make the claim, just not under the state's stand-your-ground law.

The appellate court ruled that the new statute didn't abolish claims of self-defense under Florida's common law, but only modified them to the extent provided for specifically by the legislature. Stated differently, the common law remained in effect except for those who were not engaged in unlawful activity and who were in a place where they had a right to be. Since John's unlawful behavior made the new statute inapplicable to his case, any claim of self-defense he wished to make would be judged under the common law, with its duty to retreat.

The appellate court then went further and examined the facts of John's case to see if he had fulfilled his duty to retreat under the common law. It decided that he had. At the time of the shooting he was surrounded and his back was literally against the grill of his truck with all his paths of escape blocked by one of four hostile aggressors. In short, he was facing an unlawful threat of death or serious bodily injury from four men, and his back was literally "to the wall." The appellate court determined he had met his burden of showing that he tried to avoid the use of deadly force because there "was no duty to retreat where a defendant had retreated to the wall or retreat would be futile."[12]

Based on the facts, the appellate court also found that when John fired the shots that killed Sean and Garrett he was acting not out of hostility, malice, or ill will, but with intent to save himself from death or serious bodily injury. He didn't have the requisite murderous intent to support a murder conviction and could not be found guilty of second degree murder. The court didn't set him free, however, because it was unsure whether a jury might convict him of manslaughter. It set aside the two murder convictions and sent the case back to the Palm Beach County Circuit Court for a new trial to determine his ultimate fate.

The point to be made is that stand-your-ground statutes are limited to persons and situations described specifically in the statute, and other situations that do not meet the statutory language continue to be governed by the common law with its duty to retreat. It is important to understand clearly how stand-your-ground statutes amend the common law.

10

CASTLE DOCTRINE

THREATS ON ONE'S PROPERTY

Gibraltar, Michigan, sits on the Detroit River about twenty-five miles southwest of Detroit and is home to about 5,000 people. The residents within its 3.9 square miles have set aside enough land for two nature parks. Karen Koch is one of its daughters. During the 1969–1970 ice hockey season she played goalie for the Marquette Iron Rangers in the United States Hockey League, becoming the world's first professional woman hockey player, receiving the handsome sum of forty dollars per game. She was let go though for repeatedly disobeying the coach's orders by taking off her facemask during the games in order to better see the hockey pucks flying at her head. They make them tough in Gibraltar.

Martin Randolph owned a home just south of Gibraltar between the main part of town and the Lake Erie Metro Park. He was an average sized man, athletic looking, and a Wayne State graduate. Thirty-one years old, single, and friendly, most women found Marty attractive. Three years before the incident, he and a friend started a real estate appraisal company and built it into a good business. He wasn't rich but he lived comfortably alone as a bachelor with all he needed and pretty much all he wanted. Life was good.

Marty's house was a pleasant looking Cape Cod on a rectangular shaped lot of about two and one-half acres. Several large white ash trees provided good shade in the summer and spectacular colors in the fall. Yew shrubs stood near the house's front door like sentinels guarding the entrance. A driveway led from the road to an oversized detached garage and a short narrow walkway led from there to the house. When Marty bought the place he thought he would tear down the garage and build a new one attached to the house. Then he decided to keep it and fix it up instead. He was glad he did. The garage became something of a local hangout. It seemed like there was always someone stopping by and staying awhile. Although Marty complained about it for appearances sake, truth be known, he liked having his friends around, liked having the company.

Not being married, Marty turned his garage into a comfortable man cave that was the envy of all his friends, all his male friends at least. He didn't worry about nicks and dings to the woodwork, stains on the countertops, scuff marks on the floors. It was a garage after all. Empty beer bottles sat in the corner trashcan as long as he felt like leaving them there. He kept the garage heated in the winter and cooled in the summer. He had two parking bays, both clean and tidy, one for his Ford F-150 pickup truck, the other for his pride and joy, an orange 1969 *Dukes of Hazzard* Dodge Charger. He spent a small fortune restoring the car to its original condition, painting it the obligatory orange, polishing it compulsively with expensive waxes, and never, absolutely never, driving it if there was salt on the roads.

There was a moderately sized storeroom in the garage that became the centerpiece of Marty's man cave. He sheet-rocked the walls, painted them dark, hung two huge TVs on them, installed a bathroom, built a bar, threw some rugs on the floor, and threaded the needle with used furniture nice enough to discourage lounging in dirty clothes, but "broken-in" enough so people didn't feel guilty about taking liberties, now and then, like putting one's feet up on the coffee table.

The garage became something of a private club for Marty's friends. When they dropped by, and they came quite often, they almost always ended up in the garage. On the weekends the place drew people like bugs to a spotlight. There was always somebody around shooting the breeze, joking good naturedly, usually at Marty's expense, laughing, admiring the Dodge Charger, poking into his stuff. There was a refrigerator in the storeroom that Marty kept well stocked with Stroh's and Bells beer. The rule was if you took one then you owed one. Most people followed it. The TVs were usually tuned to a sporting event, and most times a pretty interesting conversation could be had for the asking. In short it was a fun place to be, the kind of place where you could relax and just mess around without anybody caring too much about what you did.

One Friday evening in August, Marty and a couple of friends were in the storeroom having a beer and talking baseball. The conversation turned to dinner and someone thought it a good idea to fire up the barbecue. The decision made, Marty went about setting up the gas grill, one of his friends went to get groceries at the store, and the other started making phone calls to spouses and girlfriends. The charcoal was lit nicely and people were already there when the grocery buyer got back with the food.

About a half hour after they began grilling, John Bolling, one of Marty's high school classmates, showed up with a man named Ralph Costanza. Bolling lived in Gibralter and was familiar to everyone in the group. Constanza, on the other hand, was a stranger, an outsider from Detroit who worked with Bolling. He and Bolling had driven down from the city that afternoon, bar hopping the entire way, and both men were a little unsteady on their feet.

Jane Turley was standing next to Marty at the grill gently "critiquing" his barbecue skills when John and Ralph walked up to them. Jane knew John but not Ralph. A product of the Midwest, she was independent, self-assured, savvy, and had a great sense of humor, a woman who loved having a good time, but who also knew how to set limits for her "men folk." She smiled inwardly when she saw Ralph. Her first thought was of a Chippendale's dancer. He was wearing loose shorts and a tight T-shirt. His stomach was flat and he had the physique of a bodybuilder. He was obviously proud of it.

"Hey pretty lady, how about throwing a couple extra burgers on the grill for me," Ralph said in Jane's direction.

Jane turned to Marty, grinning, and raised her eyebrows. Surely this guy was pulling her leg. "Nice to meet you too. I'm Jane Turley," she said, smiling and extending her hand to Ralph. He shook her hand, but didn't let go of it right away, instead holding on, rubbing his thumb against the back of her hand a bit too long and a bit too friendly.

"I'm Ralph Costanza. Nice to meet you, sweetie. Could you put on some food? I'm dying of hunger here." He was grinning from ear to ear, oblivious to Jane's discomfort.

John saw Jane tense up and watched the smile fade from her face. He knew she didn't think of herself as anybody's "pretty lady," or "sweetie," except perhaps for Will Bonney, her husband. John also knew she wasn't impressed by Ralph's attempt at some sort of intimate hand massage. He tried to move everybody past the awkwardness. "Hey, Jane … Martin. Good to see you guys. How's Will?" he asked looking at Jane.

"Will's good," she said. "He's inside somewhere, probably watching the Tigers. How've you been?"

"I'm good. The job's good. Sam's good. It's all good," he said, referring to his wife Samantha.

"Where is Sam?" Jane asked, emphasizing the word "is," glancing in Ralph's direction, her face betraying her real question, why are you here with this guy?

"She's at her parents. Her father's sick. Nothing serious but she wanted to go see him."

Ralph interrupted, "All this is great. Glad to hear the job's good, you're good, your wife's good, everybody's good, but if nobody's going to give me anything to eat, can you at least tell me where the piss house is?"

"Uh ... It's inside the garage," Marty said. "Just go through the overhead doors to the back of the building. Follow the sounds of the television. The bathroom's in the television room on your left."

Ralph walked off toward the garage doors.

Jane turned to John. "What's up with your friend?" Jane asked, jabbing her thumb over her shoulder at Ralph, not caring if he heard her, making it clear she wasn't happy, irritation in her voice.

"Too much beer," John said.

"Yea, well too much asshole too. If he's going to act like that, tell him to cook his own damn food. And you'd better keep him away from Will. Will won't be impressed by the tight T-shirt and the pecs," she said. Jane didn't usually swear.

Marty, also unhappy with Ralph's attitude, joined in the conversation. "We're all good friends here, John. Maybe it'd be better if you took your friend Ralph someplace else."

"He's not a bad guy. He's just a little beered up. I've probably had a bit too much myself. Let me grab a bite to eat and I'll get him out of here. Do you have any coffee?"

"I'm not sure staying's a good idea," Marty said. "Your friend doesn't fit, John, and I don't want any more of what I just heard. We'll be here for a while. Why don't you take your friend somewhere else and come back if you want?"

Jane looked at Marty, who was looking at John, who was looking at Ralph as he walked into the garage. Marty wanted Ralph gone, but it didn't seem to be registering with John. Ralph disappeared into the garage and John looked back at Marty as if there was something more to be said. Marty didn't speak. He just looked back at John and the silence between them became uncomfortable. "He needs more than coffee, John," Jane said finally.

John looked away. "OK, I get it," he said. "The coffee isn't for him, it's for me. I shouldn't be driving and I need something to eat. We'll find something in town."

Marty blew out his breath and relaxed his shoulders. He liked John and didn't enjoy asking him to leave.

"Well, you're right, John," he said. "You probably shouldn't be driving. I don't want you getting stopped by the cops. We'll get you something to eat, but no more beer, and I'll go make some coffee. Then please get him out of here."

"OK, I will. I'll talk to him right now and if he says anything we'll forget the coffee. I'll just leave," John said.

"And keep him away from me," Jane added.

"Don't worry, I will. Is there anything already cooked?" John asked.

"I doubt it with this crowd, but maybe in the storeroom," Jane said.

"OK, we have a plan," Marty said smiling. He gave John a friendly punch in the shoulder as he stepped past him to go make coffee, letting him know things were all right between them.

John went into the storeroom and met Ralph just coming out of the bathroom. Somehow, along the way, Ralph had gotten himself another beer. There was no food in the man cave and John guided Ralph out of the garage toward the grill where Jane was cooking more burgers and hot dogs.

"Looks like the bitch got the message," Ralph said.

"Hey Ralph, c'mon. She's good people and she's doing us a favor. You want to do the cooking?" John asked.

"I wouldn't mind sticking something in her oven. It looks kinda hot," Ralph said loud enough for Jane to hear him.

"C'mon Ralph, these are my friends."

"Yea, well, they're not mine, a bunch of hillbilly losers," Ralph said waiving his hand dismissively. "Don't worry about your princess. She's not worth it."

John didn't like the way Ralph was talking and started to say something, but then decided not to. Ralph had a mean streak in him, particularly when he'd been drinking. John had seen it before. There was no need to risk a confrontation. His chances of getting Ralph out of there were better if he didn't challenge him.

"Look, Ralph. Let's get a quick bite to eat and get out of here. We'll find a better place in town," John said.

"Hey, you're the one who wanted to come here. Besides, there's a lot of great looking pussy here."

"Not quite, Ralph. There's a lot of great looking married women here who love their husbands," John tried.

"Can't hold it against them."

"The people I really wanted to see didn't come anyway, and this crowd is a pretty tightly knit group," John said. "Let's just eat and go."

Ralph stopped eyeing Jane and turned to look at John. There was a blank expression on his face and his eyes were cold. "Somebody say something about me?" he asked.

"Well, about us," John lied. "It's my fault. Apparently, you had to be invited to be here, and I wasn't. A guy made a point to tell me and suggested we go, but I don't care about that. It would just be better if we left."

Ralph's gaze locked on John, making him uncomfortable. His eyes were suspicious, perhaps even a little hostile.

Jane turned from the grill and looked in their direction. "Hey, guys—food's ready," she said, transferring hamburgers and hot dogs from the grill to rolls on two paper plates.

Ralph acknowledged her message by pointing his beer bottle at her. He looked back at John. "Screw 'em," he said. "Let's go eat."

Marty was inside his house in the kitchen, and the coffee was almost done when he heard the back door open and saw Jane walk through it. She didn't look pleased.

"Hey, Marty. I just came to tell you that Will and I are leaving," she said, flipping her hand, an edge in her voice.

"What happened?" Marty asked.

"I've had it. John's jerk friend just grabbed my ass," she blurted out. "I cooked their damn food to get them out of here. This guy just stands there staring at me, and when I tell them it's done, he walks over, gets his plate, and as he walks by he starts feeling up my butt. I almost hit him, but that would have made it worse. You know Will. There'd have been a fight. I mean what the hell. I'm so pissed," she said crossing her arms and staring out the kitchen window.

"Ahh man, Jane. I'm really sorry. I thought we had this taken care of. I'll go get rid of him."

Jane unfolded her arms, looking uncomfortable. "Whatever you do, don't tell Will. I don't want him punching this guy's lights out. Part of me would enjoy it, but it's not worth it. Women have to deal with this crap all the time. We'll just go home."

"OK, I got it, Jane. I don't want any trouble either, but this is my house and you guys are my friends. I'm not going to allow it. I'd like you to stay, but either way John's friend is out of here, now."

"Well, you do what you've got to do, but I think it's best if Will and I just leave. No hard feelings. Maybe we'll see you next week. Take care." Jane turned and went out the door.

Martin stood there in the kitchen, his anger building. The coffee maker sizzled, announcing the brewing cycle's end, bringing him back from his thoughts. He was furious about what Ralph had done, but he took time to calm down, he wasn't going to lose his temper. He moved about the kitchen deliberately, retrieving a large thermos from the cabinet, rinsing it out with fresh water, pouring in the coffee, carefully putting cream and sugar into containers, and placing them onto a tray with the thermos.

He looked out the window and saw John and Ralph talking in front of the garage. Ralph had a beer bottle in his hand, something he'd asked John not to let him do. John's arms were extended in front of him, palms up, asking for something. Marty picked up the tray and walked out the kitchen door.

He carried the coffee toward the garage intending to put it on a table in the storeroom near one of the televisions before talking to Ralph. As he got closer to the garage he began to hear what John and Ralph were saying.

"So, if we leave now, we can get back to the city just about the time the pubs get going," John said.

"Any women?" Ralph asked.

"Hi guys," Martin interrupted. "Leaving?"

John turned his head. "Hey, Martin. Yea, I was thinking we should start back to the city. Thanks for the food, man. It was great."

"Nah, I'm not ready just yet. Couple of more people I'd like to talk to," Ralph said.

"Well, leaving now is not a bad idea. Much later and the cops will be out in force. Friday night, you know," Marty said.

"You gotta problem with me staying?" Ralph challenged.

"Yes, as a matter of fact I do," Marty said. "This is a private party. I'm OK with you getting something to eat and having a beer, but now I think it's time for you to go."

"If you think you're big enough to throw me out, I suggest it," Ralph said. Marty looked at him, thought to himself that didn't make any sense, he wanted to say, I suggest you try it. The guy was drunk and mean.

Ralph waited for Marty to answer. He ran his eyes up and down Marty's body, slowly, dismissively, and then he added, "You touch me little man and I'll kill you." He shifted his beer bottle to his left hand, reached into his pocket with his right hand, and grabbed something inside it.

My God, he's got a gun, Marty thought. I'm standing here holding a coffee tray and this guy is thinking about shooting me.

"C'mon Ralph. Let's go," John pleaded. "We don't need this."

Ralph glanced at John. "I'm not taking any crap from this asshole." He kept his right hand in his pocket and locked eyes with Marty, and then he bent down, placed the beer bottle in his left hand gently on the driveway. "So what's it going to be little man?" he said, as he straightened up.

Marty needed to slow this thing down. It was moving way too fast in the wrong direction. "Well, I guess it's going to be me taking this coffee into the garage," he said. He stepped past Ralph and continued on his way toward the garage, terrified the sound of a gun would be the next thing he heard, and the last thing he heard.

"That's what I thought," Ralph spit at Marty's back. Then he looked at John. "I'd have broken his damn skull. We can stay as long as we want."

Marty made it through the garage door and let out his breath, grateful nothing had happened. Several people were inside the storeroom lounging around, talking, and watching Detroit Tigers baseball. He was glad he was carrying the coffee tray, because it helped to steady his hands. He walked over to a small table in the corner of the room and set down the tray.

"Hey, Marty, my man. What's up? You look kinda pale. You feeling OK?" His friend, Mark Markota, got up from a chair and came over to where Marty was standing. Mark was a local pharmacist and a good guy.

"I'm OK, Mark. Thanks. Got a sudden headache. I'll be OK in a minute. Want some coffee?"

"Yup, think I will, thanks." Markota picked up a Styrofoam cup and began to make himself a cup of coffee.

Marty walked across the room, took a set of keys from his pocket, and opened the door to a small storage closet near the storeroom entrance. He went inside the closet, shut the door behind him, and leaned back against it. He closed his eyes, breathed deeply, and thought about what had just happened. Maybe he'd overreacted to Ralph's threat. It was hard to believe the man would really try to kill him. On the other hand, he thought Ralph had a gun in his pocket. Why would he be carrying a gun in his pocket? Maybe he should call the cops. But telling the cops that a man was threatening to kill him seemed a little melodramatic. Maybe before he did that he should ask Ralph to leave one more time. That seemed reasonable. That way he'd know for sure if the cops were really necessary.

His plan in place, Marty stepped away from the door and turned to leave when he spied the metal cabinet and thought of the M-1 carbine inside it. Should he take the rifle? What would happen if he asked Ralph to leave and the man had a gun and went crazy? If Ralph started shooting some of his friends were likely to get hurt, some of them may even be killed. He couldn't let that happen. He took the M-1 out of the cabinet, loaded it, and wrapped it in a blanket. He grabbed a couple of fishing rods and wrapped them in the same blanket leaving parts of the rods visible, making the whole thing look like a bunch of wrapped-up fishing rods.

He left the closet and went into the garage carrying the fishing rods and the rifle. When he reached the overhead doors he unwrapped the blanket, took out the carbine, and leaned it against the wall in the corner, next to the door. He put the fishing rods in front of it and arranged the blanket around them until he was satisfied it hid the rifle. Then he walked out the door onto the driveway. He saw Ralph and John leaning against a parked car and went over to where they were standing. John looked nervous. Ralph looked angry.

"So where's the burger cooker?" Ralph asked.

"Huh, oh she's gone home," Marty said, smiling at Ralph. "Look Ralph, I'm sorry if I said anything earlier that offended you. I didn't mean it. Really. I apologize. I'm not sure how we got cross-wise. What I was trying to say is that we're a pretty small group of very close friends, and today is a special get together we hold every so often, kind of like a family reunion. I wanted to keep it that way. Does that make sense?"

Ralph looked back at him, his arms across his chest, leaning back against the side of the car. "It does. We're all one big happy family. So you want me to leave, is that it?"

"Yes, that's it. I'm asking you to please leave. Join us another time, but today is just for family and friends."

Ralph catapulted off the car hitting Martin in the chest with both hands knocking him off his feet. Marty fell down hitting the back of his head against the ground. John jumped between them tucking his head and wrapping his arms around Ralph's waist. He tried to push Ralph back against the car while Marty got back on his feet. "Jesus, Ralph. What are you doing? We don't need this."

Ralph ignored John's attempt to restrain him and focused intently on Marty like a big cat about to strike its prey. He moved forward, realized John was holding him back, and grabbed John by his shoulders breaking John's hold on his waist. Ralph stood John up and punched him squarely in the face, sending him to his knees. "That son of a bitch is a dead man and so are you if you don't get out of my way," he screamed.

While Ralph was dealing with John, Marty got to his feet and staggered toward the garage. His head was still foggy from the blow he'd received. When he reached the garage door he looked back and saw Ralph standing over John who was on the ground, blood running down his face. Ralph looked up, saw Marty looking at him, and yelled, "You're next, you son of a bitch." Then he reached into his pocket and started toward Marty.

Marty turned and reached for the rifle in the corner of the garage. Releasing the safety and raising the rifle to his shoulder, he turned back and stepped onto the driveway. Ralph was already there, the barrel of Marty's gun almost hitting him in the chest. There was fury on his face and something black in his right hand. Marty pulled the trigger quickly, three times. Ralph was dead before he hit the ground.

Martin Randolph was tried and convicted of second degree murder and possession of a firearm during the commission of a felony.[1] The prosecutor argued that he had failed to retreat when he could have, and that such failure defeated his claim of self-defense.

NO REQUIREMENT TO FLEE FROM THREATS IN ONE'S HOME

There are several important public policy considerations involving the duty to retreat. One of them is that life is more important than space. Space can be reoccupied, if abandoned, life once taken, is gone forever. So if there's a choice to be made, the law in duty to retreat states prefers that space be given up and life be preserved, and that is true even where an innocent person is threatened unlawfully, intimidated and pushed forcibly from his or her peaceful occupation of the space. But what if the space to be given up is in one's own home? Must an innocent person retreat when attacked where he or she lives?

As a general proposition, all states say that there is no duty to retreat in one's own home. We know it as the Castle Doctrine. A man's home is his castle, a place of refuge, a place he or she can feel safe and can protect from outsiders.[2] The Castle Doctrine grants people a privilege of non-retreat in their homes, a right to stand and face an intruder, and to use deadly force, if necessary, to protect their home against external threats.[3] Historically, the doctrine is a reaction to the common law duty to retreat, a rejection of the idea that a person must flee if attacked in his or her own home. U.S. Supreme Court justice Benjamin Cardozo described it by saying, "it is not now and never has been the law that a man assailed in his own dwelling is bound to retreat. If assailed there, he may stand his ground and resist the attack. He is under no duty to take to the fields and the highways, a fugitive from his own home."[4]

The Castle Doctrine is easy to describe, difficult to apply, because what it covers isn't the same in every state. Some states interpret the doctrine very narrowly, limiting the right to resist without first retreating to areas inside the actual dwelling space of a person's home. Other states interpret it more broadly to include areas outside someone's actual living space. Some states even include areas away from the homeowner's property. In short, there is a general consensus among the states about what the Castle Doctrine is, but little agreement about how to apply it.

FEAR AND THE CASTLE DOCTRINE, CONFUSING THE THREAT WITH PROPERTY RIGHTS

The fear that judges have of self-defense being used to mask murder has led them into deep legal swamps over how to interpret the duty to retreat as part of the Castle Doctrine. Some of it would be funny were the circumstances not so serious. What happened in Florida is a good case in point. In 1965, a live-in boyfriend attacked a Florida woman in her home, and the boyfriend ended up dead.[5] The woman was tried for murder, and the critical issue was whether, under the circumstances, she had a duty to retreat from her home, the prosecutor arguing that she should have left it before using deadly force. The woman defended herself based on Florida's Castle Doctrine, claiming that she had no duty to retreat in her own home. The jury convicted her of manslaughter and she appealed her case to the Florida Supreme Court.

The Supreme Court overturned her conviction, deciding that the dead boyfriend was a guest in her home. As a guest he was on the premises legally, but once she told him to leave his legal status changed and he no longer had a legal right to be there. He was, in effect, a trespasser, and if he attacked her the Castle Doctrine would apply, exempting her from a duty to retreat in the face of his assault. The court's legal reasoning focused on the victim's property right, his right to be on the premises, rather than on the threat he may have presented.

The case set the stage for a 1982 Florida case in which an enraged husband attacked his wife in their Florida home, and she killed him with a gun. The woman was tried for murder with the same legal arguments being made as were made in the 1965 case. The prosecutor argued that she had a duty to retreat and the defendant argued that she was exempt from such duty under the Castle Doctrine. She was convicted and appealed her conviction.

This time the Florida Supreme Court held the woman did have a duty to retreat before resorting to the use of deadly force. The court stated that the Castle Doctrine was intended to protect people in their homes against external attacks by invaders, burglars, intruders, trespassers, people coming from outside the home who had no legal right to be there and guests who had been invited into the home, but refused to leave it when asked. Since the woman's husband was legally entitled to be in the home, the Castle Doctrine didn't apply to her circumstances and she had a duty to retreat in the face of her husband's threats.[6] When read together, the two cases meant that Florida allowed women to invoke the Castle Doctrine if attacked by their live-in boyfriends but not by their husbands. So much for encouraging marriage.

The mess got worse. First, the court extended the Castle Doctrine to cover a person's workplace, ruling that an employee had no duty to retreat while at work.[7] Then it said a man's car was not his castle,[8] so a person occupying a car or truck had a duty to retreat in the face of an attack, notwithstanding the fact that many people work out of cars and the backs of trucks. Then it said that a person driving to work had a duty to retreat, but a person who had already arrived did not. Of course, that raised the question of when does a person arrive at work, inside the building, inside his or her actual workspace, in the parking lot, in the parking lot but in the car, in the parking lot but out of the car, etc. Not satisfied with work arrival times, the Supreme Court examined whether a person attacked by a co-worker had a duty to retreat and decided he or she did because the co-worker had a lawful right to be on the premises. So if an angry client threatened you at work you could take immediate action to defend yourself. But if a fellow employee threatened you at work, you had to look for a path of escape.[9]

In 1999, the Florida Supreme Court appeared to tire of this nonsense and revisited its earlier decision about a woman's duty to retreat in her own home when faced with a deadly threat by her husband or by some other person with the "right" to be there.[10] This time it reached the rather unremarkable conclusion that imposing a duty to retreat in such circumstances would limit the woman's ability to protect herself.[11] It overturned its previous decision and said there was no duty to retreat under Florida's Castle Doctrine. Well, it said it was overturning its previous decision. Well, it kind of overturned its previous decision. Well, not really.

Despite the case's headline saying "there is no duty to retreat from the residence before resorting to deadly force against a co-occupant or invitee," the Supreme Court went on to say the woman did have "a limited duty to retreat within the residence to the extent reasonably possible."[12] Apparently, she didn't have to actually run out of the house before using deadly force to keep from getting killed or injured, but she did have to run around inside it to the extent it was "reasonably possible," of course.[13]

Finally, in 2005, the Florida legislature moved to end the legal chaos codifying the Castle Doctrine as part of its self-defense law. Title XLVI,

Section 776.013 (3) of Florida statutes now makes it clear that a man or woman facing a deadly threat in their home from anyone, no matter the person's property right status in the premises, has no duty to retreat. They may employ deadly force if they reasonably believe it is necessary to avoid death or great injury, or to prevent the commission of a forcible felony.

To be fair, Florida is not the only state that has gone through these kinds of legal gyrations. Judges feel strongly about maintaining the idea of necessity in self-defense cases and they worry that any modification of the duty to retreat will be used to justify murder. The U.S. legal landscape is littered with decisions about the Castle Doctrine that are difficult to understand much less to comply with. The confusion and arbitrariness surrounding these decisions helped to expand the "true man" doctrine, to permit a person threatened with deadly danger to stand and meet it without first having to retreat.

PROTECTED GROUND AND CURTILAGE

Although statutory codifications of self-defense law have helped to clarify the Castle Doctrine, the states continue to have their differences in how it is applied. A key difference involves the question of what area the Castle Doctrine protects? In other words, where on the property is a person exempted from the duty to retreat? Is it defined by geography, the property's boundary lines for example, or by function, where the person actually lives, or by some other standard?

In the absence of specific statutory language, the Castle Doctrine attaches to what is known as "curtilage,"[14] an area in and around the home where daily living activities occur. Curtilage is often discussed in the context of Fourth Amendment cases, because the law recognizes greater individual privacy inside this protected area.[15]

Unfortunately, there's no uniform standard for determining the boundaries of what constitutes a dwelling's curtilage. It depends very much on the statutes and the court decisions of the state where you live. At a minimum, curtilage includes the space where you carry on the day-to-day business of living, eating, sleeping, resting, and where you keep your clothes, that sort of thing. In most states it includes a bit more,[16] but how much more varies widely. In some states, curtilage includes outbuildings on the property, garages and sheds.[17] In others, it includes the yard around the house,[18] a garden,[19] or a porch attached to the house.[20]

Other states define curtilage by describing what it doesn't include, a street in front of the building,[21] a common area,[22] a driveway,[23] a parking lot.[24] Curtilage has been found to be anywhere on your property[25] and has included areas you don't own. For example, Ohio courts have suggested that if you are sleeping in a tent in the woods you have no duty to retreat if another camper in a nearby tent threatens you with violence.[26]

THE POWER OF PRECEDENT

Marty Randolph's trial for killing Ralph Costanza was decided on the question of what is included in the curtilage of a home under the Castle Doctrine in the state of Michigan. To begin, Michigan is a duty to retreat state, so unless he was exempt under the state's Castle Doctrine, Marty had a common law duty to retreat before resorting to deadly force to defend himself.

The confrontation between Marty and Ralph evolved over time, the tension building, until it exploded with little warning in a final act that ended with Ralph being killed. As we have seen before, in duty to retreat states it's not so much about the final act of deadly violence as it is about the events leading up to it, and the point when the deadly danger arguably was apparent enough to warrant the shooter's retreat from the area. If one goes back in the chain of events far enough, there is almost always a point in time when the shooter could have turned away and sought to avoid the confrontation, but didn't perhaps because the danger wasn't fully formed in his mind or wasn't recognized as being deadly, or the path of escape was deemed too risky or for some other reason. In Marty's case that point in time came when he was inside the storage closet in his garage leaning against the door. Ralph had threatened to kill him and had reached into his pocket in a manner that convinced Marty he had a gun. Marty had several options as he stood there in relative safety. Among them, he could have called the police, gone into his house, left the area, sought help from his other guests, or simply stayed where he was. He chose none of them, but rather prepared himself for a confrontation with Ralph. He got a rifle and pre-positioned it near the garage doo, in case there was trouble, in case Ralph became violent. The placement of the rifle alone meant he knew deadly danger was possibly afoot. Unless the Castle Doctrine placed him in an area where he was exempt from retreating in the face of such danger, he had a duty to retreat before confronting Ralph with a rifle.

The Michigan Supreme Court had to determine, as a matter of Michigan law, whether Marty's garage was part of the curtilage of his home. If it was, then he had no duty to retreat and his case would be sent back for a new trial. If it wasn't part of the curtilage, then Marty did have a duty to retreat and his murder conviction would be upheld. Unfortunately for Marty, the Supreme Court could find no prior case that decided an outbuilding was part of the home's curtilage and it declined to use Marty's case as a way to expand the definition of that term to include them. It decided instead to follow Michigan precedents regarding what areas were included in his property's curtilage. It held that Marty's garage was not part of the dwelling's curtilage and hence was not covered by the Castle Doctrine. It upheld Marty's conviction.

Just as the specific language of stand-your-ground laws affects the duty to retreat in states that have enacted them, so too do the statutes and case decisions about a state's Castle Doctrine. In the absence of specific modifying language, common law self-defense, with its duty to retreat in the face of danger, will likely apply to determine the shooter's fate.

11

DE-ESCALATION

STEPPING OFF THE PATHWAY TOWARD VIOLENCE

Yaffa and Richard Ballinger didn't get along very well. Yaffa tried to make the marriage work but Richard drank too much, and if he wasn't drinking he was doing drugs. Whenever Richard went on a serious drinking binge, or lost a couple of days on drugs, she would kick him out of their South Philadelphia apartment. After a while he would say he was sorry, beg for forgiveness, promise to never do it again, and she would take him back. For a time things would be better, but then he would start drinking again, or doing drugs, and the ritual would repeat itself.

Yaffa cared deeply for Richard, but no matter what she did she couldn't seem to break the cycle of his misbehavior, forgiveness, and then more misbehavior. It finally reached the point where she gave him an ultimatum. He had to clean himself up, she said. She told him to get some help, do whatever he had to do to control his addictions, she would help him, but she wasn't going to keep going down their current path.

Richard listened and nodded, told her he understood, said he would change, promised he was done with all that. But their history got in the way. They'd done this before, issued warnings and ignored them and made promises only to break them. It had happened so many times that Richard didn't really believe this time would be any different.

Richard's next episode came a few weeks later. He got high and didn't come home for days. There was no real reason for it, nothing good, nothing bad, he just felt like getting hammered. Yaffa was beside herself with worry. When he finally showed up she was relieved, and then she became furious. She began to see Richard in a different light. She decided that he didn't respect her, didn't think she was important, otherwise he would have at least tried to fix himself. She realized how unhappy she was and promised herself that she was going to do something about it.

She told Richard to get out and take whatever he wanted with him. She called her brother, David Simon in front of him, and asked him to come stay with her for a few days. That got Richard's attention. David was very protective of his sister and he didn't like Richard much. David had tried several times to convince Yaffa to leave Richard. He even offered to pay once for their divorce.

David's involvement in their troubles was something new in Richard's mind. Yaffa had never called David when she'd kicked him out before, much less invite him to come stay with her. She knew how much David disliked him. More importantly, she knew that he knew of David's dislike, and so she had always kept their troubles away from David, at least up until now. Richard also knew that David would be only too happy to come stay with Yaffa, and that while he was there they would talk more about a divorce. He began to worry that maybe this time Yaffa was serious about him leaving.

Still it was hard for Richard to think Yaffa might actually divorce him. He knew she was angry right now, but thought she would cool down eventually and take him back. He might have to tone it down a bit, but in the end it would be ok, it always was. He decided she needed some space, some time to miss him, so he used the kitchen phone to call a friend and arranged to stay at the friend's apartment for a few days.

Yaffa was standing in the living room, watching him, when he hung up the phone.

"I'm leaving for work, but I want you gone when I get back," she said.

Richard started to respond, but she had turned and was already part way out of the door. He winced as the door closed with a bang behind her. He finished his coffee, went to the bedroom, and threw some clothes into a suitcase. Then he straightened up the apartment, hoping it would be seen as a peace offering, and, without leaving a note, went to stay with his friend.

When Yaffa came home that evening she was relieved to find that Richard wasn't there. She'd spent much of the day distracted, thinking about him, about what was important, about their future together. She thought maybe she loved him enough to accept his flaws, but decided that was foolish. Becoming a junkie's wife so he could satisfy his cravings wasn't her dream, she was better than that, and it wasn't the answer to their problems. Late in the afternoon she decided her marriage was over, called an attorney, and made an appointment to see her the next day about a divorce.

David arrived at the apartment around 7 o'clock that evening. He carried his suitcase in one hand and a small black plastic case in the other. Yaffa knew what was inside the plastic case. She'd seen David carry his pistol in it before, but that was about the extent of her knowledge of guns. She wasn't concerned about it being in her apartment though, because David was very safe with the pistol and she trusted his judgment. If he thought he needed it, that was good enough for her.

"Hey, Dave," she greeted him. "Thanks for coming. Sorry for asking."

"Not an issue, Yaffa. Sorry it's come to this."

"He was gone again. Several days. Drugs. I didn't know where he was," she said. With David, it was all she needed to say. He knew Richard. "I'm not going to take it anymore."

"You shouldn't have to, Yaffa, but you know, this isn't the first time."

"I know, I know," she said, frowning. "But this time it's going to be different. I've already made an appointment to see a lawyer. I'm done. It's over. Put your stuff in the spare bedroom and come to the table. I made dinner for us and it's ready." She turned and walked back into the kitchen.

David took his suitcase into the spare bedroom. Yaffa doesn't seem that upset, he thought. He was a little surprised by her business-as-usual attitude and by the fact she'd contacted a lawyer. Maybe this time it would be different. He opened the suitcase, took out a couple of shirts, hung them in the closet so they wouldn't wrinkle, picked up the gun case, and went back to the dining area near the kitchen. He sat down at a small round dining table and put the gun case on the chair next to him. He pushed the chair under the table until the gun case disappeared beneath the overhanging tablecloth. Yaffa was busy in the kitchen putting food on plates.

"You need any help?" he asked.

"No, everything's done. Don't get up. It's ready."

"So, you alright?"

"Yes, I'm fine. I don't know what I'll need for the lawyer tomorrow, but I guess I'll find out. I never thought I'd be doing this."

"You'll be fine, Yaffa. You're a good person. It'll work out. What was it this time, cocaine?"

"I don't know. And you know what, I've thought about it, and I really don't care. I've done my best to make our marriage work and I failed, and now I'm done. I'm not going to take any more of this. It's time to move on."

"I'm sorry, Yaffa. I really am. But I'm really not surprised. I was never a big fan of Richard's. The only thing I never understood is why you stayed with him so long."

"I know. I just thought I could change him. There's a lot about Richard I like when he's not drinking, or high on drugs. I thought I could fix his problems, but now I know I can't. I'll get over it."

David watched Yaffa set silverware and two plates of spaghetti and meatballs on the table. Then she brought two salads, some more plates, French bread, and olive oil. She brought some napkins and two glasses of water. Then she sat down.

David noticed how steady she was. There was no furrowed brow of worry, no anger, no tears, she wasn't questioning herself. She's calm, he thought, that's good, she's made her decision. He knew Yaffa was a thinker. She pondered deeply, taking time, sometimes too much time he thought, to mull over things she thought were important. But when she made her decision it was final. Once she knew what she wanted to do, she never looked back. She just kept moving ahead until the task was done. David expected there would be difficult days ahead for Yaffa, but in a way the hard part for her was over. Inside he was happy. Richard was a millstone around his sister's neck, and she was finally going to get rid of it.

They had just about completed dinner when there was a knock on the door. David wondered if he should answer it, but before he could speak Yaffa was already on her feet, wiping her hands on a napkin, and walking toward the door. She looked through the door's peephole to see who was there.

"Shit, it's Richard," she said. David turned to see her open the door and Richard standing there, a goofy grin on his face, the one that said he'd been drinking. He stepped past Yaffa into the hallway, but when he saw David, his face darkened. The two men locked eyes but Richard gave no sign of recognition. He turned to face Yaffa, ignoring David as if he wasn't there, as if he didn't exist.

"I need to get the last of my stuff and I wanted to talk to you," he said.

"OK, you can get your stuff but please do it quickly and then leave. I don't want to talk to you," she said.

"It's not going to hurt to talk a bit, Yaffa. I screwed up. I'm sorry."

"Yes you did, Richard. But talk isn't going to help this time. Please just get your stuff and leave." Yaffa walked back toward the kitchen and Richard followed her into the living room.

"Yaffa, I said I'm sorry. I love you," he said.

"Richard, I said I don't want to talk to you. We're not doing this again. You made your choice and I wasn't it. You chose drugs, so I'm done. Please just get what you want and leave. If you keep at me I'm going to call the police."

"But this doesn't make any sense. I didn't …" Richard stopped when David stood up from the table, the sound of his chair scraping against the floor. David walked into the living room and stood beside his sister. His right hand was down by the side of his leg. In his hand was a revolver, its barrel pointed toward the floor.

"Yaffa asked you to leave, Richard. It's pretty clear she doesn't want to talk to you, at least not tonight. So please take whatever you want and go," David said.

Richard looked at David, looked at the gun in his hand, and then looked at Yaffa. "What's going on? What is this, Yaffa? What's he doing here? Why does he have a gun in our apartment? You going to have him shoot me with his gun, Yaffa? Is that what you want? The big man going to shoot me with his big gun?"

"Please Richard, just leave," she said.

"I'm not going anywhere, goddamn it. I want to know why he's here with a gun. You afraid of me, Yaffa? You think I'm going to beat you up or something?"

"I'm not afraid of you, Richard. I just want you to leave."

"So this big man here, with his big gun, is he supposed to make me leave Yaffa?" Richard asked, nodding toward David. "The big man with the big gun. Or maybe he's afraid of me? Is that it? You're not afraid of me, but he is. You afraid of me, Davey boy? You going to use your big gun to make me leave?" Richard taunted. He was working himself into a rage, growing more and more angry as he spoke.

"You know what, big man with the big gun?" he persisted. "I've wanted to kick your ass for a long time. Maybe its about time I did." He looked down at the pistol in David's hand. "You're a dipshit, with your big gun. I don't care if you have a big gun. I have a gun too. What do you think about that, dipshit?"

David looked at his sister. "Call the police, Yaffa," he said. "Just call the police and let them take care of it."

Yaffa turned and went into the kitchen. She picked up the phone and dialed 911. A dispatcher answered almost immediately.

"My husband is in my apartment and I can't get him to leave. Can you send someone?" she asked. The dispatcher began immediately to ask her questions.

Richard and David stood in the living room listening to Yaffa talk to the dispatcher. Richard glared at David. "Well dipshit, looks like the cops are coming. Now you've got to decide whether to use your big gun to hold me for the cops or make me leave. You going to hold me?"

"No, Richard. I'm not going to hold you. You're free to leave anytime you want. In fact, I wish you would."

"I figured as much. Underneath it, you're a chicken-shit. Why don't you put your big gun away before you hurt yourself, asshole?" Richard appeared about ready to explode. His face was red, his breathing was heavy, and his hands were balled into fists.

David lowered his eyes breaking eye contact with Richard. He said nothing, turned away, and walked over to the dining room table. He sat down, put the revolver back in the gun case, snapped it shut, put the case back on the chair, and turned his back toward Richard. Yaffa was repeating their address for the dispatcher.

"That's right, dipshit, walk away," Richard said. "While you're shitting your pants, don't shoot yourself with your big gun," he snarled. He gave the middle finger to the back of David's head, and then he walked down the hall to their bedroom.

Yaffa hung up the phone.

"Are they coming?" David asked.

"He said they'd send somebody right away. Maybe by the time he gets here Richard will be gone."

"Maybe."

"I'd better go see what he's doing."

"I wouldn't do that, Yaffa. He's pretty angry right now. Just let him be. Hopefully, he'll get whatever he wants and leave. If he takes something that's not his, we can deal with it later, when he's sober. The important thing right now is to get him out of your apartment."

Yaffa sat down at the table and started rubbing her fingernails with her thumb, a habit she had when she was nervous. They could hear Richard moving around in the bedroom. The dresser drawers opened and closed. Then the closet door slid open. David thought Richard was probably getting more clothes.

"I don't know what he's looking for," Yaffa said. "I looked around when I got home and most of his clothes were gone."

"I'm not sure he's after anything. I think he probably came back because he wanted to talk to you," David said.

The closet door in the bedroom slammed with a loud bang causing both of them to jump. Yaffa put her hand to her mouth and looked at David, her eyes wide with realization.

"David, he kept a shotgun in the closet. I don't know if he took it earlier or not," she said.

"Well, we'll just have to see. You don't want it for anything, do you?" he asked.

Yaffa shook her head. She didn't believe what she'd just heard. "Of course I don't want it. What would I do with a damn shotgun? What the hell are you talking about, David? You've got a gun, now maybe he's got a gun. This is getting crazy. I'm going to see what's he doing," she said, standing up and walking away from the table.

"Don't argue with him," was all David could say before she disappeared around the corner on her way to the bedroom.

Richard was coming at her through the bedroom door. The only thing in his hands was the shotgun, a short-barreled pump.

"David, he's got the gun! He's got the gun!" Yaffa shouted.

The sound of her voice seemed to trigger something in Richard. He grabbed the shotgun's fore end, ratcheted it back, and slid it forward. The unmistakable sound of a pump shotgun slamming home the bolt, chambering a round, filled the hallway. Yaffa tried to block Richard as he came toward her, but Richard was much bigger and she was no match for him. He used the shotgun, holding it across his chest with both hands, to push her roughly out of the way.

David heard his sister yell, followed almost immediately by the sound of the shotgun. He's going to kill her, he thought, grabbing the gun case off the chair. He opened it, took out the revolver, and stood up from the table, just as Richard entered the living room holding the shotgun in both hands diagonally across his chest.

The two men were about fifteen feet apart. Richard saw David begin to point the shotgun in his direction, but before he could fire, David raised his revolver and pulled the trigger three times, rapidly. The sound of gunfire boomed through the apartment. Two of the shots struck Richard in the chest. He staggered, bent his knees, and sat straight down onto the floor. Blood started to soak through the front of his shirt.

Yaffa ran to the kitchen and dialed 911. This time the dispatcher kept her talking on the phone until the police and ambulance crew arrived. Richard was placed on a gurney and rushed to the hospital, but he never regained consciousness. He died from the two gunshot wounds to his chest.

David cooperated with the police, answered their questions, and described how the incident occurred. Yaffa backed up his story. When the investigation was over the prosecutor for the Commonwealth of Pennsylvania charged David with murder and David claimed self-defense. He said he shot Richard to keep from being shot himself. At David's request, a judge, sitting alone without a jury, decided the case. The judge found David guilty of voluntary manslaughter and sentenced him to from five to ten years in prison.[1]

INTRODUCING A GUN INTO AN ARGUMENT

The introduction of a gun into a verbal argument is never a good idea because it increases the likelihood of a deadly confrontation. It not only incites resentment and anger, but also creates a reasonable fear of imminent deadly danger that can trigger the use of deadly force against the man holding the gun leading to unwanted, fatal consequences.

The judge who tried David's case felt that David's introduction of a revolver into the discussion between Yaffa and Richard was a highly provocative act because it changed what was essentially a verbal disagreement between spouses into a very dangerous encounter, one in which Richard faced an imminent threat of death or serious injury. While

David may have thought he was protecting his sister, nothing in what had transpired between Richard and Yaffa indicated that she was in any danger. No words, no gestures, nothing to suggest that Richard was about to attack her physically, much less kill or seriously injure her.

The gun's impact on Richard's behavior was immediate and profound. Before Richard saw the gun he was pleading with Yaffa to discuss their problems, saying he loved her, apologizing for his bad behavior. After he saw the gun he was very angry, hostile toward both Yaffa and David, taunting them, insulting them, and threatening David. There was no need for a gun and it served no useful purpose, but it did provoke Richard. The judge concluded that while David did not have murderous intent when he killed Richard, introducing the gun was misbehavior, provocative, and at least partly responsible for Richard's death. In his mind it extinguished David's right of self-defense and made him guilty of voluntary manslaughter.

WALKING AWAY FROM A CONFRONTATION

On appeal the Pennsylvania Supreme Court looked at the same set of facts and came to a different conclusion. It reversed the trial judge's decision, set aside the conviction, and set David free.

The Supreme Court said there were two confrontations that evening. The first one occurred when David stood by his sister's side with the revolver in his hand, and the second one occurred when Richard confronted David with the shotgun. The court focused on David's conduct between the two confrontations and found behavior that made David's shooting of Richard during the second confrontation an act of self-defense.

As Yaffa talked with the 911 dispatcher during the first confrontation, David bore the brunt of Richard's anger. He still had the revolver in his hand, but he didn't point it at Richard and he didn't threaten to use it against him. He engaged neither verbally nor physically with Richard despite Richard's taunts and threats. Instead, he told Yaffa to call the police and let them handle it and then he walked away from Richard, went to the dining table, and put the gun away. He did nothing further until he heard Yaffa shout that Richard had a gun and thought Richard was about to kill her.

The law of self-defense recognizes that a person who starts a fight may, at some point, decide that he or she no longer wishes to continue it, that it would be better to stop and end the confrontation peacefully. It allows for, and even encourages, such behavior. A man whose misbehavior has forfeited his right of self-defense may revive it through subsequent good behavior, provided his subsequent conduct shows clearly his desire to end the confrontation. In other words, if the initial attacker abandons his attack and by word or deed shows that he wants to seek peace, his effort to stop the fight, to cease hostilities, must be respected, and if the victim of his initial assault then turns the tables on him and attacks him violently, he may respond with deadly force, if necessary, to defend himself.[2]

David's situation is a good example of how the law works. The trial court was correct when it concluded that David's introduction of a handgun into the argument between Yaffa and Richard was a highly provocative act. There was nothing to suggest that Yaffa was in any danger, and the only purpose of a handgun at that point was to intimidate Richard into leaving the apartment. Had the first encounter escalated into a shootout, with no intervening good behavior on David's part, the Supreme Court likely would have agreed with the trial judge and upheld David's manslaughter conviction.

That's not what happened, however. David, by his behavior, quit the first confrontation. He stopped his hostile behavior toward Richard and walked away from him ending the confrontation. In response to Richard's threatening behavior, he told Yaffa to call the police and let them take care of it and then he turned his back on Richard and walked to the table where he put his gun back in its case. His behavior de-escalated the confrontation, lowering tensions rather than increasing them, thereby making physical violence less likely. The law says such behavior is good behavior because it shows that David no longer wished to fight and was trying to end the confrontation peacefully.

When Richard left the living room and went into the bedroom, David did not pursue him but remained sitting at the table, his gun stored in its carrying case. The confrontation was over. The misbehavior in brandishing the gun before Richard was erased by his good behavior in putting it away. The law resets the relationship between them as if the misbehavior had not occurred. They were in the same position, relative to each other when Yaffa first opened the door and let Richard into the apartment. Neither of them was guilty of any misconduct.

The second confrontation occurred because Richard decided to turn the tables and use the shotgun to intimidate David. He got the shotgun out of the closet and went back to confront David in the living room. His behavior wasn't a continuation of their prior encounter in which David was the aggressor threatening him with the revolver. It initiated a new encounter in which Richard was the aggressor threatening David with the shotgun. The behavior of each participant is judged as if the first confrontation hadn't occurred. In the second confrontation, when Richard began to point the shotgun at David, it triggered David's right of self-defense, switched the light on, and permitted him to shoot Richard and subsequently claim he acted in self-defense.[3]

ENDING AGGRESSION IN GOOD FAITH

There are four factors that must be present for a person to redeem himself from prior misbehavior and revive his or her right of self-defense. First, the person must act in good faith to end all hostile acts toward the victim. His behavior must clearly indicate that he no longer wishes to participate in the confrontation. He may walk away, cast aside a weapon, offer an apology, declare the matter over, or engage in any other behavior that indicates a good faith desire to avoid further conflict in favor of peace. The possibilities of such behavior are endless. It can be anything so long as it shows clearly the person wishes to end the argument peacefully.

COMMUNICATING EFFECTIVELY ONE'S DESIRE FOR PEACE

Second, the person must not only cease his or her aggressive behavior and seek peace, but also must communicate his or her intent to do so, clearly and effectively, to the other combatant. Communicating one's intent to abandon the fight shows sincerity and good faith and helps to allay the victim's fear of further attack.[4] The best way to communicate the desire to withdraw from a fight is to verbally express the desire for peace, words heard by others as well as by the adversary. The intent to abandon a confrontation can also be communicated effectively by one's actions so long as they show clearly one's desire to end the fight. Turning one's back and walking away from an adversary, as David did to Richard, certainly does it, but so too do other kinds of behavior. Again, it can be anything as long as it signals that the threat is over.[5]

The burden for making sure an adversary understands one's desire for peace falls on the person seeking to de-escalate the encounter.[6] He or she is said to have failed to withdraw effectively where the communication is unclear or not understood. A person who fails to withdraw effectively from the fray remains responsible for his or her misbehavior and may not claim self-defense if such misbehavior promoted, prolonged, or contributed to the circumstances that led to another person's death.

NO NEW MISBEHAVIOR

The third element that must be present for a person to erase prior misbehavior is the absence of any new misbehavior. Once a person has successfully withdrawn from the confrontation and erased his prior misbehavior through subsequent good behavior, the relationship of the parties is reset and they are back on equal footing. Any subsequent confrontation between them must be judged anew by the facts of the new encounter and by the role each party played in bringing it about. If the person who redeemed himself from prior misbehavior is free of any new misbehavior during the subsequent encounter, then he or she may respond with deadly force, if necessary, to avoid a threat of death or serious injury.

UNEQUIVOCAL INTENT TO WITHDRAW

Fourth, and finally, for the right of self-defense to revive, the words and/ or acts meant to communicate that a person wants to abandon the fight must be clear and unequivocal. They cannot be subject to interpretation. A verbal statement announcing one's intent to abandon the fight is important because there is less chance of misinterpretation, and there is a clearer record of what the person was thinking. Behaviors alone can be sufficient if their meaning is clear as they were in David's case, but there is always the danger they will be misinterpreted or that they will remain ambiguous.

Good faith intent to withdraw, clear communications, no additional misbehavior, and unequivocal meaning. These are the four elements that when coupled with good behavior will erase a person's prior misbehavior and permit him or her to withdraw effectively from a confrontation, and reclaim the right of self-defense. That is what the Pennsylvania Supreme Court found had occurred in David's case. He abandoned the first confrontation and redeemed himself only to have Richard turn the tables and threaten him with the shotgun. Because David was without fault in provoking the new confrontation, he had the right to defend himself with deadly force against Richard's threat of deadly violence.

FAILING TO WITHDRAW EFFECTIVELY FROM A CONFRONTATION

It's worth taking a look at another case to see how the four elements of effective withdrawal from a confrontation might play out. Gina Lombardi and Wendy Anderson were lovers who lived together in Village, Oklahoma, near Oklahoma City. Their relationship was volatile, sometimes calm, sometimes stormy, and during one of their frequent storms, Wendy killed Gina.[7]

It started at a supermarket. The couple quarreled over a welfare check, and soon they were screaming and swearing at each other, disturbing the other customers. The store manager called the police who arrived quickly and managed to lower the argument's volume, if not its profanity.

Gina decided that she was going to end the relationship with Wendy and phoned her mother to come pick her up at the store. When her mother arrived, Gina asked the police to come back with her to her and Wendy's apartment so that she could remove her personal belongings. The police obliged and they left the store.

Gina was at their apartment packing her clothes in her mother's car when Wendy arrived from the store. Wendy approached Gina and asked if she would reconsider her decision to leave. She said she loved Gina and wanted her to stay. She promised to work out their differences, apologized for her behavior at the supermarket, and asked for forgiveness. Gina wasn't interested in working things out. She'd made up her mind, she said. She wanted to leave. She asked Wendy to leave her alone and stay out of her way while she packed the rest of her things.

Wendy followed Gina when she went to put the last of her things into the car and asked her again if she would reconsider and stay. Gina lost her temper, grabbed a small claw garden rake laying in the trunk of her mother's car and lashed out at Wendy with it. The tines of the rake struck Wendy in the face, just below her left eye, causing four deep claw marks, two of them bleeding. A police officer intervened and separated the two women. Wendy went back inside their apartment to take care of her face and Gina finished packing the car and then she left with her mother.

When Wendy finished cleaning and covering her wounds she got into her car and drove toward the part of town where Gina's mother lived. About half way there she spied Gina and her mother in the car several blocks ahead of her and began to follow them. Her mother was driving and Gina turned around in the front seat and looked at her. She knew Wendy was following them.

A bit farther down the road Gina's mother turned the car into the parking lot of a police station and parked. Wendy was right behind her and spotted an open parking space on the street in front of the police station. She parked her car in the open space and went to the parking lot. When she was almost to their car, the front passenger door flew open and suddenly Gina emerged with the garden rake in her hand. She was very angry, swore at Wendy, and said she was going to kill her. She stepped toward Wendy and raised her arm to strike her with the rake. Wendy turned and ran out of the parking lot, along the sidewalk to her car. Gina ran after her, the garden rake in her hand.

When Wendy reached the car she fumbled open the passenger front door, reached into the glove compartment, and removed a pistol she kept there. Then she turned to face Gina who was just a few steps away and closing fast. Gina tried to hit her with the rake and Wendy tried to grab it. She missed but caught Gina's arm and the two women began to struggle, pushing and shoving each other, until they found themselves in the middle of the street. Gina was enraged, screaming and swearing at Wendy and trying to hit her with the garden rake. Suddenly, there was a gunshot. Gina stiffened and fell to the pavement. She died of a single gunshot wound to the head.

Wendy was tried and convicted of murder in the Oklahoma courts. She claimed she shot Gina in self-defense trying to prevent her own death or serious bodily injury. The prosecutor argued that she misbehaved by continuing to pursue Gina after Gina had made it clear that she didn't want to reconcile with Wendy and after she had asked Wendy to leave her alone. He said that by doing so Wendy prolonged the confrontation and contributed to the circumstances that led to Gina's death, disqualifying her from claiming self-defense.

Wendy's lawyer argued that her behavior in the police parking lot, turning her back and running away from Gina, showed that she intended to abandon the fight and end the confrontation. Gina understood that Wendy wanted to stop fighting because Gina had to run after her to prevent her from escaping. He said that Wendy's good behavior at the police station erased any previous misbehavior and allowed her to claim a right of self-defense. The prosecutor countered this argument by saying that if such was the case then Wendy failed to communicate her intent clearly to Gina.

There are important factual differences between Wendy's case and David Simon's case. David's behavior reduced tensions by increasing the physical distance between himself and Richard. He turned his back and walked away from Richard to the dining room table, giving Richard more physical space, thereby reducing the chances of a fistfight. He also created a temporal pause in the chain of events, a period of time when the two parties were separated with neither person being in a position to harm the other. The confrontation was effectively over.

Wendy's behavior did just the opposite. Throughout the chain of events, up until the very end, she increased tensions by reducing the physical distance between herself and Gina, approaching her in the bedroom, following her to the car, following her to her mother's house, and seeking repeatedly to engage her in conversation, conversation Gina didn't want to have. Moreover, there was no perceived pause in the confrontation, no period of separation. It was just one long chain of hostile interactions, a series of incidents one after another, each connected to the one preceding it.

In addition, there is a question of whether Wendy's behavior in running away from Gina in the parking lot signaled clearly her desire to end the confrontation peacefully. The fact that Wendy ran when she saw Gina with the garden rake doesn't mean necessarily that she intended to end the matter. If that had been her intent she could have told Gina she didn't want to fight anymore, or given up and said she wouldn't bother her anymore, or she could have run into the police station, or when she reached her car she could have jumped in and locked the doors, started the car, and driven away. She didn't do any of these things. She ran to the passenger side of the car, opened the glove compartment, and got a gun. Then she turned to face Gina. Her retrieval of the pistol could have meant that she was frightened and trying to defend herself against what she thought was a deadly threat, but just as easily it could also have meant that she was trying to arm herself so she could win the fight. In other words, she ran not to lower the risk of confrontation, but to ensure that when it occurred she would emerge the victor.

The reason why Wendy ran to the car is unclear. Maybe it reflected her desire to end the fight, but maybe not. Her behavior can be interpreted either way, and there is nothing to clarify which interpretation is correct. There was no pause in the chain of events to suggest that her flight from Gina in the parking lot was not just a continuation of her repeated efforts to pursue her. If Wendy intended to withdraw from the confrontation with Gina, unlike David Simon, she failed to communicate it effectively and failed to create a break in the chain of events leading to Gina's death. She remained responsible for her misbehavior, was barred from claiming she acted in self-defense, and her conviction was affirmed. Sometimes running away is not a sign of a person withdrawing from the fight, but rather of a person seeking tactical advantage to win it.

12

MISTAKE

MISJUDGMENTS

Midland, Texas sits astride Interstate 20 in west Texas on the southern-most part of the Great Plains. It was established in 1881 when the Texas and Pacific Railroad decided a place midway between Fort Worth and El Paso was as good a place as any for its trains to stop. It's a bustling city of about 120,000 people. Southwest of Midland, fifteen or twenty miles down Interstate 20, lies Odessa, its sister city. Midland has been in the news in the last few years because the Bush family chose to live there. President George H. W. Bush and First Lady Barbara Bush lent their names to the place, then their son President George W. Bush and First Lady Laura Bush called it home, two presidents, one town.

It was Friday evening in west Texas, the day after Thanksgiving. Odessa residents Sara Healy, her sister Michelle Healy, and their friend Katherine Engler, met up for a girls' night out. They had nothing particular in mind except to enjoy a bit of the long weekend. After the usual back and forth about where to go, they decided to see what was happening at the Zodiac Club, one of Odessa's local watering holes. So they piled into Sara's car and Katherine drove them down South Dixie Boulevard toward the nightclub. Katherine was behind the wheel because Sara forgot to bring her glasses and wasn't wearing her contact lenses. Katherine parked the car near South Dixie and East Murphy Streets, locked it, and the three women walked the two blocks to the club.

They got there just as the evening crowd was starting to build. People were coming through the door in twos and fours, fanning out to tables, and grabbing spots at the bar. Michelle managed to snag a table and they settled in. A waiter appeared out of nowhere and they ordered drinks amid the usual conversation about work, families, and the holidays. As more people arrived the place grew noisy and the three women found themselves competing to be heard over the background noise of a busy bar. Soon enough they became part of it, relaxed, happy, enjoying the evening.

"Well, well, look at this. It's the Healy sisters. Out slumming?" came the question.

Sara stiffened recognizing the voice. It was her husband, soon to be ex-husband, Ted Michelson. She looked up and there he was, standing between her and Katherine's chair. Another man she didn't know stood beside him. Ted was looking at her with the smile that told her he was anything but happy to see her. She shifted in her chair to better see him. Her first thought was that he looked like the same old Ted, the man she fell in love with, handsome, not too tall, a day-old beard, jeans, cowboy boots, and a buttoned shirt with an open collar. He had a beer in his hand. His friend wasn't quite as good looking or as well dressed, but she expected that. Ted liked people around him who didn't detract from his own luster.

"I see you've got the bitch with you," he said looking at Michelle.

"Hi Ted," Sara said. "We just came out for a couple of drinks. I didn't know you were here."

"Well, I am so let's be clear about that. I've been here an hour or so. You got here after me. I didn't follow you. I have no interest in seeing you. I wouldn't waste my time."

"I understand. I'm not looking for any trouble. We'll have our drinks and then we'll leave. There's not going to be any problems."

"Maybe not with you, but I don't think I can trust the bitch here," Ted said nodding in Michelle's direction. "She'd like nothing better than to sick the police on me, isn't that right, bitch?"

"That's right Ted. I'd like nothing better," Michelle said, holding Ted's gaze, defiant, angry eyes flashing. Michelle was nothing if not tough. "In fact big boy, if you don't leave us alone. I'm going to call over the bouncer and tell him about the court order. Then I'm going to call the police." She broke eye contact with Ted just long enough to pick up her cell phone from the table. She looked back up at him, her thumb poised over the dial pad.

"Whoa!" Ted's friend said. "We just went from zero to sixty in about two seconds. Let's ease off, lady."

"C'mon Ted," Sara said. "Let's not do this. We don't want any trouble. We're going to leave."

"You do that, Sara." Ted looked down at her. "I don't want you anywhere near me." He turned his head toward Michelle and pointed his finger at her. "And let me tell you something, bitch. You mess with me and I'm going to whip your ass just like I did the last time. It don't matter to me. I'll find your ugly ass, and when I do it won't be just your arm. You got that, bitch?" he said, jabbing his finger at her.

"I got it, big boy," Michelle said. She dialed 911, put her thumb on the send button and held the phone up so Ted could see the number on her screen. "You get this?"

Ted moved as if he was going to hit her, but his friend grabbed his shoulder. "C'mon Ted. We don't need this crap. Let's get another beer." He tugged gently on Ted's shoulder. "C'mon, screw them. C'mon." Ted raised his middle finger to Michelle, broke eye contact, turned his back, and walked back to the bar with his friend.

"Well, that was fun," Katherine said.

"What an asshole," Michelle said.

"Yea," Sara said. "I can't believe I married that guy. And how long it took me to realize what a jerk he is." She was talking to Michelle and Katherine but her eyes were fixed on Ted's back as he walked away.

"You know, Michelle, you embarrassed him in front of his buddy with that 911 stuff," Sara said. "He won't let that go. It will eat at him. He'll drink a couple more beers and then he'll be back. So let's just get out of here." She was tapping her fingers compulsively on the arm of her chair, fearful of what might happen if Ted lost his temper.

Michelle sensed her sister's fear. She had seen the nervous tapping before. Despite her bravado, she was afraid herself. "OK," she said. "Let's go. It's not going to be much fun if we stay here anyway." She reached down and picked up her purse from the floor near the leg of her chair, her movement triggering Katherine to do the same. Sara continued to watch Ted as if she thought he might turn around and come back to the table. Michelle stood up, grabbed her sister's arm, and the three women left the bar.

Once she was out of the nightclub, Sara began to relax. She grew more at ease the farther away she got from Ted. Michelle tried to distract her from thinking about her soon to be ex by asking where they would go next. Katherine said there was another Zodiac Club in Midland that was better than the one in Odessa, and they decided to go there. Katherine got behind the wheel, they found the entrance to I-20, and headed toward Midland.

Sara sat in the back seat and couldn't keep from thinking about Ted. She was afraid of him, afraid of his family and of what they might do to her. They were nice enough people in public, the men handsome, the women attractive with ready smiles and good wishes. But underneath their public personas there was a meanness of spirit and a sense of entitlement that made them angry and dangerous people. Ted and his sister, Cecile, were particularly bad, both of them subject to fits of rage, both capable of sudden violence against others.

She thought about the first time she called the police when Ted beat and threatened to kill her and how nothing happened. Her call for help had made things worse. The police came, the court issued an order requiring Ted to stay away from her, but he ignored it, found her, and then he really hurt her. She hadn't been able to leave the house for days, too ashamed of the way her face looked. Rather than seek help again from the police, she took to staying out of Ted's way, and she was always on the lookout for signs of his displeasure, like a poker player looking for tells. For the most part she was successful, but not always, and when she missed a signal that he was unhappy she paid heavily for her mistake.

About six months before their girls' night out, she took their two children, went to live with Michelle, and filed for a divorce. A few days after she left Ted, she and Michelle returned to the apartment to get some of her things. Ted was there when they arrived. He let them in and said nothing while Sara filled suitcases and trash bags with clothes. When she tried to leave, he wouldn't let her. He asked her to come back, and when she refused, he blocked the door. Michelle tried to intervene and told him to back off. He hit her with a baseball bat breaking her arm. She and Michelle went to the hospital where the doctor put on a cast. Then they went to the police station to file a complaint against Ted. The judge issued an order and the police served it on Ted, commanding him to stay away from her and Michelle. He ignored the order, ignored the police, and harassed the both of them—leading to absolutely nothing.

Sara continued to work her job as a social worker. One of her duties was to make home visits to her employer's elderly clients. Not long after the incident with the baseball bat, she was visiting the home of an elderly couple when she glanced out of their front window and happened to see Ted and his sister, Cecile, sitting in Cecile's car parked on the opposite side of the street. Ted got out of the car, walked across the street to her car, which was parked in the client's driveway, opened the door, and got in behind the wheel.

Sara went outside to see what he was doing. When she walked up to the driver's side of the car, Ted lowered the window. She saw an ignition key in his hand and couldn't imagine where he got it. He said he wanted her to come back, blaming Michelle for keeping them apart. She had poisoned Sara's mind against him, he said. Sara told him that Michelle had nothing to do with it. She said she was just tired of being hit and that she wanted a divorce. She asked him to please leave her car alone. Then she made a big mistake.

She reached through the car window and tried to grab the key in Ted's hand, but she wasn't fast enough. He grabbed her hand and held it fast. Then he raised the window. She tried to use her other hand to stop it, but he grabbed that one too, and held it just long enough to trap both hands in the closing window. Then he started the car, backed out of the driveway, and drove down the street. Sara tried to keep up, running alongside the car, but he accelerated and she lost her footing. The car dragged her down the street. Her arms felt like they were being torn off, and she screamed for help as loud as she could. Ted slammed on the breaks, jolting her to a stop. Then he asked her again if she would come back to him. The pain in her arms hurt terribly, her pants were torn, one shoe was missing, and her foot was bleeding from being scraped against the pavement. She struggled to her feet, looked him in the eye, and lied.

Yes, she told him, she would come back to him, but she wanted to get her shoe. It was laying in the middle of the road. He lowered the window freeing her hands. Sara fell to her knees and rested her head against the car door. She rubbed some of the pain out of her wrists. Ted was talking to her through the window but she didn't hear what he was saying. All she could think about was getting away. She reached up with one hand and grabbed the open window frame. She leaned against the door and slowly pulled herself to her feet. Her wrists hurt and her foot stung, but otherwise she didn't think she was hurt seriously. She told Ted she would go get her shoe and get into the car, but when she was a few steps away she turned and bolted for her client's house.

She ran as fast as she could, and she thought she could make it. She had a head start and Ted wasn't much of a runner. She figured he would turn the car around and drive after her rather than get out and chase her on foot. She believed it would give her enough time to reach the house. Sure enough, Ted tried to make a U-turn, but the street's narrow width and a parked car made it impossible for him to get all the way around. He had to stop, back up, and then go forward again to get by.

Sara ran across the lawn and was almost to the old couple's front steps when she heard the revving engine of another car. It was Ted's sister, Cecile, sitting in her car on the other side of the street. Cecile pulled out of her parking space and angled the car to intercept her. Sara kept running. She reached the steps, ran up them, opened the front door, and looked back. Cecile was pointing a gun at her through the driver's window. Sara heard two or three shots and the thud of bullets hitting the front of the house. She ducked through the door, closed it, and locked the dead bolt. She used the client's telephone to call the police. They came in a matter of minutes, but by the time they got there both Ted and his sister were gone. The police took statements from Sara and from the homeowners, but they didn't arrest Ted.

At Michelle's insistence Sara trudged once more to the local court and filled out another bunch of forms about Ted, this time including Cecile. The judge issued another restraining order against both Ted and Cecile, ordering them to stay away from Sara. They ignored it. Indeed, they seemed to take delight in showing up wherever she was, taunting her with their presence, with the law's inability to protect her. She called the police, but Ted and Cecile were always gone when they arrived. After several calls she knew that in the cop's eyes she was the problem, not Ted. They thought she was a whiner, a weak woman who saw threats where none existed.

As she rode along in the back of her car, Sara thought about how she'd done everything they'd told her to do, to stop Ted from coming after her, but none of it had worked. She was alone with two children to care for, her job her only source of income, and the law unable or unwilling to help her. She thought she'd never have bought the gun if someone could keep Ted away from her. She knew she wasn't strong enough to stop him from hitting her, and she was terribly afraid of the beatings. The gun was in the car's glove box. She'd only had it for two weeks and she needed to learn how to shoot it better. The car bumped suddenly and broke her train of thought. They were entering the parking lot of the Zodiac Club in Midland.

They found a spot in the parking lot, checked their makeup, and went into the club. It was in full swing, with lots of music, lots of loud talk, and lots of laughing people. They pushed their way through the crowd to the bar, and after a bit of hand waving at the bartender, ordered drinks. Three unattached women in a crowded bar, it didn't take long before the men were chatting them up. The earlier incident with Ted faded into the past and they became part of the scrum: drinking, talking, laughing, accepting some dance offers, rejecting others. After an hour or so they started to drift into separate conversations with different people and agreed to meet by the door at 11:30 p.m.

Abby Blevins and her friends were at the Zodiac Club celebrating her birthday. It had been a long, hard week for her and she wasn't in the best of moods. A particularly annoying co-worker, who was trying to pick her up, didn't help. Using the bathroom as an excuse, she extracted herself from his awkward advances and headed toward the bar.

Nobody really knows how it all started and it isn't really important to what followed, but somehow Abby and Michelle got into a fight near the bar. It began as a shouting match, but escalated quickly into pushing and shoving and then into a fistfight. Other club patrons stepped in to stop it, but before they did Michelle had been hit over the head with a beer bottle and Abby had a fat lip from being punched in the face. The beer bottle broke when it hit Michelle's head, cutting her scalp, sending blood streaming down her face onto her shirt, making her appear more injured than she really was. Katherine was close by talking to a friend, heard the commotion, and saw Michelle with a bloody face. She grabbed Michelle's hand and guided her to a side door near the bar and they both exited the club.

They stepped outside into another parking lot on the opposite side of the building from where they had parked Sara's car.

"You OK?" Katherine asked, reaching into her purse and handing Michelle a handkerchief to help her stem the bleeding from her head.

"Yes. I think so. It's just a lot of blood. I think I need some stitches."

"I'm going to find Sara and we'll get you to a hospital. Are you going to be OK?"

"I'm alright. I'll stay here a minute and see if I can stop some of this bleeding. I'll meet you at the car."

"Just stay here. I'll be right back." Katherine tried to go back into the bar through the side door, but it was locked from the inside. Shaking her head, she looked at Michelle. "Be right back, just stay here," she said again. She walked toward the front of the building and disappeared around the corner.

Michelle pressed the handkerchief against the cut on her head. It didn't hurt that much, but the amount of blood was scary. It seemed to be everywhere. She started to follow the way Katherine had gone when she heard the side door open. A woman, resembling vaguely the woman she'd fought with in the bar, came out the door. She had an angry look on her face. When she saw Michelle she charged her, pushing her in the chest and causing her to stagger backward.

"You bitch," she screamed. "You hit my sister."

Michelle was bigger than her attacker and she didn't let anyone push her around like that. She grabbed the smaller woman by the shirt and threw her to the ground. "Back off woman or I'll kick your ass," she said.

Maybe it was the shock of being thrown so quickly to the ground or the blood streaming down Michelle's face or the angry look in her eyes, or maybe it was all of them, but Abby's sister made no move to get up. She averted her eyes and became quiet. Michelle stared at her briefly and then turned and walked away toward the front of the building.

As she rounded the corner Michelle saw Katherine near the front door surrounded by a half dozen angry people. They were shouting at her and she was shouting back. She walked toward the group intending to fetch Katherine and go to the hospital. Abby's sister ran past her and joined the group around Katherine. She said something to Abby who Michelle recognized as the person she'd fought with. Several heads in the group leaned in to hear what she was saying. Then she pointed at Michelle and everyone seemed to forget Katherine. All eyes turned and focused on her bloody face.

"You come to get some more, ugly bitch?" Abby shouted.

"No, I've come to get my friend and leave," Michelle said.

"Well, you're not going anywhere until this is finished."

"It's finished," Michelle said. She moved toward their car signaling Katherine to join her.

"It's finished when I say it's finished, bitch. What's the matter, you afraid?" Abby shouted, but Michelle and Katherine ignored her and kept walking. Abby followed them, hurling invective, and cussing at their backs trying to provoke a response. Her friends trailed along behind watching to see what might happen. Abby ran ahead of the two women, turned, and blocked their way. Her friends streamed around both sides of the three of them and lined up behind Abby.

"I'm going to kick your ass," Abby yelled. Several people behind her joined in, "That's right, girl," "You go, girl."

Michelle let out a deep breath of resignation. "Alright, I'm done," she said. "I've been hit over the head with a bottle, attacked by baby sis here, screamed at, called all sorts of names, and now you want to fight? OK, you've got a fight, but let's get something straight, baby girl. There's nobody out here to hit me over the head when I'm not looking and nobody's going to come rushing in to save your ass. You got it? So you want to fight, baby girl? Let's go," Michelle said, raising her right hand, fingers motioning for Abby to join her.

Michelle's gesture unnerved Abby making her think about what she'd started. This woman was waiting, unafraid, angry, and ready to fight. There wouldn't be any more cussing, no more threats, no more bravado. Suddenly a fight didn't seem like such a good idea and Abby wasn't sure she wanted to go through with it. She stood still, trying to think of a way out, searching for the words to save face. Her friends behind her sensed her hesitation. Someone said "What a bitch." Somebody else shouted, "Let's kick their asses."

Inside the club a stranger walked up to Sara who was sitting at a table away from the bar, talking with a man who'd asked her to dance.

"Hey lady, your friend just got into a fight over by the bar."

"Who? What happened?" Sara sat up in her chair.

"I don't know, but she's covered in blood."

Sara immediately thought of Ted. She knew it. He'd followed them intent on exacting revenge for Michelle's 911 comments. She knew he wouldn't let it go. He hated Michelle too much.

"Where is she?" Sara asked. "How bad is she hurt? Has anyone called the police? Has anyone called an ambulance?"

"I don't know any of that stuff. I didn't hang around," the man replied.

"Where is she?" Sara asked again, standing up and grabbing the man's arm to keep him from leaving, looking around the bar for Michelle and Katherine.

"I don't know. She went outside," the stranger said.

Sara let go of his arm, picked up her cell phone, and hurried toward the front door. She was afraid Ted would follow Michelle outside, catch her in the parking lot, and beat her until some dark desire inside him was sated. She knew from experience that's how it went.

She went quickly out the door, and seeing no one nearby ran to her car, but there was no one there either. She started back toward the nightclub when she thought of the pistol in her glove box. She knew she couldn't stop Ted if he was determined to hurt Michelle like when he hit her with the baseball bat. She rummaged through her purse, found her extra car key, opened the door, and retrieved the pistol. She shoved it into her pocket and ran back into the club looking for Michelle.

She couldn't find Michelle or Katherine, but near the bar it was clear that something bad had happened. People were talking quietly, nodding their heads. There was a space in front of the bar where blood and broken glass littered the floor. There was a woman there with a broom cleaning it up. Sara asked her what happened.

"A woman got hurt pretty bad," the woman said.

"How?"

"I don't know. Somebody hit her with a beer bottle. I just saw her bleeding. It was all over her face."

"Where did she go?"

"She and another woman went out that door," the woman said pointing to the side door near the bar.

"Thanks," Sara said, walking toward the door. She went through it and found herself in another parking lot on the other side of the building. Again, there was no one there. She hurried toward the front of the building, rounded the corner, and saw a small group of people off to her left. She heard someone in the group shout, "Let's kick their asses," and ran in that direction.

She recognized Michelle and Katherine by the color of their clothes and rushed to where they were standing. When she got closer, she was shocked by what she saw. Michelle's hair was matted with blood. There was more blood running down her face, down her neck, staining her white shirt. Sara had never seen so much blood before. She thought of

Ted again. She knew if he thought he could get away with it, he wouldn't hesitate to kill Michelle. Michelle looked hurt, and Sara thought she needed to get to a hospital immediately.

Sara grabbed Michelle's arm with both hands and looked at her bloody face. "Oh my god, Michelle! Are you all right? Who did this?" she asked. Without waiting for an answer, she swiveled her head and scanned the crowd looking for Ted and Cecile, knowing that if she could find Ted, Cecile wouldn't be far away. Without her glasses, she was having trouble in the dark picking out their faces. "Michelle, who did this to you," she asked again, this time shouting, as if Michelle couldn't hear her.

Sara's behavior alarmed Katherine. Her eyes were bulging and she was gulping air like she'd just finished a difficult workout. Her head was swiveling back and forth, looking for something, or someone. Katherine heard someone say, "What's up with her?" She's terrified, Katherine thought, she's really terrified.

"Sara, it's OK. It's OK," Katherine said, trying to calm Sara down.

Sara screamed at Michelle again, "Who did this to you?"

Michelle, unsure what was going on with her sister, pointed in the general direction of the people blocking their way. Sara followed her finger and saw a couple in front. She thought they were Ted and Cecile. The man she thought to be Ted was reaching into his pocket. He pulled something out that was black and started to raise it toward her. She thought it was a gun in his hand. "Let's get that bitch," he said. Sara pulled the gun from her pocket, aimed it at him, and pulled the trigger.

The sound of the gunshot startled the crowd, flushing it like a covey of quail. "She's got a gun," somebody screamed, and people started moving in all directions. Some dropped to the ground, others ducked behind cars, and some got into them and drove away. Sara stood there, shaking uncontrollably, the gun in front of her, pointing at nothing, because everyone but her, her sister, and Katherine was gone. Abby lay dead on the ground, a bullet hole in her forehead.

Katherine grabbed Sara's arm. "Come on, Sara. We've got to get out of here before they come back." Sara was confused and started running toward the street, but Katherine stopped her. "No Sara, this way, the car is this way."

Suddenly, a man appeared in front of Sara and shouted at her, "Give me the gun. Now!" Sara threw the pistol at his feet, but kept on running toward the car. Michelle was already there. Katherine got behind the wheel and the two sisters climbed into the back seat. Katherine started the car, backed out of the parking space, and drove toward the exit. Another man appeared in front of the car with a gun yelling at them to stop. Katherine kept going and he jumped out of the way. A shot rang out shattering their car's right rear window, but no one was hurt, and soon they were racing out of the parking lot and into the night.

Ted Michelson and his sister, Cecile, were not at the Zodiac Club in Midland that night. They never left Odessa. There was a man in the group with Abby, who looked a bit like Ted, and he had a black flashlight in his pocket. He told the police the shooting started when he took out the flashlight to shine in Sara's face. Sara was tried and convicted of murder and sentenced to fifty years in jail. She appealed her conviction. [1]

THE THEORY OF TRANSFERRED INTENT

In 1576, an English court tried a man for shooting an arrow, intending to kill his enemy but missing and instead killing another man, an innocent man, who'd done nothing wrong, and against whom the archer harbored no ill will. [2] The archer had no desire to hurt the victim much less kill him. His arrow simply hit the wrong man.

It was clear the archer shot the arrow deliberately and willfully. His intended target was also clear. It wasn't the man he killed. Self-defense wasn't an issue because the archer wasn't threatened when he let the arrow fly. The English judge who tried the case decided to focus on why the archer shot the arrow, and he concluded the archer let it go intending to kill one man, but killed another man by mistake.

The judge reasoned that although the archer had no malice, hostility, or ill will toward the man he actually killed, he did have murderous intent to kill someone, and he acted to do so. Moreover, he thought that since it made no difference to the dead man whether or not he was the person the archer intended to kill, it should make no difference to the law. The important thing was that the archer did want to kill someone and managed to do it. On that basis, the English court found the archer guilty of murder, and thus was born the doctrine of transferred intent.

INTENT FOLLOWS BEHAVIOR, WHEREVER IT LEADS

The idea behind the doctrine of transferred intent is that a person's intent follows his or her act to its conclusion, whatever that conclusion may be. Stated differently, people are responsible for what they set out to do intentionally and for the results they achieve. Thus, if a person acts intentionally to do good for one person, but instead does good for another person, his intent is still to do good, and it is said to have moved from the one he intended to help to the one he actually did help. Likewise, if a person acts intentionally to do bad to one person, but instead does bad to another person, his intent is still to do bad and likewise moves from the person he wished to hurt to the person he actually did hurt. Either way, the law will hold the actor accountable for the results he or she was able to achieve. In the archer's case he intended to kill unlawfully another human being, and he did so by shooting the arrow. His murderous intent, coupled with the act that produced a death, made him guilty of murder.[3]

TRANSFERRED INTENT IN SELF-DEFENSE CASES

How does the doctrine of transferred intent apply to claims of self-defense? As we have seen, the shooter's intent is critical in determining whether a self-defense claim is valid. If the shooter acts with murderous intent, that is malice, hostility, or ill will toward the victim, then he or she is guilty of murder. On the other hand, if the shooter acts with good intent to avoid death or serious injury to himself or to someone else, then he or she acted in self-defense. So what happens if the shooter acts with good intent, but achieves a bad result, namely killing someone other than the person threatening him or her with deadly danger? As with the archer, the doctrine of transferred intent moves the shooter's intent, in this case good intent, from his intended target to the unintentional target. The shooter's good intent prevents him from being convicted of murder because although the outcome was bad his intent was still good when he performed the act that produced the unintended result.

To illustrate, let's look at the self-defense claim of a man named Peter Smith.[4] Clarence Williams had a younger brother named Bob who most people considered a hothead, a person easily provoked to violence. One day Peter said something that offended Bob and Bob responded by threatening to shoot Peter the next time he saw him.

About three weeks after the threat, Clarence and Bob stopped at a local gas station to fill up Bob's car. They pulled in to an open pump and were surprised to find Peter pumping gas in front of them. Bob jumped out of his car and walked toward Peter. Clarence shouted for his brother to stop.

Peter heard Clarence's shout behind him and turned to see Bob coming his way. Bob clenched his fist and screamed at Peter that he was going to put him "in the ground." Clarence caught up with Bob and grabbed his arm just as Bob was reaching into his pocket. Clarence tried to pull Bob away, but Bob resisted and they struggled.

Peter thought Bob was reaching for a gun. Fearing that he was about to be shot, he opened the door of his truck and retrieved a 20-gauge shotgun. He managed to load the gun just as Bob broke loose from Clarence's grip and charged at him. Peter raised the shotgun and fired, hitting Bob. Some of the pellets also struck Clarence, who was directly behind his brother.

Peter was charged with two counts of aggravated assault, one for shooting Bob and one for shooting Clarence. The jury found Peter not guilty of aggravated assault against Bob because it believed that Peter reasonably feared Bob was about to attack him with a gun. His intent when he fired the shotgun was not to kill Bob but to save himself from harm. At the same time, it found Peter guilty of shooting Clarence because Clarence posed no threat at the time he was shot. Peter appealed the conviction, arguing that if his intent was good with respect to Bob, it was also good with respect to Clarence.

The Georgia appellate court, using the same approach as the English judge in the archer's case, focused on what Peter intended to do when he shot at Bob, and whether his intent somehow changed with respect to Clarence. In other words, did the fact that some of the shotgun pellets ended up hitting Clarence by mistake change the purpose or reason for why they were shot? The court decided that it did not, citing a one-hundred year old Georgia case that said, "If, in consequence of an assault upon himself which he did not provoke, the accused shot at his assailant, but missed him and the shot killed a bystander, no guilt would attach to him if the assault upon him was such as would have justified him in killing his assailant."[5] In short, Peter's good intent followed his act of self-defense, although with respect to Clarence, the outcome was bad. The Georgia appellate court vacated Peter's conviction for shooting Clarence.

MISTAKEN ASSESSMENTS AND REASONABLENESS

The concept of transferred intent is generally accepted throughout the United States. If a person acts with good intent, but achieves a bad result, it doesn't invalidate his or her claim of self-defense. But what happens if the person acts with good intent but achieves a bad result, but in the mistaken belief that he or she faced deadly danger when no such danger existed? Does the good intent still transfer to the victim and protect the shooter from criminal liability? The answer is yes, it does, and that brings us back to the case of Sara Healy and the shooting of Abby Blevins.

Sara fired her pistol after misjudging both the facts and the nature of the threat. She thought she was shooting at Ted Michelson, her estranged husband, a violent man who had beat her and broke her sister's arm, but she wasn't. She thought her target had pulled a gun from his pocket and was about to shoot her and Michelle, but he hadn't. She thought she was facing an imminent threat of death or serious injury, and based on that feared for her life, but she wasn't. Finally, she aimed at the man she thought was Ted but missed him and mistakenly killed Abby Blevins, a woman she didn't know and had never met. It's hard to imagine how she could have been more wrong.

People acting in self-defense are not required to have perfect judgment, but they are required to have reasonable beliefs. The question of whether Sara could use deadly force in the situation in which she found herself depends on the answers to two questions. First, if everything she thought was true, was in fact true, would those facts have led a reasonable person to fear that he or she was in imminent danger of death or serious injury? In other words, if Ted Michelson had been there in the parking lot with a gun in his hand, having done to Sara and Michelle all the things Sara knew he had done, would those facts cause a reasonable person in Sara's place to fear that he or she was in deadly danger? If the answer to that question is no, then Sara's claim of self-defense for shooting Abby fails because her fear wasn't reasonable even if everything she thought she saw in the parking lot was in fact true. If the answer to that question is yes, then the second question becomes important.

The second question asks if the mistakes Sara made in judging the facts and the nature of the threat were reasonable mistakes. Put another way, were they the kind of mistakes that a reasonable person would make if faced with the same facts and circumstances? Deciding this question involves the same process we have seen repeatedly. If the jury believes a reasonable person would make the same mistakes that Sara made, then Sara's mistakes are reasonable and she may claim self-defense. If the jury believes a reasonable person would not have made the same mistakes, then Sara's mistakes are not reasonable and she may not claim self-defense.

Whether the shooter's behavior is reasonable is determined, at least in part, by the nature of the relationship between the shooter and the victim. Evidence of that relationship plays an important role in the jury's deliberations. In Sara's case, the trial judge prevented her from telling the jury about her relationship with Ted and about her past experiences with him because Ted was not at the Zodiac Club that night in Midland. The Texas Court of Appeals believed the absence of such information unfairly shifted the evidence against Sara on both questions, that is whether her fear of danger was reasonable and whether the mistakes she made in judging the facts and the threat were reasonable. It set aside her conviction and sent her case back to the trial court for a new trial. When mistakes are made in self-defense shootings the determining factor is whether a reasonable person, in similar circumstances, would have made the same mistakes.

13

REASONABLE FORCE

KNOWING WHEN ENOUGH IS ENOUGH

It was a beautiful, warm spring night on Chicago's south side. The winter had loosened its grip and baseball talk was in the air. David "Kitch" Kasey, Maurice "Mo" Morrison, and Angelo "Angel" Delarosa were sitting on Mo's front porch arguing good naturedly, like they always did, about Chicago's pro sports teams. Kitch and Mo were in their late twenties. Angel was a little older. He was a big Chicago sports fan. Kitch and Mo said he thought any team with the word "Chicago" in it was worth following. The two of them weren't quite that dedicated. Their loyalties pretty much stopped after the Bears and the Blackhawks. They passed on baseball altogether, not enough action. They tolerated the Bulls' games, but agreed that all of them were decided in the last two minutes so why spend all that time watching them run up and down the court? The argument started because Angel wanted to go see a Cubs game.

"Man, I'm not interested in spending three hours watching the grass grow at Wrigley," Kitch said.

"Yea, count me out, booooring," added Mo. "What about a flick?"

"A flick? You wanna see a flick? Angel asked. "You've gotta be kidding me. We just snatched Andre Dawson, "The Hawk," from Montreal. The man hits, he steals, he's got a gold glove. The Cubs got a shot this year, and you want to see a flick? You gotta be nuts."

Kitch and Mo laughed. "I don't believe what I just heard," Kitch said. "The Cubs got a shot? You think the Cubs got a shot?"

"You need help, Angel," Mo said, shaking his head.

"I'm telling you, Andre Dawson's going to make a big difference. Want to put money on it?"

"I'm not taking your money, Angel," Kitch said. "If a Chicago Little League team was playing the Yankees you'd bet on Chicago. The Cubs got no chance at the playoffs. Not going to happen."

Something in the street caught Angel's attention. He got up and took a couple of steps toward the porch railing. "Let's do both," he said looking down the street. He was talking to Kitch and Mo, but his attention was focused on a man walking toward them on the sidewalk. "We'll hit an afternoon game, grab something to eat, and then go see a movie. You guys pick the flick," he said, still staring at the man on the sidewalk.

"How do you know there's going to be an afternoon game?" Mo asked.

"I just know," Angel said. He turned his head and looked back at his two friends. "Melvin Caporicci's coming down the street," he said. "I wonder what he's doing round here."

"That jerk. What's he want?" asked Mo.

"How the hell should I know," Angel said, turning back toward the street. "Probably looking for something to steal. The guy's a thief. He still owes me fifty bucks for the Dallas–Bears game last year."

"Kiss that fifty good bye," Kitch laughed. "You got about as much chance of getting any money from Caporicci as the Cubs have of getting into the playoffs." Kitch winked at Mo, proud of his twofer, busting Angel's chops about not getting paid and at the same time taking a shot at the Cubs. Mo grinned back. Sometimes picking on Angel was just too easy.

"I wonder what Caporicci'd be doing if you owed him fifty bucks?" Kitch asked Angel, smiling at Mo.

"Probably be bouncing your head on the pavement," Mo suggested to Angel's back, upping it a notch.

"Yea, right," Angel snarled. "It kind of ticks me off. I think I'll go see if Mr. Caporicci's gonna pay up?" Angel walked down the porch steps to the sidewalk and started for Caporicci. Kitch and Mo looked at each other and grinned. "This is going to be good," Kitch said.

Caporicci stopped on the sidewalk a couple of feet from Angel. "Hey, Angel, how's it going?"

"Hey, Mel," Angel said.

Back on the porch Kitch's eyebrows shot up in surprise. "Mel?" he mouthed silently to Mo. Mo grinned and shrugged.

"Mel, I need to ask you for the $50 you owe me for the Dallas-Bears game. I need the money."

"Ah man, I ain't got $50 on me."

"Well, you've got to have some of it, Mel. That was from last fall and I really need to get my money," Angel said, spreading his arms in front of him, palms up, pleading.

"Angel, I haven't got it. How about next week? Let me see what I can do after I get paid," Mel said, shaking his head, waiving his hand, and shooing Angel away like a bothersome housefly. The gesture irritated Angel.

"Every time I ask you for my money Mel, you say let me see about it next week. But next week never comes. I want my money." When Angel said it he dropped his hands and moved his right foot back a half step.

Mel caught the movement and his eyes flickered. He'd been on Chicago's streets too long not to know what was coming. He put both hands into his jacket pockets, relaxed his shoulders, and sighed. He stood quietly looking at Angel like a man who knew he was wrong and was ready to admit it.

Something about the way Mel was behaving bothered Kitch. It wasn't like him. Mel didn't give up like that for anybody. Kitch looked at Mo, who apparently had seen it too. Mo was leaning forward in his chair, no longer smiling, on alert, sensing trouble, watching carefully the goings-on in front of him. He stood up and walked to the top of the porch stairs, never taking his eyes off of Angel and Mel. Kitch stayed in his chair, and stared at the two men on the sidewalk. He wasn't smiling either.

Mel's left hand came out of his jacket pocket. He held it close across the front of his body, elbow bent, palm up, a reasonable man engaged in a friendly conversation. He smiled. "Look Angel, I know I lost the bet, but I haven't got the $50 right now and …" He paused, looked away as if searching for the right words, looked back, lowered his voice, and locked eyes with Angel,"… and I don't know if I ever will." He dropped the smile and his words came out cold and angry.

There it is, Mo thought, the Melvin Caporicci I know. He started down the porch steps.

The words hit Angel like a slap in the face and he reacted impulsively. His right arm shot out at Mel's head connecting with nothing but air, Mel sidestepping easily out of the way. He threw another punch and Mel sidestepped that one too, but he grabbed Angel's arm as it passed him and used Angel's momentum to throw him off balance. Angel staggered two or three steps down the sidewalk, his arms flailing, trying and managing, just barely, to stay on his feet. Angel wasn't in Mel's league as a street fighter. Like a matador in a bullring, Mel had parried Angel's punches with one hand, the other still in his pocket. Angel was game, however. Recovering his balance, he turned to face Mel, ready to try again.

Mel smiled at him, dismissive of Angel's fighting skills. Then his right hand came out of his jacket pocket holding a semi-automatic pistol. "So, you still want to fight, you son of a bitch?" he snarled.

Mo saw the gun and ran toward the two men. Mel glanced at him, but kept the pistol trained on Angel, apparently unconcerned that Mo was approaching. When Mo was almost to the sidewalk, too close to miss, Mel pointed the pistol at Mo and calmly shot him in the chest. Feeling the impact, but no pain, Mo instantly changed direction but kept running, past the two men, a look of disbelief on his face. Angel froze in place, unable to move, trying to understand what had just happened. He couldn't believe Mo had been shot.

Finished with Mo, Mel turned back to Angel, the gun steady in his hand, pointing now at Angel's chest. He pulled the trigger again. "I'm shot," Angel cried out, and he too started running in the same direction as Mo.

Both wounded men ran down the sidewalk looking for cover, something they could put between them and Mel's gun. Mel watched them go, prepared to leave them alone, then he changed his mind for some reason and ran after them.

Kitch watched the whole thing from the porch. He was stunned and confused. It had all happened so fast and yet Mel had acted so casually, like it was no big deal, just another day shooting a couple of guys in the chest. Kitch was having trouble processing it and he was slow to react. When he finally understood clearly what Mel had done, and realized that Mel was now chasing his friends down the street with a gun, he bolted from his chair and ran after them knowing he had to do something quickly to stop Mel before he killed them.

Mo ran past a stranger on the sidewalk, Angel, right behind him, blood soaking the front of both their shirts. The stranger stopped walking, a look of concern on his face, surprised by the two bleeding men running by him. Then he saw Mel with a gun in his hand and understood. He pulled out his cell phone. "What are you doing?" he shouted at Mel. "I'm calling the cops."

Mel stopped running, looked at the stranger, pointed his pistol at him, and fired. He missed. The stranger ducked, like he was dodging a rock rather than a bullet, scurried between two parked cars, and started running across the street.

"You calling the cops, you calling the cops," Mel screamed at him as he moved quickly along the line of parked cars, looking for an easy shot at the stranger. He reached the same gap the stranger had taken, ran into it, and raised his pistol to fire at the back of the fleeing man. While he focused on shooting the stranger, Mo and Angel were able to escape. The stranger's actions probably saved both of their lives.

Kitch was running up the street after Mel, saw him shoot at the stranger, and then run between two parked cars. Mel was looking across the street and didn't see Kitch coming. Kitch didn't hesitate. He ran straight at Mel, lowered his shoulder, and crashed into his side, putting everything he had behind it like a linebacker crushing an unsuspecting quarterback. The impact threw Mel into one of the parked cars, snapping his head against a fender. Kitch held on, using his weight to push Mel as hard as possible into the car, driving Mel's head into the fender and cushioning his own collision. The crack of Mel's skull hitting metal left no doubt about how hard the hit had been. Remarkably, Mel was still on his feet, but he was clearly hurt. He reeled, his eyes unfocused, his left hand moving awkwardly, pawing the air as if reaching for something to grasp. He staggered to the sidewalk and fell on his face.

Cushioned by Mel's body, Kitch emerged unhurt from the impact. He jumped on Mel's back as he lay on the sidewalk. Mel still had the gun in his right hand. Kitch grabbed the hair on the back of Mel's head, pulled it up, and slammed his face into the sidewalk. He did it again. Mel let go of the pistol and moved his hand slowly to his face. Kitch grabbed the pistol from the sidewalk, shoved it into Mel's back, and pulled the trigger.

Mel flinched and then stopped moving. He was bleeding badly from the injuries to his face and from the gunshot wound to his back. Kitch got off him, and stood up. He pointed the gun at him. "You son of a bitch," he screamed. "You shot my friends. You no good son of a bitch," he screamed again, louder.

Mel began to move, slowly, like he was trying to get his hands underneath him, to push himself up. The movement startled Kitch. He tightened his grip on the pistol and shuffled his feet. He extended his arms more forcefully toward Mel, as if that would somehow make the injured man stop moving. He reached down, grabbed the back of Mel's jacket, shook it, "Stay down, goddamn you. Stay down," he shouted.

Whether he couldn't hear Kitch, or he was too groggy to understand, Mel didn't stop moving. He seemed to gather strength from the sound of Kitch's voice, a man regaining consciousness after having been knocked out. He moved his leg and lifted his knee as if he was trying to kneel. His arm was pawing the air again as if he was reaching for something to help him get up, but his movements were slow, like he was very tired. Kitch reached down, grabbed the back of his head again, pulled it up, aimed the pistol at the base of his skull, and pulled the trigger. Mel stopped moving.

Kitch left Mel on the sidewalk and went looking for Mo and Angel, fearing what he would find. He passed a dumpster in an alleyway and threw the gun into it. He searched the neighborhood but didn't see Angel or Mo. He entered a building where two of his friends lived and went to their apartment. He told them what had happened and what he had done. At one point he laughed about it nervously.

After escaping from Mel, Angel and Mo had separated, each running in a different direction, unaware of Kitch's attack on Mel. Angel eventually passed out, weakened by the loss of blood, unable to go any farther. Somehow he crawled into some bushes in front of a house, in a strange neighborhood, before he lost consciousness. Mo staggered on, not as badly hurt, determined to save himself. As luck would have it, he came upon a man parking his car. The man drove Mo to the nearest hospital. The police later found Angel and took him to the same hospital. Both men survived their wounds.

Melvin Caporicci didn't survive his injuries. He died on the sidewalk. David "Kitch" Kasey was convicted of murder by a Cook County judge sitting without a jury and sentenced to twenty-five years in prison.[1] He appealed his conviction.

DEFINING REASONABLE FORCE

The U.S. Code of Federal Regulations describes deadly force as "that force which a reasonable person would consider likely to cause death or serious bodily harm. Its use may be justified only under conditions of extreme necessity, when all lesser means have failed or cannot reasonably be employed."[2] It's as good a description as any, and a good place to start thinking about the reasonable use of deadly force. Note the central role of necessity in the definition, limiting the use of deadly force to situations involving "extreme necessity, when all lesser means have failed or cannot reasonably be employed."

There are times when the employment of deadly force in self-defense situations is simply unreasonable either because it is too much force or because deadly force isn't necessary to contain the threat. Take for example the shooting at the Red Stripe Food Market in Richmond, Virginia. The confrontation in that case ended with the would-be robber on the floor, wounded, submissive, and with Jason Donohue standing over him, a broken revolver in his hand. The robber was contained, subject to Jason's control, and no longer a threat to anyone in the store.

Yet some of its patrons, the people he had threatened, urged Jason to shoot him again, to make sure he didn't get up and continue his rampage. Had Jason listened to them and done as they asked, his actions would have been unreasonable because shooting the gunman was no longer necessary to contain the threat. He was already disarmed and disabled. There was no deadly danger that warranted a deadly response.

REASONABLE FORCE AND THE NATURE OF THE THREAT

The reasonable use of deadly force is linked closely to the nature of the threat depending on whether it's deadly, whether it's imminent, and whether alternatives exist to avoid its employment. Whether the force used was appropriate arises often in situations where a deadly threat once present has begun to lessen, diminishing over time to the point where it is no longer deadly, no longer imminent, or an alternative emerges making deadly force unnecessary. The question becomes at what point along the behavior continuum does this occur? When does the threat cross over from being deadly to being non-deadly, because the aggressor no longer has the will or the means to carry it out?

If a man suddenly stops attacking his victim and says he wants peace, then the threat is no longer deadly, and the right of self-defense is extinguished. Victims in these situations must decide quickly, whether the deadly threat is really gone, or whether it still exists, whether the aggressor's behavior means he has given up or whether it is just a ruse designed to give him or her some sort of advantage. Unless the threat is still deadly, still imminent, and there are still no reasonable alternatives to avoid it, the use of deadly force against him is prohibited because it isn't necessary.

THE THREAT MUST BE DEADLY

For reasonable force to be used, the threat must be deadly, or at least appear to be deadly. There must be some unlawful, violent behavior that puts the physical safety of the intended victim in danger, risking his or her death or serious bodily injury. Fistfights are a good example of the interplay between a threat's deadliness and what force may be used to counter it, because as the fight progresses, the danger evolves usually to become more deadly or less deadly.

Let's revisit the fistfight between Mike Brighton and Bobby Randall in Meridian, Mississippi. The beginning of the fight was pretty normal, pretty routine as far as fistfights go. Bobby punched Mike without warning, enabling him to get the upper hand quickly. He knocked Mike against the side of his truck and kept punching until Mike fell to the ground. So far nothing unusual. The fight was unlawful, violent, but still most likely to end without anyone being hurt seriously. It certainly didn't warrant Mike responding with deadly force at that point in time, because there has to be more than the prospects of a black eye or a bloody nose to kill a man.

But the fight went on and Bobby continued to press his advantage, even after it became clear that Mike was no longer able to resist. Bobby achieved dominance over Mike, and then he went beyond it to a level of violence that unless stopped, was likely to kill Mike or seriously injure him. He crossed over the point on the violence continuum that separates non-deadly from deadly threats. His behavior suggested murderous intent and it triggered Mike's right to defend himself with deadly force to stop the attack.

THE DANGER MUST BE IMMINENT

The use of reasonable deadly force also means the threat must be imminent, a right now kind of danger that requires a person to act instantly to avoid it. If there's no behavior threatening immediate, unlawful violence then there's no need to act immediately with deadly force to counter it.

Judy Ann Taylor, the North Carolina woman who shot her sleeping husband in the head, is a case in point. The question in her trial was whether the dangerous and endemic threat against her, absent any behavior suggesting immediate unlawful violence on Floyd's part, allowed her to use deadly force in the present to avoid a deadly threat in the future. The decision in that case, one that is uniformly followed by all states, except in cases of spousal abuse, is that deadly force may not be used unless an act of unlawful deadly violence is present. There must be some behavior that poses an immediate, right now threat of death or serious bodily injury. Judy's killing of her husband while he slept was an unreasonable use of deadly force because at the time of his death he was not behaving in a way that put her in imminent deadly danger. In the Code of Federal Regulations language there was no "extreme necessity" for her to shoot him.

Another case illustrating the link between imminent danger and deadly force involved two Vietnamese men from Kent County, Michigan. Let's call them Thanh and Bao. The two men lived together in an apartment. Bao allegedly stole a gun from a man named John. John and several of his friends went to Thanh and Bao's apartment seeking to recover the gun. They broke into the apartment, found both men at home, and beat them savagely. They never found the stolen gun. Before leaving the apartment, John told Thanh and Bao that he intended to kill both of them the next time he saw them. He threatened to get another gun and "take care" of them permanently.

Two days after the beatings Thanh and Bao were hunting in the woods when they spotted John. He was alone, walking ahead of them, carrying a pistol in a holster on his belt. He didn't know that Thanh and Bao had spotted him. The two men were frightened because they suspected John knew they were in the woods and was stalking them, intent on carrying out his promise to kill them. They feared he would discover their location, double back somehow, sneak up behind them, and shoot them. Rather than let that happen, they decided to strike first. They hurried along a side trail, got in front of him, found a good place to hide, and waited until he came into view. When John passed by the place where they were hiding, the two men shot him several times in the back. They were tried and convicted of first-degree murder.[3]

The use of reasonable force almost always becomes an issue when someone is shot in the back. Turning one's back on an opponent normally means either that the person doesn't know his adversary is present or that the person is aware of the adversary's presence but doesn't wish to engage with him. Either way, the use of deadly force to kill the person whose back is turned is not justified.

The judge, who tried Thanh and Bao, concluded there was no imminent threat because there was no evidence to show that John knew the two Vietnamese men were in the woods. He described Thanh and Bao's behavior as "what might be called a preemptive strike on a man who had previously beaten them and threatened them, and shot him in the back before he could come around and bother them again. Whatever else it may be, a preemptive strike is not, under Anglo-American law, any form of self-defense."[4] The Michigan Appeals Court agreed with the trial judge's view of the case, reiterating that preemptive strikes have no place in the law of self-defense.

Notwithstanding repeated judicial decisions to the contrary, defendants continue to rely on endemic threats to justify the need for present action in the absence of contemporaneous, violent behavior to avoid death or serious injury at some point in the future. Judges, for their part, continue to remain steadfast, ruling again and again that prior threats and future danger in the absence of present unlawful deadly violence do not justify the use of deadly force. The exception that proves the rule is spousal abuse cases, where the abuse is long-standing and particularly egregious, but such cases are relatively rare. It is a safe bet to assume that a court dealing with a reasonable use of deadly force issue will demand some contemporary violent behavior as a precondition for finding its use reasonable.

THERE MUST BE NO ALTERNATIVE TO THE USE OF DEADLY FORCE

Finally, for the use of deadly force to be reasonable there must be no easy path of retreat, no reasonable, non-deadly alternative to the killing. Once again, Thanh and Bao's case is instructive. Their encounter with John in the woods was admittedly a potentially dangerous situation. John was armed, perhaps looking for them, perhaps not. Either way, Thanh and Bao knew where John was and they also knew that he might be a danger to them. Still they were safe because John didn't know they had seen him and he didn't know they were there. There was no need for them to respond immediately, they had time to assess the danger, and there were several ways to avoid it. They could have remained out of sight until John was gone or turned around and left the area or called the police. They were in a position of safety with several easy non-deadly alternatives they could have employed rather than using deadly force. They simply decided not to take any of them, preferring to lie in wait and shoot John in the back. The use of such force was unreasonable because the availability of alternatives made it unnecessary. [5]

REASONABLE FORCE WHEN WITHDRAWING FROM DEADLY ENCOUNTERS

Determining whether the use of deadly force is reasonable can be particularly challenging in situations where the initial aggressor withdraws, or attempts to withdraw, from the confrontation either by abandoning the contest or by being no longer willing or able to pursue it. It isn't always easy to tell if an attacker has withdrawn from the fight and if he or she really does desire to seek peace. For example, let's assume there's a confrontation and one of the parties turns his back on his opponent and walks away. Normally, such behavior is seen as a sign of the person's intent to end the quarrel, but it doesn't have to mean that. What if walking away enables the person to position himself better tactically or allows him to rest before resuming the fight or permits him to create a ruse that places his adversary at a disadvantage or gives him time and space to arm himself with a weapon? These behaviors escalate the confrontation increasing the likelihood of further violence by setting conditions for further attack that benefit the person employing them. How does one determine what behavior is sincere and what behavior is not?

Wendy Anderson's trial for killing Gina Lombardi outside the police station in Village, Oklahoma, illustrates one way of thinking about the problem. It looked at Wendy's behavior to see if it was consistent with intent to withdraw from the confrontation. The critical question in that case was: Did Wendy run to her car intending to withdraw from the fight or did she run to the car to improve her position in the dispute by retrieving a pistol? If her intent was to run to the car to get away from Gina, her behavior, grabbing the pistol from her glove box and turning to meet Gina was inconsistent with that goal. Behavior consistent with getting away from Gina would have been for her to run into the police station or lock herself inside her car or drive away or at least tell Gina that she didn't want to fight anymore. Unfortunately for Wendy, her behavior in running to the passenger side of the car, retrieving her pistol, and turning to face Gina suggests she didn't want to withdraw from the confrontation, but rather to win it. At the very least it made her intent unclear and she paid the price for that ambiguity.

INCONSISTENT DEFENSE THEORIES: AVOIDING A MURDER CONVICTION

The best way to determine whether Kitch used unreasonable deadly force is to look at how he tried to defend himself against the charge of murder. At Kitch's request, his trial took place before a judge, sitting without a jury. That meant the judge would decide both the facts of the case and the law he would apply to them.

Kitch offered what is known as inconsistent theories of defense. His primary objective was to avoid a murder conviction. His first theory argued that he was not guilty of any crime because he acted in self-defense. Mel, he said, posed an imminent threat of death or serious bodily injury to him and to others. When he shot Mel his intent was not to kill him but to save himself and others from the deadly threat that Mel posed. If the judge believed his argument, then he would be found not guilty of any crime and set free.

Kitch's second theory of defense was a backup in case the judge didn't believe his first theory. It argued that he killed Mel deliberately, but it was on the spur of the moment, in the heat of passion, as a result of having seen Mel shoot Bo and Angel. If the judge believed that argument then he would be found guilty of manslaughter and his time in prison would be much shorter.

The two theories are inconsistent, one arguing that Kitch is innocent and the other arguing that he's guilty, but not of murder. Taken together, he was saying to the judge, I'm not guilty of murder because I acted in self-defense, but if you don't believe that, if you believe I acted with an evil heart, then I'm still not guilty of murder because when I killed Mel, I acted in a sudden rage, out of uncontrollable anger because Mel shot my two friends. Such arguments are common in criminal trials and judges will examine each one carefully, on its own merits, in light of all the facts.

The judge could reject both of Kitch's arguments and find him guilty of murder or he could agree with his first defense theory and find him not guilty of any crime because he acted in self-defense, or he could reject that idea and agree with his second defense theory and find him guilty of voluntary manslaughter for killing Mel in the heat of passion. Judges maneuver through this kind of legal terrain routinely in criminal cases and it was one of the reasons Kitch wanted a judge, not a jury, to decide his case.

The judge in Kitch's case focused on the second gunshot to the back of Mel's head because it was the killing shot. The first shot injured Mel seriously but didn't kill him. At the time the second shot was fired, Mel was lying on the ground, obviously injured, perhaps unconscious. He was not fully alert and capable of aggressively resisting Kitch, who was standing over him, holding the gun, in complete control of the situation, and clearly angry about what he had just witnessed Mel do to his friends.

WHERE THE AGGRESSOR IS DISARMED

Kitch first argued that he killed Mel in self-defense because Mel was threatening him and others with imminent death or serious bodily injury. The judge believed that Mel was clearly a deadly threat. He had already shot two men and had tried to shoot a third when Kitch intervened. It was reasonable for Kitch to fear for his own life and for the lives of others when he tackled Mel, knocked him to the ground, and took away his gun.

His beliefs were reasonable, however, only as long as Mel posed a deadly danger. Once Mel was rendered incapable of any further violence, of carrying out the threat, there was no longer deadly danger and it became unreasonable for Kitch to fear for his life.

The law is well settled in situations where an aggressor loses his weapon. It assumes the deadly danger has passed. It is over and with it the need to respond with deadly force. It doesn't matter how the aggressor loses the weapon. Once it's gone, the use of deadly force against the aggressor is prohibited unless it is clear, for some other reason, that the threat continues to be deadly, imminent, and there are no alternatives to avoid it. The prohibition exists even where an attacker "loses" his weapon by using it up trying to kill the victim, firing all of his bullets, for example, as occurred in the Red Stripe Food Market shooting. The inability of the shooter in that case to continue his rampage because he ran out of bullets still protects him from the use of deadly force against him. Another example is a woman who threw a knife at her boyfriend, missing him, whereupon he drew a gun and killed her. Once the knife left her hand and missed the target, the deadly threat was over and the use of deadly force against her was unreasonable, making the shooter guilty of murder.[6]

WHERE THE AGGRESSOR IS RENDERED INCAPABLE OF COMMITTING FURTHER VIOLENCE

Deadly force may not be used against a person who has been rendered incapable of committing deadly violence. That, too, is considered excessive. Whether the person is incapacitated from having been subdued or by weakness, injury, exhaustion, or any other reason, the result is the same. Whatever deadly danger he or she once posed no longer exists. It has passed, or become non-deadly, making the use of deadly force an excessive, unnecessary, retaliatory act.

At the time Mel was shot in the back of the head, he had been slammed into a car, had his face smashed into the sidewalk, lost his pistol, been shot once in the back, was probably only semiconscious, and was unable to stand up. He was unarmed, rendered incapable of further attack, and no longer posed a deadly threat to Kitch or to anyone else. Shooting him in the head at that point was unreasonable and excessive because it wasn't necessary to avoid an imminent threat of death or serious bodily injury. The judge rejected Kitch's claim of self-defense because deadly force was not needed to control Mel's behavior in his then current condition.

DEADLY FORCE USED IN THE HEAT OF PASSION

That left Kitch's second defense theory, that he killed Mel in the heat of passion, seized by an uncontrollable fit of rage at seeing Mel shoot his friends. The applicable Illinois manslaughter statute states: "A person who kills an individual without lawful justification commits voluntary manslaughter if at the time of the killing he is acting under a sudden and intense passion resulting from serious provocation by ... [t]he individual killed."[7] "Serious provocation" is behavior sufficient to excite a sudden and intense passion in a reasonable person.[8]

There are two requirements for "heat of passion" to exist: a serious provocation and sudden uncontrollable emotions. Watching someone shoot your friends qualifies easily as a serious provocation that can create intense emotions in the observer, emotions that take control of reason and cause a person to act spontaneously, on impulse, on the spur of the moment. Such impulsive behavior is the best indicator of crimes involving the heat of passion. This was probably Kitch's strongest defense, because clearly he had grounds to argue that when he saw Mel shoot Bo and Angel, he flew into a fit of uncontrollable rage and killed him.

The law says heat of passion is not an enduring state of mind. It doesn't have a long shelf life. It appears suddenly, burns very hot for a short period of time, and then quickly disappears, and cooler heads prevail. As noted in the Illinois statute, it is "sudden and intense," meaning it is fleeting and subsides with the passage of time. Had Kitch fired the fatal shot just after he and Mel crashed into the parked car, when they were first grappling on the sidewalk, when Kitch's adrenalin was at its peak, after struggling for control of Mel's pistol, his claim of uncontrollable rage might have been much stronger, possibly strong enough to convince the judge that he shot Mel in the heat of passion. As it was, the shooting didn't happen that way. It happened after Kitch took the pistol away from Mel, shot him in the back, got to his feet, and stood over him for some period of time, pointing the gun in his direction. By then, Kitch had complete control of the situation and he maintained it long enough in the judge's mind for his rage to subside, for the heat of passion to cool. The judge rejected his heat of passion argument, noting "There was sufficient time in my opinion for any type of adrenaline to drain after you have the man down. There's no rhyme, there's no reason why, [after the first shot,] with no one fighting with [defendant,] with no one doing anything to indicate that there's going to be any further struggle by the victim, he shoots him in the [head] with what appears to be cold blood. Doesn't appear to be any excited passions or anything,"[9] The judge also rejected Kitch's second defense theory and found him guilty of murder.

In many respects, Mel was in the same position as the man with the blue baseball cap at the Red Stripe Food Market. He'd been shot, his weapon taken away, and he'd lost a fistfight with the man who'd shot him. He had been rendered incapable of further violence, was lying on the floor, or in Mel's case on the sidewalk, with his captor standing over him holding a gun. He no longer threatened anyone and the deadly danger had passed. At the Red Stripe Food Market, Jason Donohue held his fire. In Mel's case Kitch did not and that is the difference between being set free and being convicted of murder based on the excessive use of deadly force.

14

THREATENED

GOING TO A DANGEROUS PLACE

It was near the end of a long week at the store. Gary Gorham was busy when the telephone call came.

"It's for you, Gary."

"Uh, OK thanks. Hello."

"Gary, it's Sallie. God, I hurt so much." The words came out in a flood of tears, more a plea for help, than a statement of fact. Gary's hand tightened around the phone. Sallie Henderson was his little sister.

"Again, Sallie?" he asked.

"Gary, I don't know what to do," she sobbed. "I really hurt."

"Can you get out of there?"

"He's in the garage right now, but it really hurts my side to move. It even hurts to breathe. My face is all messed up. I can't breathe very well," she sobbed.

"Jesus, Sallie. I'll be right over."

"I don't know, Gary. I'm really scared." She was crying hard, losing control.

"Sallie, does he know you're on the phone?"

"I don't think so. I heard the door close when he went out. I haven't heard him come back in again. Please help me."

"I will Sallie. I'm on my way. Don't tell him you called me. I'll just show up like I always do, just dropping by on my way home from work."

"I don't know, Gary. He goes crazy when he gets mad."

"Sallie, I'm coming over. I'll be there as soon as I can. Just don't say anything to him." Gary hung up the phone, told his boss he was leaving, grabbed his jacket, and rushed out of the store. He got into his car and drove toward his sister's house.

No matter where in Maryland you're driving during rush hour, the roads seem to be crowded, even in Wicomico County, especially if you want to get somewhere quickly. Normally, Gary didn't let it bother him. He relaxed, listened to the radio, went with the flow. Tonight was different. He wanted to be at his sister's house as soon as possible. He was anxious and worried knowing what he would find when he got there, knowing she would need help. He tightened his grip on the steering wheel, cursed under his breath, and tried to maneuver back and forth between the lanes, willing cars out of his way as he pushed through the 5 o'clock traffic toward Sallie's house.

As he crept along Gary thought about how Sallie and Harry had been married only two years. In the beginning it looked like a great marriage, a good fit, making Gary happy to see his sister happy. About six months into it the abuse started, beginning with a slap across the face. The first time there were no marks, saving Sallie the embarrassment of having to explain them. The second time she wasn't so lucky. Harry beat her with his fists leaving her with a black eye and black and blue bruises on her arms and around her neck. Gary talked to Harry after that one, making it clear he had no right to treat Sallie that way, threatening consequences if it didn't stop. Harry had been contrite, apologizing for what he'd done, promising it would never happen again, but it did, again and again. He hurt her physically, betrayed her emotionally, and every time Sallie would call Gary, and his heart would break.

The abuse got worse over time. About a year into their marriage Harry beat Sallie so badly that she complained to the police and they arrested him. Harry cried, pleaded with her not to send him to jail, asked for a second chance, promised never to hit her again. She relented and told the police she wouldn't testify against him. They let Harry go, but the beatings continued.

Not long after the arrest Gary saw a pistol in Harry's waistband under his shirt. He talked to one of Harry's friends about it and learned that Harry carried it routinely and was prone to reach for it when he was angry or felt threatened. The friend laughed, shook his head, and told Gary that he recently took a shotgun away from "old Harry" because he was drunk and ranting about shooting Sallie. He'd never really shoot her, of course. It was just Harry talking. Gary didn't think it was funny.

He begged Sallie to leave Harry, repeatedly, offering to help her, promising to do whatever she wanted if she would just get out of the marriage. He even tried to force her hand by telling their mother about the beatings. Their mom reacted as he knew she would. She spoke with Sallie forcefully, and at length, about respect, dignity, and safety. All it really accomplished was to close Sallie down. She stopped talking to Gary, accused him of violating her confidence, and didn't call him the next time Harry beat her. A friend who saw the bruises called to tell him she'd been hurt. That really worried him because it left him totally in the dark, not knowing if or when she might need his help. Just as important, it left Sallie with no one to turn to.

Despite Gary's best efforts nothing seemed to work. For some reason he couldn't fathom, out of some loyalty he couldn't comprehend, Sallie stayed with Harry and endured his beatings. Finally, understanding that he was powerless to stop the abuse, and unable to convince her to leave, Gary decided all he could do was just be there for her, listen to her when she cried, help her when she would let him, and hope she would come to her senses before Harry killed her. So he stayed close to her, provided support, and kept his mouth shut about Harry, ashamed he couldn't stop what was happening.

Gary reached the turnoff to Sallie's house and took it. The traffic wasn't as bad on the side streets. He picked up speed, driving as fast as he dared, rolling slowly through the intersections, keeping an eye out for traffic and the police. He thought about Sallie's phone call to the store. It wasn't like the others. In the past, she'd tell him what happened, accept his sympathy, and decline his offers of help. This time she sounded frightened and asked him to help her. That was different. He wondered if Harry had finally gone too far, if maybe this time things would be different.

Gary saw nothing amiss when he pulled into Sallie and Harry's driveway. Their cars were parked in their usual spots. Everything looked normal, no signs of a scuffle in the yard, no sounds of a fight coming from inside the house. It seemed peaceful enough.

He parked his car behind Harry's, got out, and walked to the front door. He had a key to the house and let himself in, just like he always did. It was a ritual. He'd open the door, rap his knuckles against it as he crossed the threshold, and call out his name announcing himself to everyone inside. He followed his usual practice as if he didn't know what Harry had done.

"Harry, Sallie. It's me, Gary." He looked to his right into the living room and saw Harry sitting there in a chair watching television.

"Hey, Harry, what's up?"

Harry didn't look up from the television. "Not much," he said.

"Where's Sallie?"

"Upstairs in the bedroom."

"She busy?"

"I wouldn't know." Harry shrugged his shoulders and his eyes stayed glued to the television. He lifted a beer bottle to his lips, his message clear, he didn't know where Sallie was, didn't care, and didn't want to talk to Gary. Typical, Gary thought.

"OK, I'll just run up and find her," Gary said cheerfully, keeping it light. He glanced over at Harry and started up the stairs. Harry looked up at him for the first time, his face registering disapproval, but he made no move to stop him.

At the top of the stairs Gary turned left and walked the short distance to the master bedroom. The door was open. He entered the room and saw Sallie in bed, lying on her side, facing him. Her eyes were closed, but when she heard his footsteps she opened them and reached out to him.

Gary tried to smile but he was stunned by the damage Harry had done. Sallie's left eye was swollen almost shut and beneath it a large bruise covered her cheekbone. Her face was puffy and Gary could see dried blood on her teeth from a cut somewhere inside her mouth. The right side of her face appeared swollen, like it had been slammed against the wall. Her forearms were beginning to show black and blue marks and her fingernails were torn and broken from trying to protect herself. That was just the damage Gary could see, who knew how much she was hurt inside.

"Jesus, Sallie ... Jesus."

"I thought he wasn't going to stop," she sobbed. "He just kept hitting me. He wouldn't stop."

Gary took her outstretched hand, looked away at the sight of her swollen fingers and broken fingernails, trying to keep his tears at bay, feeling intense pressure growing in his chest. He knew his emotions were starting to get the better of him.

"Jesus, Sallie. You can't stay here. We've got to get you out of here. This time you've got to go. We've got to stop this. He's really hurt you. You're my sister, Sallie. I love you. Please, Sallie. He's going to kill you," he pleaded.

"I know," she whispered.

"Then please Sallie, let me get you out of here." Now the tears were running down Gary's face. "For God's sake, let me help you."

She looked at him, squeezed his hand, and nodded, "OK, Gary. OK."

They talked a bit longer, Sallie thick lipped, Gary straining to control himself. They agreed to a plan. She would gather up some of her belongings, enough so she wouldn't have to come back, and leave that night, and he would help. Gary would go get his SUV to carry them and take her to their mother's house where she would be safe. They would deal with her car and with Harry later. Right now the goal was to get her safely out of the house. Their plan in place, Gary left the bedroom to go get the SUV while Sallie stayed in bed, hoping to avoid Harry until Gary returned.

Gary walked downstairs. Harry was still sitting in the same place watching television. He looked up, caught Gary's gaze, and held it, challenging him as if to say so what're you going to do about it? Gary held his gaze, and stared back. The air between them was thick with hostility.

Gary wanted to take revenge for his sister, bludgeon Harry to within an inch of his life, make him hurt like he'd made Sallie hurt, but he stopped himself. A fistfight now would jeopardize the plan to have Sallie leave, something he had been trying to do for months. Nothing was more important than getting her away from there. So he choked down his anger, dropped his eyes and looked away, like a scolded child, and then he turned and walked toward the front door. Harry smiled. "That's what I thought, you chickenshit," he said, as Gary walked out the front door.

Gary drove home to get the SUV. When he told his wife Carol about Sallie and the plan to spirit her away from Harry a worried look crossed her face.

"I don't know, Gary. I'm not sure that's such a good idea. I don't want you getting hurt."

"I'm not going to get hurt. It'll be all right. I've got to get her out of there."

"Why don't you call the police? Ask them to go with you. That way if there's trouble they can take care of it."

Gary thought about that. It was probably the right thing to do. Harry would be furious at the thought of Sallie leaving and he would probably try to stop her. He was drinking and that would make a confrontation more likely. There was also the problem of his gun. The police could certainly help with that. On the other hand, he hadn't talked to Sallie about involving the police. It wasn't part of the plan and it might spook her. The last time the police got involved it didn't end up well. He had to avoid anything that might cause Sallie to back out of leaving. He decided not to call them.

"I think it will be ok," he said. "If I show up with the cops Sallie might decide not to come. Remember what happened the last time. Harry cried and she crumbled and nothing changed. I don't want that to happen again. I've got to get her out of there before he kills her."

"I don't want you getting hurt," Carol said. "I don't like him. He's a mean guy and it's only a matter of time before he hurts somebody. Call the cops."

"I promise I'll call them if anything happens. I just don't want to show up with them and have her decide not to leave. I can't let that happen, Carol."

"I don't like this," Carol said, but she turned and walked into the kitchen knowing it was time to let him mull it over. Perhaps he would change his mind. Sometimes he did, but not this time.

Gary thought about Harry. He was pretty sure he would try to stop Sallie from leaving, and there was no telling what he might do. Gary walked into the bedroom, went into his closet, and retrieved an M-1 carbine he kept there. He liked the carbine because it was small and easy to handle, even inside a car. He loaded a magazine and put it into his pocket. Then he carried the rifle, barrel down, along the side of his leg to hide it from Carol and left the bedroom. He picked up the SUV keys and walked out the front door. "I'll be back in a bit," he called in Carol's direction. "Be careful," she replied from the kitchen.

Once outside, Gary took the magazine out of his pocket, inserted it into the carbine, and chambered a round. He put the safety on, opened the SUV's back door, and laid it on the back seat. He sat behind the steering wheel, reached into the back, and moved the rifle around until he was satisfied he could reach it quickly. Then he started the car and drove away.

When Gary reached Sallie's place he noticed Harry's car was gone. He left the rifle where it was and entered the house calling out his sister's name. She answered from the master bedroom. Gary looked around but Harry wasn't there. He went upstairs and found Sallie putting some clothes into a plastic garbage bag. She moved very slowly, obviously in pain, lifting clothes from the bureau drawer and dropping them into the bag.

"He's gone?" Gary asked.

"Yes, about fifteen minutes ago. I don't know where he went or when he'll be back. Let's hurry and get out of here," she said.

They packed hurriedly, carried Sallie's things downstairs, and loaded them into the SUV. Gary made sure nothing interfered with the rifle. Sallie didn't take very much, choosing what she needed rather than what she wanted, more interested in getting away. It was almost dark when they finished. They got into the car and Gary drove down the street toward the main highway. They were out of the neighborhood and half way to her mother's house when Sallie stiffened in her seat.

"Damn it, Gary. I forgot my wallet. I've got to go back."

"What? Are you sure?"

"I'm sure. I left it on the kitchen counter when I unplugged my phone."

"You need it tonight? Can't we get it later?"

"No, Gary. I really need to get it now. Everything is in it. My driver's license, my credit cards, my ATM card. I've got no money. We've got to go back. If Harry finds it, it would be just like him to destroy everything. Please turn around."

"Aw mannnn! I knew this was too good to be true." Gary slowed the SUV, checked the rear-view mirror, made a U-turn, and headed back toward Sallie's house.

When they arrived Harry's car was parked in its usual spot. The light was on over the front door and multiple lights were on inside the house. The last thing they'd done before leaving was turn them all off. Gary looked at Sallie.

"He's looking for you, Sal. Let's just forget it. We're out of here. We can get it tomorrow when we come back to pick up your car."

"I don't want to come back tomorrow. It'll be all right. I'll just run in and get it and come right back out."

"Sallie, you know it's not going to work that way. By now he knows you're not there. He knows you've taken your stuff and as soon as he sees you there's going to be a problem. I don't want you getting hurt, and I don't want to get into a fight. I'll come back tomorrow with the cops and get the wallet."

"Gary, I don't want the cops. I've got to face him sometime. It might as well be now. It will just take a minute. He'll try to get me to stay, but I promise not this time, and if he comes after me I'll tell him you're out here and will call the cops if I don't come right back out. He's afraid of the cops."

Gary looked at her, silent, unconvinced.

"I just want my wallet and for this to be over. I don't want to have to deal with him again tomorrow," she continued.

He relented against his better judgment. "OK, I'll come with you."

"No, I rather you didn't. It will just provoke him. When I come out of the house I just want to get out of here as fast as possible. I'll be right back, I promise." Sallie shifted in her seat, making ready to open the door.

"OK, Sallie. Just don't argue with him. If he starts to argue or does anything, just turn around and leave. Forget the damn wallet, OK?" Gary took his cell phone out of his pocket and laid it on the dash, ready to keep his end of the bargain.

Sallie reached over and squeezed his hand. "I promise," she smiled. Then she pushed open the door to get out of the car.

Gary looked toward the house expecting the front door to open, thinking Harry must be watching them from the living room alerted by the SUV's headlights shining on its windows. Sallie stepped around the car door and started to close it.

Gary caught the flash of movement near the back of the SUV out of the corner of his eye. Suddenly, Harry was there pushing Sallie aside, and grabbing for the car door. He missed the handle but managed to keep the door from closing. He grabbed the door again and pulled it open. He reached under his shirt with his other hand.

Gary thought immediately of Harry's gun, turned in his seat, grabbed the M-1, and released the safety. Then he saw the gun in Harry's hand as it came out from under his shirt. Gary pointed the M-1, like a pistol, and pulled the trigger, twice, in rapid succession. Both shots hit Harry in the chest. The first one seemed to stagger him backward, the second caused him to sit down on the ground and then roll onto his side.

Gary picked up his phone and called 911. Then he jumped out of the car and tried to help Harry. There was a .45 caliber semi-automatic pistol on the ground beside him. He tried to stop the bleeding but couldn't. Harry died on his way to the hospital.

Gary was tried and found guilty of second-degree murder. He appealed his conviction claiming that the trial court had failed to adequately describe the law of self-defense to the jury.[1]

IGNORING THE THREAT

Gary's behavior, returning to the house with a gun to help Sallie, became a major issue at his trial. Gary asked the judge to tell the jury that he "had a right to arm himself in anticipation of an assault and the privilege of going wherever he had a lawful right to go," meaning, of course, that it was OK for him to ignore the threat posed by Harry and take a gun with him when he went back to help Sallie move out of the house. The judge refused to give the requested instruction, and it became the central issue in Gary's appeal.

When Gary went back to his sister's house he knew a violent confrontation with Harry was possible, maybe even likely. There were too many danger signals for him to ignore. Harry was drinking and likely to challenge Sallie if she tried to leave. He was violent, having already injured Sallie and shown his willingness to fight Gary if he tried to help her. He also carried a pistol and had a reputation for drawing it when he was angry. Finally, he had threatened to shoot Sallie on at least one occasion. There was no question but that Gary understood that going back to his sister's house might be very dangerous. Why else take the rifle?

The issue at trial, in its simplest terms, was whether Gary behaved reasonably when he armed himself in anticipation of danger and went to the place where he knew the danger was likely to be. Was such behavior reasonable or was it a provocation, misbehavior that disqualified Gary from claiming self-defense in connection with Harry's death?

ARMING ONESELF IN ANTICIPATION OF DANGER

The first question is whether it is misbehavior to arm oneself in anticipation of danger. For purposes of the discussion let's assume Gary possessed a concealed carry permit so we can dispense with any state and local laws regarding the carrying and transport of firearms.

It's not unlawful for a person, in the absence of any threat, to possess and carry a firearm for purposes of self-defense. The U.S. Supreme Court recognized self-defense as one reason why individuals have a right to bear arms under the Second Amendment of the U.S. Constitution.[2] The idea of being armed and ready to defend oneself against the possibility of a deadly threat, however remote, is also one of the reasons a majority of states have enacted concealed carry laws.

If it is lawful to arm oneself to defend against an unknown or unexpected threat, then it is certainly lawful to arm oneself to defend against a known one, one that places a particular individual at risk. Indeed, there are situations when arming oneself under such circumstances is a reasonable and prudent thing to do. Thus, the act of arming oneself in anticipation of danger is not by itself misbehavior that extinguishes the right of self-defense.

There is also no general prohibition against taking a firearm anywhere one may wish to go, with some exceptions. Many states have enacted statutes that prohibit firearms in specific locations: for example, courtrooms or schools, and private individuals may choose to prohibit firearms on their property, but there are no blanket bans against possessing and carrying a firearm, as long as one behaves lawfully. In Gary's case, there was nothing to prevent him from taking the M-1 with him when he went to help his sister move out of the house.

THE PRIVILEGE OF GOING WHEREVER ONE HAS A LAWFUL RIGHT TO GO

Freedom to move about lawfully is also an individual constitutional right guaranteed under the Privileges and Immunities Clause and the right of people to assemble peacefully under the First Amendment of the Bill of Rights. The law permits a person to go about his business, do as he chooses, visit any place he wishes, so long as he behaves legally. And that is true even if his actions put him at risk of deadly danger.[3] For example, there are unsafe places in most American cities where visits, particularly by strangers, are unwise, even potentially dangerous but that doesn't stop people from going to them if they're willing to accept the risk.

The ability to move about freely applies not only to places where the danger is endemic, drug-infested neighborhoods for example, but also to places where the life of the prospective visitor is threatened directly. To illustrate, suppose a man threatens to kill you if you set foot on a certain street corner. It's probably not the smartest thing in the world for you to go there. The law, however, says you can, if you want to, so long as you behave legally, and if you're attacked while you're there you have the right to use deadly force, if necessary, to defend yourself.[4] If the law forbade you from going there, or penalized you for doing so, it would end up being on the side of the man trying to intimidate you by enabling his misconduct and helping him to achieve his goal to prevent you from going to that particular corner. It is but a short step to imagine the man's reason for trying to keep you away from the street corner is because it is a good business location and he wants it for himself. If the law stops you from going there because of potential danger, then it will have helped the man to evict you through unlawful intimidation. The law doesn't work that way, so you may go to the street corner as long a you're going there for a lawful purpose, notwithstanding the fact that you may be exposing yourself to a risk of being attacked violently, or even killed.

SEEKING ONE'S ADVERSARY IN A PLACE OF DANGER

Going to a place where one knows there is danger is something of a metaphor, a place of danger being more a description of a dangerous environment than a physical location. It doesn't necessarily mean going to an adversary's home turf or to the physical space where he or she might be. It is more akin to moving from a place of relative safety to a place of relative danger, or from a place where violence is less likely to a place where it is more likely. For example, a man, let's call him Fred, is alone at home when he hears a loud banging on his front door. He goes to the door, peers through the peephole, and sees Jack, a fellow employee. Fred and Jack were in a fistfight earlier that day at work. Jack is very angry. He is swearing at Fred and pounding on the door. Fred retrieves his pistol and opens the door. Jack immediately attacks him with a knife and Fred shoots him.

At his trial Fred claims self-defense and describes how Jack was angry and tried to kill him with the knife. He says that when he shot Jack he believed he was about to be killed or seriously injured. Yet why did he open the front door? He was safe inside his house with the door locked. There was no imminent deadly danger because Jack couldn't get at him to carry out his threats. What was the purpose of opening the door instead of calling the police? Obviously, it was to engage Jack, to involve him in a discussion, or confront him in some way, or attempt to resolve the dispute, or some other reason we're unaware of. By opening the door, Fred went, figuratively speaking, from a position of relative safety "to a place where he knew there was danger," and by doing so increased the likelihood of a deadly encounter. The act of leaving a place of relative safety for a place of relative danger for the purpose of engaging one's adversary is misbehavior and extinguishes Fred's right of self-defense.[5]

How does this square with a person's ability to move about freely even if it exposes him or her to the risk of deadly danger? What is the difference between good behavior, exercising one's Constitutional freedoms, and bad behavior, provoking, prolonging, or contributing to a confrontation? It is the purpose of the visit. As long as the purpose for going to a place of known danger is lawful, it is reasonable behavior, but a person may not go in search of his or her adversary. That behavior is unreasonable because it increases rather than decreases the likelihood of a fatal encounter. If there's even a whiff of suspicion that the shooter took up arms and went looking for his adversary, for whatever reason, then it's highly likely he or she will be found to have misbehaved and will forfeit his or her the right to claim self-defense in the event an adversary is killed.

Fred's situation, in our example, is very similar to the second case we looked at, the one involving Michael Bowden and his girlfriend, Sandra Lacy, in rural New Mexico. Michael was also inside his home with the door locked, safe from the threat, when a reckless driver began screeching down his driveway. Like Fred, instead of staying inside his house and calling the police, he chose to arm himself and confront whoever it was in his driveway. He moved from a place of relative safety to a place of relative danger to engage the person who created the danger, and by doing so he increased substantially the likelihood of a violent confrontation. He misbehaved and contributed to the circumstances that led to the driver's death, and for that he was held criminally liable.

Let's use Fred and Jack again to look at another example of going to a place of known danger. Assume that Jack has a reputation for being violent, and Fred is aware of it. During their fight at work the following exchange takes place.

"I know where you live," Jack screams.

"Good for you," Fred shouts back.

"You won't live to see tomorrow morning."

"You stay off my property, you hear? If I find you there you'll regret it."

As night approaches Fred begins to worry about what Jack might do. He's afraid Jack might do something to his car or maybe try to burn down the house. About 11 p.m., after his family has gone to bed, Fred loads his shotgun, goes outside, and hides in the bushes where he can watch his driveway and the front of his house.

About 1 o'clock in the morning a car drives up and parks across the street. Jack gets out of the car and crosses the street into Fred's front yard. He walks to the front of the house and looks through the window into Fred's living room. Then he moves toward the corner of the house where there's a path leading to the back patio. Fred yells at Jack to stop. Jack turns in Fred's direction, startled by the sound of his voice, and reaches inside his jacket. Fred thinks he is reaching for a gun, pulls the trigger on his shotgun, and kills him.

It is not misbehavior for Jack to arm himself on his own property. And it's not misbehavior for him to sit all night in the bushes with a shotgun guarding his house against possible danger. But the same question exists as when he opened the front door. Why did he do it? What was the purpose of him arming himself and leaving the safety of his home to go outside and lay in wait in a place where he knew there might be danger on that particular night? It was to engage Jack if and when he showed up. Once again, Fred armed himself and went from a position of relative safety to a position of relative danger for the purpose of engaging his adversary. His claim of self-defense will fail, just as it failed when he opened the door.[6]

The lesson of Fred and Jack is pretty clear. Leaving a place of safety to engage an adversary is misbehavior because it increases the chances of a deadly encounter. It contributes to the circumstances that lead to the victim's death, and for that reason the shooter forfeits the right of self-defense.

UNCERTAINTY OF WHERE ONE'S ADVERSARY WILL BE

It goes without saying that if a person doesn't know for certain that his adversary will be at a particular place he intends to visit, or thinks his adversary will be someplace else, or has no idea where his adversary is, then he hasn't misbehaved because whatever the purpose of his going to a place of danger, it wasn't to engage the adversary.

The problem, of course, is that if he encounters the adversary and a deadly exchange takes place in which he kills him or her, an argument can be made that he went there to seek out the victim. Then it becomes a matter of proof based on the evidence and a question of fact for the jury to decide.

VISITS TO DANGEROUS PLACES OTHER THAN TO ENGAGE AN ADVERSARY

Arming oneself and going to a place where one knows there is danger is never a particularly good idea because it suggests the person went there to confront his adversary and armed himself to make sure he came out on top of any confrontation. Still there are situations in which a person might want to go to a place of known danger where a confrontation might occur, and there are valid reasons for doing so despite the risk.

Let's look at our street corner example again. A valid and good reason for going there after you have been threatened is to keep your successful business going. It has nothing to do with confronting the man who threatened you, indeed you hope to avoid him, but the possibility of encountering him is inherent in going to the corner. Moreover, it is not misbehavior for you to carry a firearm with you to protect yourself against the possibility of such an encounter. As long as there is a lawful purpose, other than seeking out your adversary, for going to the street corner, you may do so, and if your adversary causes you to fear for your life by threatening you with imminent death or serious injury, then you may use the firearm to defend yourself against the threat.

ALTERNATIVES TO GOING TO DANGEROUS PLACES

Avoiding the need to use deadly force is an important part of self-defense, raising the question of whether a person must seek alternatives to going to a place of known danger. There is no requirement for a person to find alternatives for lawful behavior. Seeking an alternative may be a wise thing to do, or it may be in the person's best interest to do, but the law does not require it. So long as the purpose for going to a place of danger is lawful, and is not to seek out one's adversary, a person may go there even if an alternative might lower the risk of a confrontation. For example, hiring someone to run your store on the dangerous street corner is a good alternative if taking you out of the picture lowered the risk of violence, but you're not required to do it. You may go about your business, do as you choose, and go anywhere you want, as long as you behave legally.

APPLYING THE LAW TO GARY'S CLAIM OF SELF-DEFENSE

Gary asked the trial judge to tell the jury that he "had a right to arm himself in anticipation of an assault and the privilege of going wherever he had a lawful right to go."[7] On appeal, he said the trial judge made a mistake in refusing his request. The Maryland Supreme Court agreed with him. It said the critical question in deciding his case was not whether Gary armed himself or whether he went to a place where he knew there was danger, but rather what his purpose was for going back to Sallie and Harry's house with the rifle in his SUV. In deciding that question, the jury should have known that it was not misbehavior for Gary to arm himself against the possibility of being attacked, and that it was not misbehavior for him to go to a place of known danger if his purpose for doing so was a lawful one and not to seek out Harry. In other words, Gary "had a right to arm himself in anticipation of an assault and the privilege of going wherever he had a lawful right to go."

BUT WHY DID HE TAKE A GUN?

Some would argue that taking a gun to Sallie's house was a provocative act, an escalation of the confrontation that led directly to Harry's death, behavior akin to David Simon's introduction of a pistol into the argument between his sister Yaffa and her husband, Richard. There are significant differences, however, between the two cases.

David Simon interjected himself into the conversation between Yaffa and Richard, displayed the gun openly to Richard, and used it in an effort to intimidate him into leaving the apartment. There was no equivalent behavior on Gary's part at Sallie and Harry's house. The rifle remained out of sight until it became clear that Harry was about to shoot Gary. In fact, it is fair to assume that Harry hadn't seen the rifle and didn't know Gary had it, when he reached for own pistol.

THE DUTY TO RETREAT

You might ask what happens if Maryland is a "duty to retreat" state. How does it affect Gary's decision to arm himself and then go to a place where he knew there was danger? The answer is that a duty to retreat doesn't come into play until there is actual deadly danger.

There is no duty to retreat in the face of some possible danger in the future. The duty is triggered by an immediate, right now, threat of death or serious bodily injury. There must be some behavior on the part of an adversary that places the shooter in right now, about to occur deadly peril, making it clear that death or serious injury will occur unless immediate action is taken to avoid it. There is no duty to disarm in anticipation of a future threat, and Gary was not in imminent deadly danger until Harry reached for his gun.

There is also the question of whether, assuming Gary had a duty to retreat, there was an available path of escape and Gary had the time to take it once the threat against him became known. The threat materialized when Harry reached for the gun under his shirt. At that point, Gary, his intended target, was inside the SUV with the door closed. He had no place to go and no time to get there. There was no duty to retreat under those circumstances because there was no path of retreat available.

15

DECISIONS

SPLIT SECOND JUDGMENTS

Maggie Holder was tired and depressed driving home. She had just completed another tough day at the hospital and it was only Wednesday. Mary Bellamy, a lady Maggie knew and liked from church, had died on her shift. Mary was an eighty-four-year-old hellion with many stories and a big heart. She was just a happy person and somehow it always seemed worse when people like Mary died.

Maggie drove like she felt, listless, going through the motions without much enthusiasm, thinking about Mary. All she wanted to do was get home, change out of her scrubs, and maybe have a glass of wine with her boyfriend, David Castaway. She wanted to forget the futility of working in a hospital, because in the end, everyone died. She perked up a bit when she turned onto her street and saw David's car parked in her driveway. She and David had decided to live together about six months ago. It had worked out well and Maggie was pleased. They had an easy, comfortable relationship, and she was happy when David was around.

Maggie was almost to her driveway when she noticed two men walking on the sidewalk on her side of the street going in the same direction. She stopped and waited for them to pass in front of her before turning into her driveway. She parked the car next to David's, turned off the ignition, grabbed her purse, and headed for the house.

She used her house key to open the door and stepped into the familiar comfort of her front hallway. She laid her purse on a nearby table and reached back to shut the door. She shoved it, but it didn't close. Thinking she hadn't pushed it hard enough, she turned around to give it another push when the door flew open and the two men she'd just seen on the sidewalk burst into the hallway.

The bigger man was carrying a long screwdriver with a clear yellow plastic handle. He was about six feet tall, compared to Maggie's five feet four inches, and he held the screwdriver like a knife, handle down, point up, and thrust it at her chest.

"If you don't want to get hurt just shut up and give us your money," he said, "Now."

Maggie's first thought was disbelief. This wasn't happening, not in her home. She should have paid more attention to these two when she drove into the yard. Now she knew she needed to give them what they wanted and get them out of her house.

"My wallet's right here. You can have it," Maggie said, picking up her purse, retrieving her wallet, and offering it to the bigger man, the one with the screwdriver. "Here, take it and go."

The other man was a bit smaller than his partner, but thicker around the middle. He was bald and had the shadow of a hairline around the top of his head where he'd shaved it. He grabbed the wallet from her extended hand and began looking through it. He took out four twenties and a bunch of ones. He looked at Maggie. "This all you got?" he asked.

Maggie nodded her head. "That's all I have. Just go," she said.

"That's not all you got, bitch," the big man said, waiving the screwdriver in her face. "You got a package between your legs. Maybe we'll take some of that," he said, grinning at his partner. The bald man hesitated, and then leered at Maggie. "Yeah, maybe we will, let's see what you got."

Maggie began to panic. Her eyes scanned quickly left and right, looking for a way out, wanting to run. The front door was still open, but she had no chance of getting through it before the bigger man grabbed her. Maybe the living room, she thought. The bald man read her mind, stepped farther into the house, turned, and blocked her way in that direction. She was trapped between the two of them. She tried to remember what the instructor said about rapists in the personal safety class she took at the hospital, but her mind was blank. All she could think about was the man holding the screwdriver and gesturing for her to take down her pants.

Then she thought of the gun. Maggie had a .38 caliber Smith & Wesson revolver in her purse. She'd bought it because the hospital wasn't in the best part of town, and sometimes she worked until late into the night. There had been problems in the parking lots, assaults and robberies mostly, but several people had been mugged, one of them injured badly, and she didn't want to become another victim. So she bought the pistol, got a special purse to carry it in, and went to the range. She practiced regularly until she felt comfortable carrying the revolver with her. She thought it odd that when she needed it for the very danger she feared, she had totally forgotten it.

"OK, OK, I went to the bank on the way home," she said. "I've got some more money in my purse. Let me get it and then just go away," she said, reaching back into her purse. Neither of the two men moved to stop her, greed trumping lust, at least for the moment. Maggie began rummaging through her things.

Her boyfriend, David Castaway, was in the kitchen cutting up vegetables for their dinner salad. He heard Maggie drive into the yard, the sound of her car door slam, and then the front door opening. The voices in the front hallway were unexpected. Perhaps Maggie was bringing someone from work home for dinner. That meant more salad, he thought. The muffled voices seemed off somehow, not right, and David stopped what he was doing to listen. Then curious, he wiped his hands, tossed the towel onto the counter, and left the kitchen.

"What's up, Maggie?" he asked, walking into the living room. He saw Maggie, standing near the open front door, a terrified look on her face, her purse in her hand, and two strangers. One of the strangers was standing between him and Maggie holding her wallet. The other was standing by the front door holding a screwdriver pointed at Maggie. David realized quickly what was happening and reacted instantly.

Screaming as loud as he could, he launched himself at the robber closest to him. He lowered his shoulder and hit the man in the side, like he was slamming a hockey player against the boards. "Get the hell out of here," he screamed, as he wrapped his arms around the man's waist, pumped his legs, and drove him toward the door. The bald robber staggered, flailed his arms, and fought to stay on his feet, but David had him off balance and was pushing him through the front door. The bald man started to fall, but reached out, somehow got both hands on one side of the doorframe, and held on for dear life.

David's screaming and the suddenness of his attack confused and disoriented the robber with the screwdriver, freezing him in place as he tried to comprehend what he was seeing. He'd done this before and this wasn't how it worked. People didn't scream and attack him. They gave him money. They begged him to leave. This wasn't going the way it was supposed to.

Off balance and clinging to the doorframe, the bald robber was unable to defend himself. David's first punch hit him just below his left eye. Then came a furious pounding. Shouting curses, David threw punch after punch, hitting the man in the face, as fast as he could cock his right arm and strike. Blood gushed from the bald man's nose and he let go of the doorframe, falling through the door, onto to his back on the porch. His head hit the floor with a hollow thud, like the sound of a melon falling from a shelf.

The robber with the screwdriver realized that unless he got control of the situation quickly, he would be next on David's list. David was standing in front of him, looking down at his injured partner who was moaning incoherently. David wasn't paying attention and the taller robber didn't hesitate. He tightened his grip on the screwdriver, set his feet, and drew back his arm to stab David in the back.

Maggie saw the taller robber move and read his mind. He was going to kill David with the screwdriver. She had her hand on the revolver in her purse, but there was no time to pull it out so she pointed her purse at the man and pulled the trigger. The bullet ripped through the bottom of the purse and struck him in the side. He flinched and turned in her direction, a surprised look on his face. She pulled the revolver from her purse and fired twice more into his chest. He dropped the screwdriver and fell to the floor.

David stiffened at the sound of the gunfire. He thought the tall robber must have discovered Maggie's gun and was shooting at him. He waited for the pain and wondered where he'd been hit, but nothing happened. Instead, he heard the man fall to the floor. He looked at Maggie and saw the gun in her hand. It was moving in his direction. Confused, he looked to where she was pointing it and saw the bald robber coming through the door. His face and shirt were bloody, but he was snarling, ready for another round. Two more shots rang out and another look of surprise, this time on the bald man's face. He reached his hand to his chest, leaned back against the door jam, and slid to the floor. He sat on the floor, tipped over, and fell into the hallway at David's feet. David heard a clicking sound. *Click. Click. Click. Click. Click.* Maggie was pulling the trigger on her pistol causing the hammer to fall on empty chambers. She kept pulling it until he took the gun away from her. [1]

THE PROSECUTOR DECIDES MURDER OR SELF-DEFENSE

The conference room in the prosecutor's office was government small. Its main feature was a rectangular table in the center of the room. Eight chairs surrounded the table. It wasn't like the conference rooms found in private law offices with pictures on the walls and credenzas for refreshments and windows with views of the city. There were no windows here. This room was in the middle of the building, its walls adorned with black scuff marks made by careless people. Yet in its shabbiness, the room still commanded respect because great power resided here. It was the place where government officials met to decide which of the county's citizens they would try to put in jail.

Ronnie Johnson, known as RJ, arrived first for the 10 o'clock meeting. A detective in the city's major crimes division, RJ was the lead investigator in the Maggie Holder shooting. He'd been a police officer for about twenty years and he'd seen just about everything there was to see. He was an average sized man, but a very athletic one, a man who took care of himself knowing he might need every ounce of strength he had at any time. Like most detectives, he started out as a patrolman, a job that often made him the first police officer on the scene after some horrific event. He'd seen all manner of injury and death, people beaten, burned, hit by cars, knifed by friends, overdosed on drugs, just about anything one person can do to another, or to themselves. He'd interviewed too many witnesses to count, and he'd been lied to by just about everyone, young and old, rich and poor, black, white, brown, or some other color, it didn't matter. Everybody lied to the police. Despite all that, he loved his job, persevered at it, and gained wisdom with experience about his work and about himself. He became a man in search of the truth, no matter where it led him. He questioned everyone and everything. It was what made him a good detective.

He entered the conference room, a thick file of papers under one arm, and sat in a chair near the middle of the conference table. He opened the file and rifled through it until he found the investigation timeline. He closed the file, put the timeline on top of it, and read through it one more time before the meeting.

Catherine McCarthy walked from her office down the hall toward the conference room, on time, ready to go. She'd reserved the room until noon and she wasn't sure that gave her enough time to go over the case, so she wanted to get started. Tall and slim, Catherine was a runner and a smart, attractive woman. She'd been a county deputy prosecutor for about ten years and she was very good at her job. She worked hard and fought hard in the courtroom, but she was a lawyer you could talk to, as long as you didn't lie to her.

She hated the violence she dealt with in her job, the senseless brutality all too familiar to most prosecutors. She refused to accept it, was actually offended by it, and if a crime involved an injured victim, she was relentless, driven, willing to let a jury decide, no matter how hard it might be to prove the case. She figured she owed the victims that much. Some of the defense lawyers thought she was over the top, too self-righteous. The good ones understood what drove her, knew it was because she thought representing "the people" wasn't just a job. It was a special trust.

"Hey RJ, how's it going?" she asked as she strode into the conference room carrying her own thick file of papers.

"OK, Catherine. Took my boy fishing over the weekend. It was good. No calls, nothing but us and a bunch of trout." RJ had learned quickly. It was Catherine, not "Cat," or "Cathy," or "Kate."

"So when are you going over to the dark side and become a rich defense attorney?" he asked smiling.

"When you guys are ready to do this stuff by yourselves. . . . I may be here awhile," she said. Catherine dropped her file on the table across from RJ, pulled out a chair, and sat down.

"I know just what you mean," RJ said. "Those state guys are always screwing something up." RJ was a municipal cop. Knocking the "staties" was fair game, unless of course you got the chance to knock the "federales." That was even better.

"Nice," Catherine said. She liked RJ. She liked working with good people, and she knew from experience that RJ was good at what he did.

"OK, what do you think of the Holder shooting?" she asked

"Looks like self-defense," RJ said.

"Maybe, but let's not encourage it. I don't like Annie Oakleys." Catherine was not a fan of guns. She'd seen too much of what they can do to people.

"Hey, did you know Annie Oakley shot a cigarette out of the mouth of a German Kaiser." RJ said. Catherine just looked at him.

"The Kaiser during World War I. You know who I mean?" he asked, raising his eyebrows, the picture of innocence.

Catherine looked down at her file, closed her eyes, took a deep breath, shook her head and let it out, looked back up at him. RJ extended his hands over the table, palms up.

"What? What?" he said.

"Where the hell do you get this stuff, RJ?"

"Innate intelligence," he said. "Old Phoeb just plinked a cigarette butt right out of his mouth."

"Old Phoeb?" Catherine still hadn't moved, but she felt a smile coming on. RJ could do that to her.

"Yea, well not really Old Phoeb. Phoebe was her real name. Phoebe Anne Oakley."

"OK, RJ. I get it. You like Annie Oakley. Can we talk about Margaret Holder for a minute? You know, the murder case?"

"You bet. Just thought you'd like to know who Annie Oakley is. You being a public servant and all, you never know when you might need it, talking to a pro-gun group, or something."

Catherine shook her head and started to laugh. "You need help, RJ. Seriously, you really need help."

"Just trying to have a dialogue here, Catherine."

"OK, you done?"

"I am."

"Can we talk about Holder?"

"We can."

"So what do you think?"

"I think it looks like self-defense."

"OK, let's go through it," Catherine said, picking up a long yellow legal pad. "Anything here that would suggest she shot them accidently?"

"Nah. Pete Steiner interviewed her boyfriend, Castaway. I talked to Holder. Both said pretty much the same thing. I gave her lots of chances to call it an accident. Asked her if she intended to shoot him. She said yes, she was trying to stop him from stabbing her boyfriend with the screwdriver. Asked her if the gun might have gone off accidentally. She said no. She shot them because she thought they were going to kill her boyfriend and rape her. She shot Balfour, the guy with the screwdriver, three times. She shot Balfour's buddy, Kelton, twice. It's pretty hard to describe five shots as an accident. She didn't hesitate with her answers. It wasn't a mistake. She intended to shoot them both."

"OK, so she gets to keep her self-defense claim," Catherine said.

"It would seem so."

"What about Castaway? What do you think of him?"

"A pretty gutsy guy. He was in the kitchen, thinks there's a strange conversation going on in the hallway, walks into the living room, and sees Maggie getting robbed, and possibly raped. He said she looked terrified. He charges at the closest guy, Kelton, beats him up pretty good, and gets him out the door. He says he thought if he could do that, the other guy might run. I asked him why he didn't go after Balfour first, since he was holding the screwdriver against Maggie, and he said he didn't know. He just thought he should get one of them out the door."

"Doesn't sound like much of a plan," she said. "You think there's more to it?"

"No, not really, but you're right. It wasn't much of a plan, but then again, there wasn't a lot of time to think about it. I think he saw Maggie in danger and he just went for the closest guy, and that happened to be Kelton."

"How chivalrous."

"C'mon Catherine, tackling Kelton was a pretty gutsy move, probably saved them from at least robbery, possibly rape, and maybe more. If Balfour had reacted quicker, we'd probably be investigating two murders, David and Maggie's. He didn't think about it. He just reacted. It happens. He said that if Maggie hadn't shot Balfour he would have been stabbed with the screwdriver. He thinks she saved his life. She probably did."

"Anything to contradict what either of them told you?"

"No, there really isn't. She said it wasn't an accident, and there's nothing to suggest it was. It's either self-defense or it's murder."

"Did she say she intended to kill them?" she asked.

"No, I asked her about that. She said she was just trying to stop them from hurting Castaway. She thought Balfour was going to kill him with the screwdriver, and she thought she was going to be raped. I think she's right about that. It looks like that was their game plan."

Catherine took a minute and looked down at her yellow legal pad. She made a note and checked off several items on her list, then looked back up at RJ.

"Anything to suggest she knew either Balfour or Kelton, or they knew her? Any bad blood there?"

"Not that we could find. Neither of these guys was from the neighborhood. She denies knowing either one. We checked at the hospital, looked over their records pretty good. Kelton had been to the emergency room a couple of times, but there's no record that Maggie had any contact with him. Balfour wasn't listed as a patient."

"How did these two guys get into the house?"

RJ looked at her, thinking it was rather obvious how they got into the house, but he answered her anyway.

"Well, let's start by saying she didn't invite them in. She drove home, went in the front door, and when she tried to close it, there they were. She saw them on the sidewalk when she drove into the driveway, so they must have come up pretty fast behind her after she got out of her car."

"How could two guys come up behind her that fast without her knowing?"

"Come on, Catherine. This woman is a nurse coming home from work. She lives with her boyfriend. She'd had a bad day at the hospital. Some woman she knew died. You really think she asked these two thugs to step into her living room?"

"I'm just asking."

"Long story short, she told us they pushed their way into the house, and we've got nothing to suggest otherwise. She didn't know either of them, and there's nothing to suggest she did. We also didn't find anything to suggest she might have had a reason to ask them into the house. There's really nothing there."

"What about Castaway? Did he know either of them?"

"Same story, nothing to suggest it."

"OK, what happened then?"

"Balfour pulled the screwdriver and demanded money. She offered him her wallet and told him to leave. Kelton grabbed the wallet and apparently didn't like what he found, so Balfour decided he was going to take it out in trade. He told her to take her clothes off. That's when she went for the pistol in her purse. She told him she had some more money in her purse and was reaching for the gun when Castaway came out of the kitchen."

"What was Kelton doing?"

"Blocking her way into the living room."

"You think she was really threatened?"

"Don't you? I mean two thugs with a ten-inch screwdriver in her house, demanding money, and telling her to take her clothes off. She's at best five feet five inches tall. Seems pretty clear to me."

"Could she have gotten away?"

"She might have tried to run, but I doubt she would have gotten very far. Balfour's got her covered if she moves toward the door. Kelton's got her covered if she goes toward the living room. She's sandwiched between these two guys, besides where would she go?"

"Bathroom, bedroom, maybe?"

"Not likely. I doubt she could have made it to the bathroom, shut the door, and lock it before they grabbed her. There was no lock on the bedroom door."

"What about Castaway. She could have run toward him."

"Maybe, but what makes you think a judge won't apply the Castle Doctrine here. She doesn't have to run in her own home."

"You sound a little sympathetic, RJ."

RJ sat back in his chair and looked at Catherine. He picked up the timeline and looked it over slowly, taking his time, making her wait for his answer.

"I don't make up facts," is all he said.

Catherine picked up her pen and circled an item on her legal pad. "What about Castaway? What was he doing there?"

"He's her boyfriend. Lives there. Moved into the place about six months ago."

"Did he have a key?" she asked.

"He did. He parked his car in the driveway, kept his clothes in the bedroom closet. He gave up his apartment when he moved in, and he's paying half the mortgage. It's his home, too."

"He started this whole thing."

"Well, he certainly took it up a notch pretty quick, but I don't think he started it. Kelton and Balfour get the prize for that one.

"Instead of pushing one of them out the door, maybe he should have got her out of there."

"I don't think he could have, Catherine. This thing unfolded quickly. It takes us longer to describe it than it did for it to actually play out. I don't know what he could have done. If he'd tried to help her escape, the two of them would have been on him with the screwdriver, and again we'd probably be looking at two murder cases."

Catherine looked down at her legal pad and made a check mark. "So why is she packing a gun in her purse?" she asked.

"She's got a concealed carry permit, had it for some time. We checked with the state and she's never had a problem, no negative reports, no "woman with a gun" calls, nothing like that. Apparently, she was low key about it. When we checked with her coworkers they described her as level headed, didn't get upset, didn't argue with the patients, cared about her work, cared about the patients. They were quite surprised to hear that she had a gun in her purse. A couple of her coworkers weren't too happy about it."

"So why did she carry it?"

"Worried about crime in the hospital parking lots, with good reason. It's a problem; robberies and muggings, a sexual assault about six months ago. It's not the greatest part of town, as you know. We put extra patrols in there, it slows down, we try to plug a hole somewhere else, it flares back up. It's not going to change until somebody does something about the public housing over there."

"I know. It's a mess."

"You got that right. Anyway, Holder works late sometimes and got the gun for protection. She goes to the range about once a month to practice. Guys at the range say she's good with the pistol, safe. They didn't have any problems with her."

"She ever tried to use it in the past?"

"No. Like I said, there are no firearms reports about her. In fact, the only thing she had was one speeding ticket. She's clean."

"What about booze? Anybody drinking?" she asked.

"Bobby Cooper was on patrol that evening. He was the first guy there. He's pretty good, been around. He got near enough to both Holder and Castaway to smell booze on them if it was there. He said he smelled nothing on her, nothing on him. I asked her if she'd had anything to drink and she said no, and I didn't smell anything on her when I talked to her. There was a glass of wine on the counter in the kitchen. Castaway said he'd just poured it, but hadn't drunk any of it. The glass looked like it was still fresh. Steiner said Castaway was emotional after the shooting, but he wasn't impaired in any way."

"So why do you think these guys picked Holder?"

"Random, I guess. They were probably in the neighborhood looking for somebody to rob and she fit the bill."

"I don't get it. Why would they barge in on her when there's two cars in the driveway? Either they had to know someone else was there or somebody had asked them to come."

"Or they could be stupid. Again, we've got nothing to suggest anyone asked them into the house. As for the two cars in the driveway, you and I both know we're not dealing with a couple of Mensa members here. These guys were looking for someone to rob, and she looked vulnerable. They made a bad choice."

Another check mark on Catherine's pad. "So what about the neighbors? They see anything?"

"One of the neighbors saw the two guys walking down the sidewalk. He's a neighborhood watch kind of guy and noticed them because they weren't from the neighborhood. That's about it."

"Did you find anyone who thought Holder and these two guys had any problems, maybe gotten into some kind of argument before she pulled into her driveway?"

"Again, we found nothing like that. We can go back and look again, but I doubt we'll find anything. The patrolmen did a good job canvasing the neighborhood. We've talked to everybody we can find who knows anything about Holder or Castaway, or Balfour and Kelton. We didn't find anything to connect them. There's also been a fair amount of media interest, as you know. The press is out there looking for stories. Jack Huff loves to publish stuff before we find out about it, and I know he's been asking around. If he had anything, he'd publish it. He hasn't."

"Glad to know we're relying on the press to do our investigations," Catherine said.

RJ started to let that pass, but couldn't. "Hey, we'll take leads wherever we can get them. If it's from a newspaperman, so be it. The bottom line is nobody has found anything that links Holder or Castaway to either Balfour or Kelton. She'd never laid eyes on them before this incident. If you know something different, tell me. I'd be happy to run it down."

Catherine pulled the legal pad toward her. Her eyes scanned down the first page. She flipped it and scanned down the second page, flipped it and scanned again. She picked up the pen, made a note, and laid it back down. She looked back at RJ.

"OK, go through it again for me."

RJ scratched his head. "OK, let me get my notes." He looked through his file and extracted several sheets of paper. He took out his pen and looked at the paper for a minute.

"OK. Here's what I believe happened. Holder drives home after work, parks the car, and goes in her front door. When she tries to close it, Balfour and Kelton push their way into her house. They're now standing in her hallway. We have found nothing to suggest she knew either Balfour or Kelton, and nothing to suggest they were in her house for any reason other than to rob her. Castaway is her live-in boyfriend, it's his home, too. The Castle Doctrine applies, she doesn't have a duty to retreat and neither does he." RJ made a check mark on his sheet of paper.

"Holder's done nothing wrong. She didn't know these people, didn't seek them out, didn't ask them to come into her house, didn't provoke them. In that regard, she's innocent of contributing in any way to bringing about this confrontation." RJ made another check mark on his paper.

"She hands over her wallet to Kelton, who apparently isn't satisfied with how much money she has. Balfour decides to take it up a notch and tells Holder to take off her pants, they're going to take some of her 'package.' Kelton thinks that's a fine idea. The two men box her in, one blocking the door, the other blocking the living room. She's now trapped between two strangers inside her house and they're demanding money and threatening to rape her. It seems to me that such behavior, under those circumstances, would suggest to a reasonable person that it was reasonable for Holder to fear that she was in imminent danger of death or serious bodily injury." Another check mark on the paper.

"She's got a gun in her purse because she's afraid of being mugged in the hospital parking lot, not an unreasonable fear, given the recent history there. It wasn't in her purse because she was expecting a visit from these two guys. She didn't arm herself to greet them when they arrived. That's where she kept it. Check." RJ made another mark.

"I know the elements of self-defense," Catherine said.

"I know you do, Catherine. I'm just trying to be thorough here," RJ said. Then he pressed on, "So Holder is sandwiched between these two thugs, with no place to go, and she's terrified. Along comes Castaway and decides to throw himself at the nearest robber. He nails Kelton, and after beating him to a pulp while his partner is too surprised to react, pushes him out the door. Balfour tries to stab him in the back with the screwdriver, so Holder shoots him through the bottom of her pocketbook, probably saving Castaway's life. It's no accident. Her fear appears to be reasonable fear, and she has no alternative at that point but to use deadly force. Check." Another mark.

Catherine made a note on her legal pad.

"OK, so here's the best part," RJ continues. "When we talk to Holder, she says, yes she shot them intentionally, on purpose. It wasn't an accident. But she says she didn't intend to kill anyone. She was trying to stop them from stabbing her boyfriend and raping her. And nobody can find anything, and we've looked hard, to contradict what she told us. No accident. Check. No ill will toward the two thugs who were trying to rob her, and no suggestion that she was trying to do anything but prevent her boyfriend from being killed and herself from being raped. Check." RJ put two more check marks on his paper and looked up at Catherine. "This is your decision, Catherine, but that's how I see it. It was self-defense," RJ said, putting the sheet of paper back into the folder and closing it.

Catherine didn't flinch. "What about Kelton? I can understand Balfour. He was going to stab her boyfriend, but Kelton wasn't armed. Why shoot him?"

"Kelton wasn't done. He was coming back for them through the door. Castaway got the better of him because he surprised him, but that doesn't mean Kelton wouldn't come back and possibly clean his clock. What was Holder supposed to do? Let Kelton and Castaway fight it out and shoot Kelton if he won. The force she used was reasonable." There was a hint of irritation in his voice.

"That's your testimony?"

"I believe that's the truth, and if I'm asked, that's what I'll say."

Catherine looked at him but said nothing. She had read all the reports, worked through the file with her own checklist, and she had come to the same conclusion, but she still wanted to be convinced it was the right one. She looked down at the legal pad on the desk, made another mark, and looked up. "But is there any chance Kelton was trying to run away?" she asked.

"None. She shot him in the chest when he was coming back through the door. He died on her hallway rug."

"So you don't think they could have got out of there. The only alternative was to shoot them?"

"That's about it. If these guys were out on the porch you might argue she had some alternative, maybe try to shut the door and lock it, but they were inside her house. There's no question, she didn't have to retreat anywhere. Besides, there was no place for her to go."

"But she had a gun, RJ."

"I know she did, but it isn't a crime to have a gun, and it doesn't make it murder."

Catherine picked up the legal pad and put it on top of her papers. "I think I know what you're going to say, but I'll ask anyway. What about the three shots on Balfour? Was it necessary?"

"Catherine, you've done shootings before. It's not like the movies. You don't always know if you've hit someone, much less how badly he might be hurt. She shot until Balfour started to fall. She thought the threat was over. Then she turned to Kelton. She did it right."

"You haven't told me anything I haven't read in the file. I don't like it, but I can't prove murder. So I won't be filing any charges against her. But now we'll have some more trigger happy cowboys carrying guns. "

"All I can say is, not while you're around, Catherine. Not while you're around."

"You know, RJ. You're a helluva defense lawyer," Catherine said, with just a hint of a smile.

RJ pushed back his chair. "Cheap shot. Lunch?"

"You buying?"

"I am."

THE PRICE TO BE PAID

There is a price to be paid in every self-defense shooting, regardless of whether there is a valid claim of self-defense. The shooter may feel elated at having survived, revolted by what has been done, remorseful for taking a life, unsure if it was really necessary, and in some cases he or she may experience post-traumatic stress.[2] Difficulty sleeping, concentrating, eating, or remembering even the simplest of tasks can also occur.[3]

There is the stress of waiting for the prosecutor to decide whether to file criminal charges. Deciding whether to prosecute the shooter for murder is a decision that is never made lightly, and never a foregone conclusion. There is always a careful review of the facts, always an examination of the circumstances by people who weren't there to determine if the killing was really necessary.

Until the prosecutor makes a final decision, the shooter remains at risk of being charged with murder. The police will interview the shooter, take his or her statement, and check it carefully for accuracy. They will find out what kind of person he is, whether he's misbehaved in the past, whether there's any reason for bad blood between the shooter and the victim. They will interview everyone who knows anything about the killing, or the parties to it, and they will collect every piece of evidence they can find that suggests how the incident happened. They work diligently, thoroughly, and the effort goes on and on until all the questions are answered, all the evidence is gathered, all the tests have been completed, and everyone is satisfied they have all the facts. It is a careful process, but draining for the one who awaits the final decision.

In the end, the investigators will give their assessment of what happened and why, and there will be a conversation, such as the one between Catherine McCarthy and Ronnie Johnson, where prosecutors and police officers check each other and test alternative theories about what happened, looking to see if they can prove murder. Then the prosecutor will make a decision based on the evidence. Its purpose is to give the victim justice, make sure the loss of life was really necessary, and if it wasn't, hold the shooter accountable. In the end, the decision is a cold, calculated one, based on what the prosecutor thinks a jury will believe. If the facts support a murder charge, the prosecutor will bring it, and the benefit of any doubt on that issue is usually given to the dead victim.

Forces outside the prosecutor's office will influence the decision. How the police investigate the case and how they present the facts are important. Prosecutors, like all professionals, respect the opinions of people who do a good job. Not surprisingly, police officers with reputations for thorough investigations have greater influence with them than those who don't. Their opinions of what happened, and why, and how they portray the shooter matter because they are the ones who will likely present much of the case to a jury.

There is also the issue of community norms. What do people in the community think about the alleged criminal conduct? Will they demand prosecution? Interestingly, in some kinds of cases many communities are not much interested in punishing violators of the law. For example, adultery is still a crime in a surprising number of states,[4] yet it is almost never prosecuted. Lack of resources is usually given as the reason, but in reality it's more about focusing on crimes that people really care about. Murder is at the top of the list. It always generates a demand for the guilty to be punished. At the same time, people tend to think a little differently about murder charges when there's a of claim of self-defense involved and the claimant is not a known criminal. An argument can be made that people in states that have enacted stand-your-ground laws are more sympathetic toward self-defense claims than people in states that continue to follow the common law and its duty to retreat. The same can be said about people in pro-gun or anti-gun communities, the politically safe path being to charge a person and let the jury figure it out in communities where anti-gun sentiment is perceived to be strong.

If the prosecutor decides to bring criminal charges, the shooter will incur significant financial costs. The price of lawyers varies from place to place and from lawyer to lawyer, and as with all things, you get what you pay for. High retainer fees are common and the total cost can be very expensive for cases that go to trial. A 2012 study estimated the average cost of defending against a charge of murder was about $75,000.[5] It is enough to destroy the life savings of many people, and is its own form of punishment, particularly where the claim of self-defense proves to be true.

If the prosecutor decides not to bring charges, or if a trial ends in a not guilty verdict, the shooter is left with the emotional cost of having taken another life, not an inconsequential thing. If the prosecutor brings a case and proves it, then the defendant will most likely spend some time in jail. How long it will be depends on the circumstances of the shooting and the laws of the state where the case is tried. That cost is imposed because, in the final analysis, a judge or jury has found that the victim's death wasn't really necessary.

NOTES

INTRODUCTION

1. Sigmund Freud, "Thoughts on War and Death" (1915), www.panarchy. org/freud/war.1915.html.

2. Michelle Jaffe, "Up in Arms over Florida's New 'Stand Your Ground' Law," 30 *Nova Law Review* 155 (Fall 2005): 158, citing Joseph H. Beale, Jr., "Retreat from Murderous Assault," 16 *Harvard Law Review* 567 (1902): 569.

3. John Miller, "Hugo Grotius," in the *Stanford Encyclopedia of Philosophy*, ed. Edward N. Zalta et al. (Stanford, CA: Stanford University, 2014), https:// leibniz.stanford.edu/friends/preview/grotius/.

4. Hugo Grotius, *On the Law of War and Peace*, trans. A. C. Campbell (London: Constitution Society), www.constitution.org/gro/djbp.htm.

5. Thomas Hobbes, *Leviathan, The Second Part,* (Eugene, OR: University of Oregon, 1999): Chapter 27, www.luminarium.org/renascence-editions/hobbes/ leviathan2.html.

6. State v. Holland, 193 N.C. 713, 718; 138 S.E. 8, 10 (1927).

7. 40 Am. Jur. 2d Homicide 134.

8. Kinderly Kindy and Kennedy Elliott, "990 People Were Shot and Killed by Police This Year, Here's What We Learned," *The Washington Post*, December 26, 2015, www.washingtonpost.com/graphics/national/police-shootings-year-end.

9. Jamiles Lartey et al., "The Counting; U.S. Police Killed 1,136 People in 2015. Will 2016 Be Any Different?" *The Guardian*, January 5, 2016, www. theguardian.com/commentisfree/video/2015/dec/30/us-police-killed-1103-people-this-year-will-2016-be-any-different-video.

10. Jamiles Lartey and Chris Phillips, "The Counting, U.S. Police Killings in 2015, Inside the Shocking Numbers in Two Minutes," *The Guardian*, January 5, 2016, www.theguardian.com/us-news/video/2015/jul/01/us-police-killings-this-year-the-counted-video .

11. Brandon Ellington Patterson, "Here Are All of the Cops Who Were Charged in 2015 for Shooting Suspects," *Mother Jones*, December 17, 2015, www.motherjones.com/politics/2015/12/year-police-shootings.

12. Matt Ferner and Nick Wing, "Here's How Many Cops Got Convicted of Murder Last Year for On-Duty Shootings," *The Huffington Post*, January 13, 2016, www.huffingtonpost.com/entry/police-shooting-convictions_us_5695968ce4b086bc1cd5d0da.

13. District of Columbia v. Heller, 554 U.S. 570 (2008).

14. McDonald v. Chicago, 561 U.S. 3025 (2010).

I. NECESSITY

1. Reed Williams, "Police, Proprietors Discuss Crime in South Richmond," *Richmond Times-Dispatch*, July 16, 2009, B1.

2. The gunfight upon which this story is based describes an attempted robbery in Richmond, Virginia, on July 11, 2009. Sources of information about the incident include Sandi Cauley, "Suspect in Convenient Store Robbery Dies," *WVTR*, July 15, 2009, www.wtvr.com/wtvr-shooting-Bright Star-food-market-090711,0,2691670.story; Reed Williams, "Man Who Fatally Wounded Robber Recounts Tense Shootout," *Richmond Times-Dispatch*, July 19,2009, www2.timesdispatch.com/rtd/news/local/crime/article/MART191_20090718-234801/280934/; Michael Martz, "Police Charge South Richmond Man in Convenience Store Shooting," *Richmond Times-Dispatch*, July 13, 2009, www2.timesdispatch.com/rtd/news/local/article/ROBBGAT13_20090713-122201/279736/; "Gun Discussions & Shooting," *Forums Forums,* forumsforums.com/3_9/showthread.php?t=28219; Williams, "Police, Proprietors Discuss Crime," B1; Reed Williams, "Richmond Store Owner Grateful for Man who Shot Robber," *Richmond Times-Dispatch*, July 15, 2009, http://www.richmond.com/news/article_1208ebdd-9ed5-54e1-bfd4-24a0c83a2852.html.

3. State v. Chisholm, 126 Idaho 319, 882 P. 2d 974 (1994); see also 21 Am. Jur. 2d Criminal Law 140.

4. Humphrey v. Commonwealth, 37 Va. App. 36, 45; 553 S.E. 2d 546, 550 (2001).

5. Smith v. Commonwealth, 17 Va. App 68, 71; 435 S.E. 2d 414, 416 (1993); People v. Randle, 35 Cal. 4th 987, 28 Cal. Rptr. 3d 725, 111 P. 3d 987 (2005).

6. 40 Am. Jur. 2d Homicide 134.

7. State v. Martin, 329 Md. 351, 619 A. 2d 992 (1993).

8. Commonwealth v. Edwards, 448 Pa. 79, 292 A. 2d 361 (1972).

9. Rasley v. State, 878 So. 2d 473 (Fla. Dist. Ct. App. 1st Dist. 2004).

10. State v. Jackson, 262 Kan. 119, 936 P. 2d 761 (1997).

2. INTENT

1. State v. Lucero, 147 N.M. 747, 228 P. 3d 1167 (2010).

2. Walter Wheeler Cook, "Act, Intention, and Motive in the Criminal Law," *Yale Law Journal* 26, no. 8 (June 1917): 645–663.

3. People v. Moore, 3 N.Y. Cr R 458; Black's Law Dictionary, thelawdictionary.org/criminal-intent/.

4. 21 Am. Jur. 2d Criminal Law, 140.

5. New Mexico Statutes Annotated, 1978, 30-2-2.

6. New Mexico Statutes Annotated, 1978, 30-2-3.

7. 40 Am. Jur. 2d Homicide 113.

8. Mundy v. Commonwealth, 144 Va. 609, 615; 131 S.E. 242 (1926).

9. Mundy v. Commonwealth, 144 Va. 609, 615; 131 S.E. 242, 244 (1926).

10. Id.

3. PROVOCATION

1. State v. Hidalgo, 668 So. 2d 1188, 95-319 (La. App. 5 Cir. 1/17/96).

2. Petrasson v. Nelson, 121 F. 3d 297 (1997).

3. Smith v. Commonwealth, 17 Va. App. 68, 435 S.E. 2d 414.

4. Matthew 5:38, Leviticus 24:20.

5. People v. Vatac, 631 N.E. 2d 373.

6. Jackson v. State, 586 So. 2d 562.

7. Kirk Johnson, "Goets Is Cleared in Subway Attack; Gun Count Upheld; Acquittal Won in Shooting of 4 Youths—Prison Term Possible on Weapon Charge," *New York Times*, June 17,1987, http://www.nytimes.com/1987/06/17/nyregion/goets-cleared-subway-attack-gun-count-upheld-acquittal-won-shooting-4-youths.html?pagewanted=all.

8. State v. Leaks, 114 S.C. 257, 103 S.E. 549 (1920).

9. Crawford v. State, 267 Ga. 543, 480 S.E. 2d 573 (1997).

4. DEADLY THREATS

1. Cook v. State, 194 Miss. 467, 12 So 2d 137 (1943). In the Cook case, the defendant used a knife to defend himself. The type of weapon does not affect the legal analysis.

2. Baze v. Com., 965 S.W. 2d 817 (Ky. 1997); State v. Cunningham, 344 N.C. 341, 474 S.E. 2d 772 (1996).

3. Foote v. Commonwealth, 11 Va App. 61, 396 S. E. 2d 851 (1990).

4. People v. Robinson, 375 Ill. App. 3d 320, 313 Ill. Dec. 672, 872 N.E. 2d 1061 (2d Dist. 2007).

5. State v. Harris, 870 S.W. 2d 798 (Mo. 1994).

6. Commonwealth v. Cary, 271 Va 87, 623 S.E. 2d 906 (2006).

7. McKee v. State, 1962 Ok Cr 57, 372 P 2d 243, 245 (1962).

8. People v. Evans, 259 Ill. App. 3d 195, 197 Ill. Dec. 278, 631 N.E. 2d 281 (1st Dist. 1994).

9. Commonwealth v. Edwards, 448 Pa 79, 292 A2d 361 (1972).

10. Cook v. State, 194 Miss. 467, 12 So. 2d 137, 138 (1943).

11. 40 Am. Jur. 2d Homicide 153.

12. Cook v. State, 194 Miss. 467, 12 So. 2d 137, 138 (1943).

5. VERBAL THREATS

1. Smith v. Commonwealth, 192 Va. 186 (1951).

2. State v. Gordon, 89 S.W. 1025.

3. People v. Gordon, 223 A.D.2d 372, 636 N.Y.S. 2d 317.

4. Smith v. State, 965 S.W. 2d 509; People v. Gordon, 223 A.D.2d 372, 636 N.Y.S. 2d 317; People v. Silva, 987 P. 2d 909.

5. People v. Gordon, 223 A.D.2d 372, 636 N.Y.S. 2d 317.

6. Martin v. Commonwealth, 184 Va. 1009, 1016-1017; 37 S.E. 2d 43, 46.

7. Commonwealth v. Cary, 271 Va. 87, 623 S.E. 2d 906 (2006); Koritta v. State, 263 Ga. 703, 438 S.E. 2d 68 (1994).

8. Flowers v. Commonwealth, 2011 Va. App. Lexis 310.

9. Fry v. State, 915 S.W. 2d 554 (Tex. App. Houston 14th Dist. 1995).

6. IMMINENT HARM

1. State v. Norman, 324 N.C. 253, 378 S.E. 2d 8 (1989).

2. Flowers v. Commonwealth, 2011 Va. App. Lexis 310, State v. Gappins, 320 N.C. 64, 71, 357 S.E. 2d 654,659 (1987).

3. Commonwealth v. Cary, 271 Va. 87, 623 S.E. 2d 906 (2006).

4. Ha v. State, 892 P. 2d 184 (Alaska Ct. App. 1995).

5. State v. Holland, 193 N.C. 713,718; 138 S.E. 8, 10 (1927).

6. State v. Norman, 324 N.C. 253, 261; 378 S.E. 2d 8, 13 (1989).

7. State v. Norman, 324 N.C. 253, 266; 378 S.E. 2d 8, 16 (1989).

8. State v. Norman, 324 N.C. 253, 264; 378 S.E. 2d 8, 15 (1989).

9. Id.

10. State v. Mize, 316 N.C. 48, 53; 340 S.E. 2d 439, 442 (1986).

7. REASONABLE FEAR

1. Humprhey v. State, 332 Ark. 398, 966 S.W. 2d 213 (1998).

2. Ellis v. State, 708 So. 2d 884 (Miss. 1998).

3. State v. Jackson, 262 Kan. 119, 936 P. 2d 761 (1997).

4. People v. Willis, 217 Ill. App. 3d 909, 160 Ill. Dec. 644, 577 N.E. 2d 1215 (1st Dist. 1991).

5. VanBrackle v. State, 179 S.W. 3d 708 (Tex. App. Austin 2005).

8. DUTY TO RETREAT

1. Lane v. State, 222 A. 2d 263 (1963).

2. Jaffe, "Up in Arms," 158.

3. Jaffe, "Up in Arms," 160.

4. Erwin v. State, 29 Ohio St. 186, 199–200 (1876).

5. Runyan v. State, 57 Ind. 80, 84 (1877).

6. State v. Gardner, 104 N.W. 971, 975 (1905).

7. Brown v. United States , 256 U.S. 335, 343 (1921).

8. Lane v. State, 222 A. 2d 263, 267 (1966).

9. STAND YOUR GROUND

1. Dorsey v. State, 74 So. 3d 521 (2011).

2. Jaffe, "Up in Arms," 160.

3. Weiand v. State, 732 So. 2d 1044, 1049 (Fla. 1999); State v Smiley, 932 So. 2d 1000, 1001 (Fla. 4th DCA 2006).

4. Thompson v. State, 552 So. 2d 264, 266 (Fla. 2d DCA 1989); State v. Rivera 719 So. 2d 335, 338 (Fla. 5th DCA 1998).

5. Section 776.013(3) Fla. Stat. (2006).

6. Rem Reider, "Media Got Zimmerman Story Wrong from Start," *USA Today*, July 14, 2013, www.usatoday.com/story/news/nation/2013/07/14/zim merman-trayvon-martin-nbc-news-column-rieder/2516251/.

7. Id.

8. Nicole Flatow and Rebecca Leber, "5 Disturbing Facts about the State of Stand-Your-Ground on the Second Anniversary of Trayvon's Death," *ThinkProgress*, February 26, 2014, thinkprogress.org/justice/2014/02/26/3332391/ trayvon-martin-years/.

9. Victor Li, "States with Stand-Your-Ground Laws Have Seen an Increase in Homicides, Reports Task Force," *ABA Journal*, August 8, 2014.

10. Section 870.01 and Section 775.082 (3d) Fla. Stat.

11. Section 790.23(3) Fla. Stat.

12. Dorsey v. State, 74 So. 3d 521, 527 (2011).

10. CASTLE DOCTRINE

1. People v. Riddle, 467 Mich. 116, 649 N.W. 2d 30 (2002).

2. 40 Am. Jur. 2d Homicide 163.

3. State v. Barraza, 209 Ariz. 441, 104 P. 3d 172 (2005).

4. People v. Tomlins, 213 N.Y. 240, 107 N.E. 496, 497 (1914).

5. Hedges v. State, 127 So. 2d 824 (1965).

6. State v. Bobbitt, 415 So. 2d 724 (1982).

7. Redondo v. State, 380 So. 2d 1107 (1980).

8. Baker v. State, 506 So. 2d 1056 (1987).

9. Frazier v. State, 681 So. 2d 824 (1996).

10. Weiand v. State, 732 So. 2d 1044 (1999).

11. Douglas A. Orr, "Weiand v. State and Battered Spouse Syndrome: The Toothless Tigress Can Now Roar," *The Florida Bar Journal* LXXIV, no. 6 (June 2000): 14, www.floridabar.org/divcom/jn/jnjournal01.nsf/Author/EEDD58C 673EC712885256ADB005D6306.

12. Orr, "Weiand v. State and Battered Spouse Syndrome," 14.

13. Id.

14. Kilgore v. State, 643 So. 2d 1015 (1993).

15. Hester v. United States, 265 U.S. 57, 44 S. Ct 445, 68 L.Ed.898 (1924).

16. 40 Am. Jur. 2d Homicide 165.

17. Pond v. People, 8 Mich. 150 (1860).

18. State v. Firzzelle, 243 N.C. 49, 89 S.E. 2d 725 (1955).

19. Doswell v. State, 34 Ala. App. 546, 42 So. 2d 480 (1949).

20. State v. Williford, 49 Ohio St. 3d 247, 551 N.E. 2d 1279 (1990).

21. Nunn v. State, 19 Ala. App. 619, 99 So. 738 (1924).

22. Com. v. Fortini, 44 Mass. App. Ct. 562, 692 N.E. 2d 110 (1998).

23. Com. v. Carlino, 449 Mass. 71, 865 N.E. 2d 767 (2007).

24. People v. Wytcherly, 172 Mich. App. 213, 431 N.W. 2d 463 (1988) on reh'g, 176 Mich. App. 714, 440 N.W. 2d 107 (1989).

25. State v. Quick, 138 S.C. 147, 135 S.E. 800 (1926).

26. State v. Marsh, 71 Ohio Ap. 3d 64, 593 N.E. 2d 35 (1990).

11. DE-ESCALATION

1. Commonwealth v. Samuel, 527 Pa. 298, 590 A. 2d 1245 (1991).

2. Id.

3. Commonwealth v. Edwards, 448 Pa. 79, 292 A. 2d 361 (1972).

4. Melchior v. Jago, 723 F. 2d 486, 493 (6th Cir.1983).

5. 40 Am. Jur. 2d Homicide, 149.

6. State v. Huemphreus, 270 N.W.2d 457, 462 (Iowa 1978).

7. Allen v. State, 871 P. 2d 79 (1994).

12. MISTAKE

1. Henderson v. Texas, 906 S.W. 2d 589 (1995).

2. Reg. v. Sauders, 2 Plowd. 473, 75 Eng. Reprint 706 (1576), 18 A.L.R. 923.

3. Fussell v. State, 187 Ga. App. 134, 369 S.E. 2d 511 (1988).

4. Smith v. State, 204 Ga. App. 173 (1992).

5. Butler v. State, 92 Ga. App. 601, 19 S.E. 51 (1893).

13. REASONABLE FORCE

1. People v. Kruger, 236 Ill. App. 3d 65, 603 N.E. 2d 743, 177 Ill. Dec. 673 (1992).

2. 10 CFR 1047.7

3. People v. Truong, 218 Mich. App. 325, 338; 553 N.W. 2d 692, 699 (1996).

4. Id.

5. 40 Am. Jur. 2d Homicide, 158.

6. State v. Eddington, 829 S.W. 2d 110 (Mo. Ct. App. ED. 1992).

7. People v. Kruger, 236 Ill. App. 3d 63,71; 603 N.E. 2d 743, 746; 177 Ill. Dec. 673, 676 (1992).

8. Ill.Rev.Stat. 1985, ch. 38, para. 9-2(a).

9. People v. Kruger, 236 Ill. App. 3d 63,71; 603 N.E. 2d 743, 746; 177 Ill. Dec. 673, 676 (1992).

14. THREATENED

1. Gunther v. State, 228 Md. 404, 179 A. 2d 880 (1962).

2. District of Columbia v. Heller, 554 U.S. 570 (2008).

3. 40 Am. Jur. 2d Homcide, 158.

4. Barnes v. State, 93 So. 2d 863 (Fla. 1957).

5. State v. Sanford, 450 N.W. 2d 580 (Minn. Ct. App. 1990).

6. Price v. U.S., 276 F. 628 (App. DC 1921).

7. Gunther v. State, 228 Md. 404, 408; 179 A. 2d 880,882 (1962).

15. DECISIONS

1. "True Stories," *Concealed Carry Magazine*, August/September 2010, 7.

2. National Rifle Association, *Basics of Protection Inside the Home* (Fairfax, VA: National Rifle Association of American, 2000) (10-09 Revised): 157–159.

3. American Psychological Association, "Managing Your Distress in the Aftermath of a Shooting," www.apa.org/helpcenter/mass-shooting.aspx.

4. Jolie Lee, "New Hampshire Senate Votes to Repeal Anti-Adultery Law," *USA Today,* April 17, 2014.

5. Terance D. Miethe, "Estimates of Time Spent in Capital and Non-Capital Murder Cases: A Statistical Analysis of Survey Data from Clark County Defense Attorneys," February 2012, http://www.deathpenaltyinfo.org/documents/ClarkNVCostReport.pdf, 8.

BIBLIOGRAPHY

CASES

Allen v. State, 871 P. 2d 79 (1994).

Baker v. State, 506 So. 2d 1056 (1987).

Barnes v. State, 93 So. 2d 863 (Fla. 1957).

Baze v. Commonwealth, 965 S.W. 2d 817 (Ky. 1997).

Brown v. United States, 256 U.S. 335 (1921).

Butler v. State, 92 Ga. App. 601, 19 S.E. 51 (1893).

Commonwealth v. Carlino, 449 Mass. 71, 865 N.E. 2d 767 (2007).

Commonwealth v. Cary, 271 Va 87, 623 S.E. 2d 906 (2006).

Commonwealth v. Edwards, 448 Pa. 79, 292 A. 2d 361 (1972).

Commonwealth v. Fortini, 44 Mass. App. Ct. 562, 692 N.E. 2d 110 (1998).

Commonwealth v. Samuel, 527 Pa. 298, 590 A. 2d 1245 (1991).

Cook v. State, 194 Miss. 467, 12 So 2d 137 (1943).

Crawford v. State, 267 Ga. 543, 480 S.E. 2d 573 (1997).

District of Columbia v. Heller, 554 U.S. 570 (2008).

Dorsey v. State, 74 So. 3d 521 (2011).

Doswell v. State, 34 Ala. App. 546, 42 So. 2d 480 (1949).

Ellis v. State, 708 So. 2d 884 (Miss. 1998).

Erwin v. State, 29 Ohio St. 186 (1876).

Flowers v. Commonwealth, 2011 Va. App. Lexis 310.

Foote v. Commonwealth, 11 Va App. 61, 396 S. E. 2d 851 (1990).

Frazier v. State, 681 So. 2d 824 (1996).

Fry v. State, 915 S.W. 2d 554 (Tex. App. Houston 14th Dist. 1995).

Fussell v. State, 187 Ga. App. 134, 369 S.E. 2d 511 (1988).

Gunther v. State, 228 Md. 404, 179 A. 2d 880 (1962).

Ha v. State, 892 P. 2d 184 (Alaska Ct. App. 1995).

Hedges v. State, 127 So. 2d 824 (1965).

Henderson v. Texas, 906 S.W. 2d 589 (1995).

Hester v. United States, 265 U.S. 57, 44 S. Ct. 445, 68 L. Ed. 898 (1924).

Humphrey v. Commonwealth, 37 Va. App. 36, 553 S.E. 2d 546 (2001).

Humprhey v. State, 332 Ark. 398, 966 S.W. 2d 213, (1998).

Jackson v. State, 355 S.C. 568, 586 S.E. 2d 562 (2003).

Kilgore v. State, 643 So. 2d 1015 (1993).

Koritta v. State, 263 Ga. 703, 438 S.E. 2d 68 (1994).

Lane v. State, 222 A. 2d 263 (1963).

Martin v. Commonwealth, 184 Va. 1009, 37 S.E. 2d 43 (1946).

McDonald v. Chicago, 561 U.S. 3025 (2010).

McKee v. State, 1962 Ok Cr 57, 372 P 2d 243 (1962).

Melchior v. Jago, 723 F. 2d 486 (1983).

Mundy v. Commonwealth, 144 Va. 609, 131 S.E. 242 (1926).

Nunn v. State, 19 Ala. App. 619, 99 So. 738 (1924).

People v. Batac, 259 Ill. App. 3d 415, 197 Ill. Dec. 370, 631 N.E. 2d 373 (2d Dist. 1994).

People v. Evans, 259 Ill. App. 3d 195, 197 Ill. Dec. 278, 631 N.E. 2d 281 (1st Dist. 1994).

People v. Gordon, 223 A.D.2d 372, 636 N.Y.S. 2d 317 (1996).

People v. Kruger, 236 Ill. App. 3d 65, 603 N.E. 2d 743, 177 Ill. Dec. 673 (1992).

People v. Moore, 3 N.Y. Cr R 458 (1880).

People v. Randle, 35 Cal. 4th 987, 28 Cal. Rptr. 3d 725, 111 P. 3d 987 (2005).

People v. Riddle, 467 Mich. 116, 649 N.W. 2d 30 (2002).

People v. Robinson, 375 Ill. App. 3d 320, 313 Ill. Dec. 672, 872 N.E. 2d 1061 (2d Dist. 2007).

People v. Silva, 987 P. 2d 909 (1999).

People v. Truong, 218 Mich. App. 325, 553 N.W. 2d 692 (1996).

People v. Tomlins, 213 N.Y. 240, 107 N.E. 496, 497 (1914).

People v. Wytcherly, 172 Mich. App. 213, 431 N.W. 2d 463 (1988) on reh'g, 176 Mich. App. 714, 440 N.W. 2d 107 (1989).

People v. Willis, 217 Ill. App. 3d 909, 160 Ill. Dec. 644, 577 N.E. 2d 1215 (1st. Dist. 1991).

Petrasson v. Nelson, 121 F. 3d 297 (1997).

Pond v. People, 8 Mich. 150 (1860).

Price v. U.S., 276 F. 628 (1921).

Rasley v. State, 878 So. 2d 473 (Fla. Dist. Ct. App. 1st Dist. 2004).

Redondo v. State, 380 So. 2d 1107 (1980).

Reg. v. Sauders, 2 Plowd. 473, 75 Eng. Reprint 706, 18 A.L.R. 923 (1576).

Runyan v. State, 57 Ind. 80 (1877).

Smith v. Commonwealth, 17 Va. App. 68, 435 S.E. 2d 414 (1993).

Smith v. Commonwealth, 192 Va. 186 (1951).

Smith v. State, 204 Ga. App. 173 (1992).

Smith v. State, 965 S.W. 2d 509 (1998).

State v. Barraza, 209 Ariz. 441, 104 P. 3d 172 (2005).

State v. Bobbitt, 415 So. 2d 724 (1982).

State v. Chisholm, 126 Idaho 319, 882 P. 2d 974 (1994).

State v. Cunningham, 344 N.C. 341, 474 S.E. 2d 772 (1996).

State v. Eddington, 829 S.W. 2d 110 (Mo. Ct. App. ED. 1992).

State v. Firzzelle, 243 N.C. 49, 89 S.E. 2d 725 (1955).

State v. Gappins, 320 N.C 64, 357 S.E. 2d 654 (1987).

State v. Gardner, 104 N.W. 971 (1905).

State v. Gordon, 191 Mo. 114, 89 S.W. 1025 (1905).

State v. Harris, 870 S.W. 2d 798 (Mo. 1994).

State v. Hidalgo, 668 So. 2d 1188, 95-319 (La. App. 5 Cir. 1/17/96).

State v. Holland, 193 N.C. 713, 138 S.E. 8 (1927).

State v. Huemphreus, 270 N.W.2d 457, (Iowa 1978).

State v. Jackson, 262 Kan. 119, 936 P. 2d 761 (1997).

State v. Leaks, 114 S.C. 257, 103 S.E. 549 (1920).

State v. Lucero, 147 N.M. 747, 228 P. 3d 1167 (2010).

State v. Marsh, 71 Ohio Ap. 3d 64, 593 N.E. 2d 35 (1990).

State v. Martin, 329 Md. 351, 619 A. 2d 992 (1993).

State v. Mize, 316 N.C. 48, 340 S.E. 2d 439 (1986).

State v. Norman, 324 N.C. 253, 378 S.E. 2d 8 (1989).

State v. Quick, 138 S.C. 147, 135 S.E. 800 (1926).

State v. Rivera 719 So. 2d 335 (Fla. 5th DCA 1998).

State v. Smiley, 932 So. 2d 1000 (Fla. 4th DCA 2006).

State v. Williford, 49 Ohio St. 3d 247, 551 N.E. 2d 1279 (1990).

State v. Sanford, 450 N.W. 2d 580 (Minn. Ct. App. 1990).

Thompson v. State, 552 So. 2d 264 (Fla. 2d DCA 1989).

VanBrackle v. State, 179 S.W. 3d 708 (Tex. App. Austin 2005).

Weiand v. State, 732 So. 2d 1044 (Fla. 1999).

LAWS AND REGULATIONS

10 CFR 1047.7
  Fla. Stat. Section 775.082 (3d)
  Fla. Stat. (Section 776.013(3) 2006)
  Fla. Stat. Section 790.23(3)
  Fla. Stat. Section 870.01
  Ill.Rev.Stat. 1985, ch. 38, para. 9-2(a)
  New Mexico Statutes Annotated, 1978, 30-2-2
  New Mexico Statutes Annotated, 1978, 30-2-3

DIGESTS AND TREATISES

21 Am. Jur. 2d Criminal Law 140
  40 Am. Jur. 2d Homicide 113
  40 Am. Jur. 2d Homicide 134
  40 Am. Jur. 2d Homicide 149
  40 Am. Jur. 2d Homicide 153
  40 Am. Jur. 2d Homicide 158
  40 Am. Jur. 2d Homicide 163
  40 Am. Jur. 2d Homicide 165

CITED WORKS

American Psychological Association. "Managing Your Distress in the Aftermath of a Shooting." www.apa.org/helpcenter/mass-shooting.aspx.

Cauley, Sandi. "Suspect in Convenient Store Robbery Dies." *WVTR*, July 15, 2009. www.wtvr.com/wtvr-shooting-Bright Star-food-market-090711,0,2691670.story.

Cook, Walter Wheeler. "Act, Intention, and Motive in the Criminal Law." *Yale Law Journal* 26, no. 8 (June 1917): 645–663.

Ferner, Matt, and Nick Wing. "Here's How Many Cops Got Convicted of Murder Last Year for On-Duty Shootings." *Huffington Post*, January 13, 2016. www.huffingtonpost.com/entry/police-shooting-convictions_us_5695968ce4b086bc1cd5d0da.

Flatow, Nicole, and Rebecca Leber. "5 Disturbing Facts about the State of Stand-Your-Ground on the Second Anniversary of Trayvon's Death." *ThinkProgress*, February 26, 2014. thinkprogress.org/justice/2014/02/26/3332391/trayvon-martin-years/.

Freud, Sigmund. *Thoughts for the Times on War and Death*. 1915.www.panarchy.org/freud/war.1915.html.

Grotius, Hugo. *On the Law of War and Peace*. Trans. A. C. Campbell. London: Constitution Society. www.constitution.org/gro/djbp.htm.

"Gun Discussions & Shooting." *Forums Forums*. forumsforums.com/39/showthread.php?t=28219.

Hobbes, Thomas. *Leviathan*, The Second Part. University of Oregon, 1999.

Jaffe, Michelle. "Up in Arms over Florida's New 'Stand Your Ground' Law." *Nova Law Review* 30 (Fall 2005): 155–182.

Johnson, Kirk. "Goets Is Cleared in Subway Attack; Gun Count Upheld; Acquittal Won in Shooting of 4 Youths—Prison Term Possible on Weapon Charge." *New York Times*, June 17, 1987. http://www.nytimes.com/1987/06/17/nyregion/goets-cleared-subway-attack-gun-count-upheld-acquittal-won-shooting-4-youths.html?pagewanted=all.

Kindy, Kinderly, and Kennedy Elliott, "990 People Were Shot and Killed by Police This Year, Here's What We Learned." *Washington Post*, December 26, 2015. www.washingtonpost.com/graphics/national/police-shootings-year-end.

Lartey, Jamiles and Chris Phillips. "The Counting, U.S. Police Killings in 2015, Inside the Shocking Numbers in Two Minutes." *The Guardian*, January 5, 2016. www.theguardian.com/us-news/video/2015/jul/01/us-police-killings-this-year-the-counted-video.

Lartey, Jamiles, et al. "The Counting; U.S. Police Killed 1,136 People in 2015. Will 2016 Be Any Different?" *Guardian*, January 5, 2016. www.

theguardian.com/commentisfree/video/2015/dec/30/us-police-killed-1103-people-this-year-will-2016-be-any-different-video.

Lee, Jolie. "New Hampshire Senate Votes to Repeal Anti-Adultery Law." *USA Today,* April 17, 2014.

Li, Victor. "States with Stand-Your-Ground Laws Have Seen an Increase in Homicides, Reports Task Force." *ABA Journal*, August 8, 2014.

Martz, Michael. "Police Charge South Richmond Man in Convenience Store Shooting." *Richmond Times-Dispatch*, July 13, 2009. www2. timesdispatch.com/rtd/news/local/article/ROBBGAT13_20090713-122201/279736/.

Miethe, Terance D. "Estimates of Time Spent in Capital and Non-Capital Murder Cases: A Statistical Analysis of Survey Data from Clark County Defense Attorneys." University of Nevada at Las Vegas, 2012.

Miller, John. "Hugo Grotius." In the *Stanford Encyclopedia of Philosophy*. Ed. Edward N. Zalta et al. Stanford: Stanford University, 2014. https://leibniz.stanford.edu/friends/preview/grotius/.

National Rifle Association. *Basics of Protection Inside the Home*. Fairfax, Virginia: National Rifle Association of American, 2000 (10-09 Revised): 157–159.

Orr, Douglas A. "Weiand v. State and Battered Spouse Syndrome: The Toothless Tigress can now Roar." *The Florida Bar Journal* LXXIV, no. 6 (June 2000). www.floridabar.org/divcom/jn/jnjournal01.nsf/Author/EEDD58C673EC712885256ADB005D6306.

Patterson, Brandon Ellington. "Here Are All of the Cops Who Were Charged in 2015 for Shooting Suspects." *Mother Jones*, December 17, 2015. www.motherjones.com/politics/2015/12/year-police-shootings.

Reider, Rem. "Media Got Zimmerman Story Wrong from Start." *USA Today*, July 14, 2013. www.usatoday.com/story/news/nation/2013/07/14/zimmerman-trayvon-martin-nbc-news-column-rieder/2516251/.

"True Stories." *Concealed Carry Magazine*. August/September 2010: 7.

Williams, Reed. "Richmond Store Owner Grateful for Man who Shot Robber." *Richmond Times-Dispatch*, July 15, 2009. http://www.richmond.com/news/article_1208ebdd-9ed5-54e1-bfd4-24a0c83a2852.html.

Williams, Reed. "Police, Proprietors Discuss Crime in South Richmond." *Richmond Times-Dispatch*, July 16, 2009.

Williams, Reed. "Man Who Fatally Wounded Robber Recounts Tense Shootout." *Richmond Times-Dispatch*, July 19, 2009. www2. timesdispatch.com/rtd/news/local/crime/article/MART191_20090718-234801/280934/.

INDEX

ABOUT THE AUTHOR

Bruce M. Lawlor retired from the U.S. Army as a Major General. While serving at the White House Homeland Security Council staff, he helped organize and was the first chief of staff of the U.S. Department of Homeland Security. Before that he served as the first commanding general of Joint Task Force-Civil Support, a joint military headquarters, tasked to support civil authorities during domestic terrorist incidents. Mr. Lawlor was the CEO of a homeland security consulting company and has worked extensively with police departments in the United States, and around the world, in both an official and private sector capacity.

Before serving on active military duty, he was a practicing lawyer with extensive experience in civil and criminal litigation. He has represented both police officers and criminal defendants, and his criminal defense work includes a murder trial, in which he argued successfully, the defendant's claim of self-defense.

Mr. Lawlor is a certified firearms instructor, who teaches self-defense both inside and outside the home. He performed research for the U.S. Army on the use of small arms and the rules of engagement for soldiers operating in heavily populated, civilian conflict areas.

Mr. Lawlor has a doctorate of science degree in engineering management, a juris doctor degree in law, and a masters in national security studies. He was a Harvard National Security Fellow and has served as an instructor at the U.S. Army War College. He also served as the director of the Center for Technology, Security, and Public Policy at Virginia Tech, in Arlington, Virginia.